Concerned Markets

Concerned Markets

Economic Ordering for Multiple Values

Edited by

Susi Geiger

Associate Professor of Marketing, University College Dublin, Ireland

Debbie Harrison

Associate Professor, BI Norwegian Business School, Norway

Hans Kjellberg

Associate Professor, Stockholm School of Economics, Sweden

Alexandre Mallard

Director, Centre de Sociologie de l'Innovation, Ecole des Mines ParisTech, France

Edward Elgar
Cheltenham, UK • Northampton, MA, USA

Published by
Edward Elgar Publishing Limited
The Lypiatts
15 Lansdown Road
Cheltenham
Glos GL50 2JA
UK

Edward Elgar Publishing, Inc.
William Pratt House
9 Dewey Court
Northampton
Massachusetts 01060
USA

A catalogue record for this book
is available from the British Library

Library of Congress Control Number: 2014943900

This book is available electronically in the ElgarOnline.com
Business Subject Collection, E-ISBN 978 1 78254 975 8

ISBN 978 1 78254 973 4

Typeset by Servis Filmsetting Ltd, Stockport, Cheshire
Printed and bound in Great Britain by T.J. International Ltd, Padstow

Contents

Figures

Tables

Contributors

Luis Araujo is a Professor of Industrial Marketing at Lancaster University Management School, UK. His research interests and publications are in the area of business markets, namely the boundaries of the firm and product-service systems. He is a co-editor with John Finch and Hans Kjellberg of *Reconnecting Marketing to Markets* (2010).

Frank Azimont is founder of the Market Shaping Institute, France. His research examines market practices where manufacturers and retailers are involved in the business of fast-moving consumer goods. His current work investigates categorization, calculative and metrological practices, and definitions of performance.

Ronika Chakrabarti is a lecturer in Marketing at Lancaster University Management School, UK. Her research interests, in line with 'market studies', seek to understand how a practice-based approach can inform market formation, bottom-up market design and representations and interventions for policy-making. To date, she has been engaged in collaborative research projects with local/international NGOs on poverty alleviation in disaster prone islandscapes and ecological/socially responsible design for people at the Bottom of the Pyramid (BoP)/Subsistence Marketplaces. She is further interested in how markets are normalized and performed. Ronika has published in *Industrial Marketing Management, Journal of Advertising Research, International Journal of Human Resource Management* and *Production, Planning and Control*.

Franck Cochoy is Professor of Sociology at the University of Toulouse Jean-Jaurès and a member of CERTOP-CNRS, France. He works in the field of economic sociology, with a focus on the human and technical mediations that frame the relationship between supply and demand. He has conducted several projects and case studies in such areas as the role of marketing, packaging, self-service, trade press and so on. His most recent articles in English have appeared in the *Journal of Cultural Economy, Marketing Theory, Organization and Theory, Culture and Society*.

Simona D'Antone is Assistant Professor in Marketing and head of the Sustainable Sourcing in the Network Environment Research Chair at KEDGE Business School, France. She graduated in Corporate Communication and Organizational Strategies and got her PhD in Marketing with distinction from the Sapienza University of Rome, Italy. She is a member of the IMP (Industrial Marketing and Purchasing) research group. Her main research interest is in cultural and social aspects of markets and consumption with specific focuses on: market shaping and its interaction with values and society, supply–demand interfaces, sustainable sourcing, anti-consumption, consumer well-being, branding.

Guus Dix is Lecturer in Social Philosophy at the Department of Philosophy of Maastricht University, the Netherlands. He studied philosophy and sociology at the University of Amsterdam. His thesis 'Governing by carrot and stick: a genealogy of the incentive' studies the mutual reinforcement of the production of social scientific knowledge about individuals and groups and the practices and institutions in which they are governed. In particular, he explores, from a Foucauldian perspective, the development of the 'incentive' as an object of knowledge and technique of power from the end of the nineteenth until the beginning of the twenty-first centuries.

Susi Geiger is an Associate Professor of Marketing at the University College Dublin Smurfit School of Business. Educated in Germany, France and Ireland, her research interests span the areas of economic sociology, industrial marketing and sales. At the moment, she is involved in a large-scale knowledge exchange project with a number of health technology companies, in a social enterprise research project and in an emerging markets project, considering issues of market making and market shaping in each setting. Susi has published widely in her areas of interest and sits on the editorial boards of *Industrial Marketing Management, Consumption Markets and Culture* and *Valuation Studies.*

Debbie Harrison is an Associate Professor of Inter-Organisational Relationships at BI Norwegian Business School, Oslo. Her research interests include the organizing of business networks, inter-organizational strategizing, and market design. Her recent research projects, focused on the intersection of innovation and market studies, include environmental equipment markets in the maritime industry. She has published her work in journals such as *Industrial Marketing Management, Research Policy* and *Journal of Business Research.*

Jürgen Hauber is project manager at the alliance of the associations for the promotion of schools in Tübingen, Germany. His research is focused on the practical organizing of different forms of coordination such as markets, networks and supply chains. In his thesis he examined the market practices to organize an exchange in interlinked markets. Currently, he works on the coordination of local networks to improve the cultural education of educationally disadvantaged children and teenagers.

Linus Johansson Krafve is a PhD Candidate at the Department of Thematic Studies – Technology and Social Change, Linköping University, Sweden. His research interests concern economic valuation practices in the public sector and their effects on the relations in and between politics, adminis-tration and citizens. His dissertation is about the design of a primary care market in a Swedish county council.

Hans Kjellberg is an Associate Professor of Marketing at the Stockholm School of Economics, Sweden. His research focuses on the practical organizing of markets. His work on market practices includes journal arti-cles in *Marketing Theory, Industrial Marketing Management and Journal of Cultural Economy*, the co-edited volume *Reconnecting Marketing to Markets* (2010) and the co-authored volume *Marketing Shares, Sharing Markets* (2012). Current projects include an interdisciplinary research program on the digitalization of consumption.

Alexandre Mallard is Director of the Centre de Sociologie de l'Innovation at the Ecole des Mines ParisTech, France. He carried out his first research in the field of sociology of science and technology. From 1997 to 2009, he worked at the social science laboratory of France Telecom Research and Development. He has led projects and surveys investigating the uses of Information and Communication Technology in the professional realm. He has conducted research on the study of selling activities, on very small businesses and on the rise of network interactions in the corporate environ-ment. His current research interests concern the social inscription of inno-vation at the crossroads between economic sociology and political science.

Katy Mason is a Reader, Department of Markets, Marketing and Management, Lancaster University Management School, UK and an AIM Management Practices Fellow. Katy's research focuses on how managers make and shape markets, the market-making devices they use to enrol others, and the practices that create and transform market boundaries. Through a number of research projects, she has studied the power of market-making devices such as business models, market repre-sentations and expectations. Recent research into commissioning for the provision of UK health and social care, and market-making at the Bottom of the Pyramid (BoP) investigates how markets are imagined and made real. Katy's work has been published in *Journal of Management Studies, Industrial Marketing Management, Long Range Planning, Management Learning, European Journal of Marketing* and *Journal of Marketing Management*.

Winfred Ikiring Onyas is a Research Associate in the Department of Marketing at Lancaster University Management School, UK. Her research focuses on how markets and global value chains are shaped in developing countries. In particular, Winfred researches on the sites where markets overlap, involving multiple and often conflicting efforts to organize and shape them. Winfred is currently researching on mobile phone-enabled financial services in Africa. Her work is published in *Industrial Marketing Management*.

Chantal Ruppert-Winkel is head of the research group Renewable Energy Regions at the Centre for Renewable Energy University of Freiburg, Germany. She has a background in forest sciences and wrote her PhD on community forestry. Her research interests are the analysis of sustainable resource use at local and regional levels; socio-economic analyses of actor networks, institutions, organizational structures and leadership; and inter- and transdisciplinary research on the socio-ecological use of renewable energies. In 2011, she had a ten-month research stay at the Department of Environmental Science, Policy and Management, University of California, Berkeley.

Annmarie Ryan is a Lecturer in Marketing at the University of Limerick, Ireland. Her research interests span both an IMP approach to business marketing as well as the relationship between business and society from a more market studies perspective. Her work is published in *Industrial Marketing Management, Marketing Theory, Journal of Organisational Change Management* and *Journal of Marketing Management*. She has presented at a wide range of conferences and workshops, including the IMP conference, European Group of Organizational Studies Conference and Interdisciplinary Market Studies Workshop.

Robert Spencer is Head of the Marketing Department and Head of the Markets and Consumption research cluster at KEDGE Business School, France. He holds a DEA in Business Studies and a PhD from the University of Uppsala, Sweden. He is a member of the IMP (Industrial Marketing and Purchasing) research group, and sits on the editorial review board of several major international journals (*Industrial Marketing Management, Consumption, Markets and Culture, Marketing Intelligence and Planning, Journal of Purchasing and Supply Management*). His research activities cover a variety of fields, including market studies from a market making and shaping perspective, consumption, industrial marketing and purchasing, sustainable sourcing, and network theory.

Ingrid Stigzelius is a PhD candidate at Stockholm School of Economics within the Sustainability Research Group (SuRe), Sweden. Her area of research is green consumption, with a particular focus on green food practices and the role of the consumer in the creation of organic food markets. Ingrid holds a Licentiate degree from the Department of Economics at SLU in Uppsala, where she studied the implementation of social and environmental standards.

Acknowledgements

Markets have become a fashionable topic of conversation both in public and academic discourse. While public attention perhaps has focused on financial markets in particular as a result of the turmoil in these markets in recent years, academics of many different disciplines have shown an interest in a wide variety of market contexts and organizing issues. In this book we emphasize the organizing of 'concerned markets'. We present a collection of ten chapters that cover a variety of highly topical 'concerned' market settings, such as health care, education and environmental markets, but which share one key similarity: they are all based on rich empirical material illustrating powerfully the many conflicts of values and interests inherent in these markets.

These chapters are invited and revised papers from the 2012 2nd EIASM *Interdisciplinary Market Studies Workshop* held in Dublin, which was organized by the editors. The theme of 'concerned markets' emerged out of our effort to select individual contributions from the workshop that fit well together while offering an interesting variation in terms of empirical sites of inquiry. All of the chapters have benefited greatly from the insightful comments of participants at the Workshop, and subsequently from the referees who provided critical, developmental comments for each during the review process. We would like to thank the following referees for all of their work: Andreas Brekke, Kimberly Chong, Liliana Doganova, Sophie Dubuisson-Quellier, John Finch, C-F. Helgesson, Thomas Hoholm, Donncha Kavanagh, Sara Lindemann, Kevin Mellet, Per Ingvar Olsen, Thomas Reverdy, Philip Roscoe, Elena Simakova and Lionel Sitz. We would also like to thank the people at Edward Elgar Publishing and particularly Francine O'Sullivan for their belief that 'concerned markets' are a topic worth exploring. Finally, we would like to extend our warm gratitude to Franck Cochoy who took on the considerable task of reading all chapters and crafting a most insightful concluding commentary to this volume.

Susi Geiger
Debbie Harrison
Hans Kjellberg
Alexandre Mallard

1. Being concerned about markets

Susi Geiger, Debbie Harrison, Hans Kjellberg and Alexandre Mallard[1]

Building markets is one of the most ordinary ways to produce society. This assertion seems both obvious and controversial. It is obvious because it quite simply accounts for what we see all around us, namely the pervasiveness of economic logic in the domain of social life. The situations in which market transactions intervene in our relationships with other people and in the course of our everyday activities multiply: shopping in malls, city centres or online is an ordinary leisure activity; students are increasingly advised to consider university education as an investment decision and universities compete by demonstrating the pay-off of a degree in salary terms; our personal conversations on social network platforms fuel the constitution of marketing databases; professional sports clubs increasingly resemble multinational companies; dinner conversation over organ donation markets or whether and how surrogate mothers should be paid for their services are commonplace; and health care issues have moved into lifestyle and technology markets, to name but a few examples.

But the assertion is also controversial. This is because to a large extent the economy and society are still considered as two complementary but nonetheless different dimensions of human affairs. The clash between social values and the economic order is a matter of ordinary perception, but also of disciplinary battle; witness, for instance, the fight between liberal economists striving for the implementation of pure competitive market coordination in all possible domains of activity and social science researchers insisting on the primacy of social order over the logic of economic transactions. The return on investment of 'human capital', as considered by Gary Becker, strongly conflicts with Karl Polanyi's conception of markets as 'embedded' in pre-existing social institutions and with Mark Granovetter's weak embeddedness position, where economic action is entangled in ongoing social relations.

Recently, a number of researchers from different academic disciplines have attempted to give deeper meaning and content to the idea that markets produce society and to go beyond its paradoxical or polemical flavour, which has in the past often led into dualist fights (Cochoy, 2012). This book gathers a series of research studies investigating in particular the emergence and dynamics of 'concerned markets': markets where, simply put, the economic and the social writ large are intricately entwined.

We propose the notion of 'concerned markets' to debate market configurations that take into account the various concerns that are associated with the unfolding of economic transactions. The vocabulary of concerns originates from the domain of political science. Such notions as 'political concern' or 'public concern' are used to point to the questions that, in modern democracies, are liable to arouse the attention of citizens or of the public authorities representing them. In contemporary dictionaries (for instance in the Oxford Thesaurus, 2nd Edition), the definitions proposed for the verb 'to concern' raise awareness of three different dimensions: (i) refer, relate to; (ii) affect, influence; (iii) worry, trouble. In markets, concerns are those things and situations that – for better or worse – are related to us, can affect us and worry us in the current context of liberal market democracies.

Political scientists have long stressed the importance of the processes through which one 'becomes concerned' by a given question. John Dewey's (1927) pragmatist perspective taught us that these processes are constitutive of the emergence of public issues, and, subsequently, of the very possibility of democratic order. In this context it is important to distinguish, as does Andrew Barry (2002), between *politics* as a set of techniques, practices and institutions, and *the political* as an index of the spaces for disagreements and negotiations.

The contemporary era, where such disagreements and negotiations engage with the complex and sometimes unexpected consequences of scientific and technological development, calls for a reformulation of the place of these processes in social and economic organizing (Latour, 2007).[2] Bruno Latour (2004) argues that the possibility to solve the problems posed by the ecological crisis that we witness will be measured by our capacity to understand the differences between the 'matters of fact' and the 'matters of concern' that characterize contemporary innovation. In other words, we should by now be fully aware that the entities that science and technology produce do not have distinctive frontiers and identities, that they cannot be clearly detached from their unexpected consequences, and that their effects on our lives are less characterized by their 'social impacts' than by the diversity of connections that they develop with other entities substantiating our everyday existence. In the indeterminacy of matters of concern, the political, the social and the economic fuse.

The extension of markets in the social sphere is an important dimension of this contemporary context, not only because markets are the primary vehicles through which challenging innovations circulate, but also because more generally, the proliferation of marketable – and marketed – goods requires an investigation of the relations we develop with them. Gradually, we learn that we are never completely devoid of the goods spawned by our (post)-modernity: we have to understand how we are related to them, how they affect us and how they trigger our worries – or how we are concerned by them. As Michel Callon (2007) showed, the production of 'matters of concern' is an ordinary consequence of the functioning of markets, and by no way a failure – to allude to the term used by economists deploring the encroachment of social and political issues into the economic arena – expressing their pathological drifts.

Rather than simply replacing or overlaying social bonds with economic transactions, markets initiate a plurality of social relations of a new kind, bearing matters of concern that should be carefully monitored. They invite us neither to reject the economic dynamics of markets nor to try to purify them from any remaining social relation, but rather to search for modalities of organization that are all the more relevant for the implementation of market exchanges. As a whole, we believe that moving the 'concern for matters of concern' from political science and risk analysis towards market studies demonstrates less the domination of an uncontrollable economic order than the increasingly intricate connections between social, scientific, political and economic issues.

In this book we collectively take this perspective of the entangling of the scientific, political, social and economic realms in and around markets as a starting point and explore a number of market configurations that are emblematic of the contemporary necessity to carefully articulate these entanglements.

THE PERSPECTIVE OF 'CONCERNED MARKETS' IN THE FIELD OF MARKET STUDIES

It is of course possible to develop the topic of concerned markets from a number of analytical perspectives that are prevalent in contemporary studies of markets. 'Market studies' refers to a large set of research works that have been carried out in the recent period by scholars from several academic disciplines, including marketing, sociology, economics, philosophy, history, political science, anthropology and so on.[3] Among other shared assumptions, these researchers acknowledge the importance of markets in contemporary society, but do not consider their development as a natural movement that would indicate an evolution of human history towards an inevitable economic order, nor as a testimony of the superior efficiency of market logics as compared with other modalities of organization of social life. Instead, they start from the idea that markets do not emerge as natural realities. Their establishment and functioning requires specific organizational processes enacted by a plurality of actors, which implies the integration of various stakes, practices, norms and values (see for instance the edited volumes by Araujo et al., 2010; Callon et al., 2007; Zwick and Cayla, 2011; Beckert and Aspers, 2011; or the special issues edited by Araujo et al., 2008 and Geiger et al., 2012). It is through the study of these heterogeneous modalities of organization that it is possible to account for the contribution of markets to the development of society.

We can now trace how we consider the notion of 'concerned markets' to complement and connect to a select number of the research trajectories that are part of the domain of market studies. As an exercise of mapping intellectual thought, we are by no means claiming our discussion to be exhaustive. Rather, we have been deliberately selective in our choice of comparators and refrain from drawing parallels from our notion of 'concerned' to other broadly economic and/or sociological frameworks emanating from somewhat different sets of ontological and epistemological assumptions.[4]

There are four research trajectories in particular that we elaborate upon. These are the Actor-Network Theory-inspired conception of markets as socio-technical *agencements* by Michel Callon and colleagues (e.g. Callon, 1998a; Çalişkan and Callon, 2009; 2010; Callon et al., 2002; Callon and Muniesa, 2005; Cochoy, 2012); Boltanski and Thévenot's (2006) theory of justification and orders of worth; David Stark's (2009) heterarchic organizing; and Neil Fligstein's (1996, 2001) work on markets-as-politics. The three different dictionary meanings of the verb 'to concern' that we mentioned above (refer, affect, worry) are used to organize the discussion.

Concern: Refer, Relate to – Markets Uncut

In all four research trajectories, the starting point is the observation that many contemporary markets differ vastly from the neoclassical market model of the determination of prices, outputs and incomes through supply and demand. This is an ideal state of relative stability that Callon (1998b) refers to as 'cool' situations. Arguably, in such situations there is no relating or referring to; buyers and sellers enter and leave the market as strangers, products and services exist only as disentangled goods in predetermined market spaces, and the boundaries of the market insulate the market space from any outside interference. Markets thus become 'spaces of calculability' (Callon, 1998a, p. 20).

Callon shows just how much investment is involved in making a market correspond closely to this neoclassical model, and just how difficult – if not impossible – it is to maintain it, using the example of Garcia's strawberry market. The effort is mainly one of framing, which Callon (ibid.) explains acts by 'allowing for the rejection of networks of relations, and thus by constructing an arena in which each entity [was] disconnected from the others.' He highlights that framing is an ongoing achievement; that is, the networks interrupted and the relations cut produce overflows, and markets will only remain 'cool' if these overflows can be either internalized or disregarded as being 'outside' the market.

As many empirical accounts have demonstrated subsequently, relations and networks in and around markets are not that easily cut. This is especially the case in situations in which multiple actors with diverse values, expectations and aims are concerned enough to 'concern themselves' with the market in question (with apologies for the tautology). If such actors proceed to relate to the market by making some of the market's overflows count, a 'hot' situation ensues (cf. Callon, 1998b). In a 'hot' market, the very core of the market's functioning – the 'economization', or disentangling of the product or service bought and sold from prior or subsequent relations in order to make it calculable – is called into question. Only significant investments can 'cool down' such situations and allow them to be negotiated in the 'orderly' way typically associated with spaces of calculability. The notion of concern works well to bring together the different issues involved in this dynamic process of heating up (through relating) and cooling down (through unmaking relations).

Similarly, we suggest that the notion of concern as relating speaks to a central issue in the work of Boltanski and Thévenot (2006, pp. 34–5) regarding the relationship between agreement and discord: namely, what it is that creates the need for justification. Here, cool markets, in the Callonian sense discussed above, imply that matters of agreement and discord are successfully handled via negotiations over price between direct counterparts (or in the extreme case, are relegated to the workings of the price mechanism). A concerned market, on the other hand, is one in which such direct counterparts are not that easily identified, to say nothing of the possibility of them reaching agreement. Instead, the co-existence of some particular actors cannot be regarded simply as a matter of coincidence, or their respective doings as largely independent of each other. In short, a concerned market is a market in which something that has previously been regarded as a mere contingency is recast as part of a situation of a defined nature – that is, a situation where actors become related. This, in turn, sets processes of justification in motion.

Following Boltanski and Thévenot's logic, depending on who or what is related, different orders of worth may be invoked as part of justification processes. Concerned markets are thus no longer bound by the particular order of worth associated with markets, in which competition occupies the central role for resolving conflicts. Instead, multiple methods of reaching agreement or encompassing disagreement come into play, such as scientific inquiry, political negotiations, legal proceedings, or civic ideas. Rather than the orderly exchange of well-defined products and services within an established infrastructure, these multiple engagements result in struggles where actors tap into different principles of justice or explanations of what is good.

What is at stake in these struggles is the delineation of some *common good* that can be used to establish a compromise (Boltanski and Thévenot, 2006, p. 336). By suggesting what and for whom something is 'common', the notion of concern as referring or relating to may be used to address how the search for such a common good and the compromise between different orders of worth is set in motion. While Boltanski and Thévenot (2006) acknowledge that several orders of worth (for instance the market, the industrial and the civic) do co-exist in many contemporary markets, raising concerns typically involves challenging this co-existence on specific counts. For example, how to shift a specific issue from being resolved with reference to the 'industrial' order of worth to being resolved with reference to that of the 'market'?

Concern: Affect, Influence – Markets, Heterarchies, Hybrid Forums

The second use of the verb 'concern' addresses how controversies around markets are potentially resolved. Concerned markets can be seen as an opportunity for coalescing, for reorganizing, for making markets better, more just and, perhaps, also more efficient. As we noted above, Boltanski and Thévenot (2006) invoke the notion of *compromise* when orders of worth clash, emphasizing that such compromises are arrived at through tests, or proofs of worth. Fligstein (2001), on the other hand, highlights power struggles and the *domination* of one group over others as the major explanation for the emergence of contextually and historically dependent market orders. Rather than the notions of compromise or domination, we prefer a perspective in which actors attempt to make multiple concerns count, through the continuous process of relating ('it's your concern as well'), troubling ('economizing in its current form is not good enough') and influencing ('you need to take our concerns into account').

The four theoretical trajectories of market studies we mentioned above provide two indications of how markets could be organized in order to build concern into the heart of the market space. Callon et al. (2009) describe *hybrid forums*; dialogical spaces where matters of concern can be identified and debated, and where they can be made measurable and calculable (or economized). Callon et al. recognize that as much as the market often leads to exclusion and inequity, it can also be a powerful space of encounter between contradictory interests if organized in such a way that it is open to the voices emanating from hybrid forums.

Callon (2009) invokes the notion of *civilizing* for this ongoing process of opening up and restabilizing market frames. Civilizing is a particular form of contest and disruption, which typically contrasts some conception of a more moral or ethical market practice with incumbent practices, and endeavours to shape the way in which actors frame a particular market and qualify its goods in socio-technological terms. This takes us beyond Fligstein's (1996) assumption that market actors direct actions toward the creation of stable worlds, while change emanates from external shocks. While raising concerns is about endogenizing issues by challenging the current way of conflict resolution, civilizing markets is about organizing the handling of such concerns. A civilized market, from Callon's (2009, p. 541) perspective, is one 'that organizes the discussion of the matters of concern produced by its functioning and the framings/overflowing that it entails.' Civilizing as an ongoing activity is important in all markets as it puts existing socio-technical arrangements 'under trial' (Callon, 2007), which in turn allows these arrangements to be adapted, adjusted and reformulated.

Another related way of resolving situations of controversy can be considered by drawing on Stark's (2009) ideas on *heterarchies* as an organizing principle to establish heterogeneous criteria for what is a good in a market. Heterarchies are about establishing 'local settlements', or an order of worth for a given market that is able to handle more than one common good. One central challenge facing such attempts is how to relate different common goods to each other. Two ways of handling this are to *prioritize* (for example 'only organizations that fulfil the following criteria will be allowed to compete in the market') or to *translate* ('what is the economic value of biodiversity').[5] These alternatives, however, also signal the often significant and ongoing investments needed in order for a market to be able to 'organize dissonance'. Making concerns count in markets is never achieved once and for all but influences every market exchange afresh.

Concern: Trouble, Worry – Controversies Ongoing

As the chapters assembled in this book witness, the search for the common good and for a governance regime that allows this common good to be realized in markets is not always easy. Many of the empirical sites reported represent highly controversial situations. This is hardly surprising, given that concerning, that is relating and affecting, heats markets up. On the one hand, the boundary between that which is taken into account and that which is not allows markets to function in the first place. On the other, that very boundary is also the origin of matters of concern (Callon et al., 2009; Latour, 2004). At the market boundary, these matters of concern, unstable as they may be, represent a rallying point for the concerned groups, who can start troubling the market space by making matters of concern visible to other market actors, and making themselves visible (and, as spokespersons, audible) through the matters of concern.[6] Boltanski and Thévenot (2006) speak of 'denunciations' when actors destabilize and trigger controversy concerning the legitimacy of the situation by drawing on an order of worth that had not been implicated in the situation previously.

If markets or their effects are troubling to someone, by virtue of it affecting them, efforts are made to relate others to this, in order to have them troubled as well, which is likely to highlight more issues by virtue of the way these others are related, how they influence others, and so on. Conversely, such efforts of concerning also necessarily serve to configure 'the other'; those elements, entities, actors and so on that either have little to be concerned about, or have reason to assume a diametrically opposed position.

It is hardly surprising, under such circumstances, that markets assume an explicitly political flavour, as emphasized, among others, by Fligstein (1996). His work on the political facet of market shaping has underscored that market orders are likely to reflect the interests of powerful groups. The specific institutions that he suggests are necessary preconditions for markets to exist, such as property rights, governance structures, conceptions of control, rules of exchange, are never neutral, but favour certain groups (Fligstein, 1996, p.658). Here, the notion of concern offers a way of appreciating this process without starting with 'powerful groups'; instead, the process of concerning produces potentially powerful groups. The classic Actor Network Theory concept of the 'macro actor' comes to mind here; however, the notion of concern emphasizes that there is no inevitability as to who this 'macro actor' may be, or what shape it may take; instead, the notion of concern helps us understand what goes together: concerns form groups – even if they are unlikely alliances formed by being subject to common influences.

OVERVIEW OF THE CHAPTERS

All of the chapters in this book share one key trait: they are based on solid empirical material which exemplifies clashes of interest or orders of worth in a variety of market settings or contexts.[7] Notwithstanding their diversity, all the market settings covered are highly topical. Specifically, the chapters take us to such settings as the upstream market for coffee in Uganda (Onyas and Ryan), the market for primary health care in a Swedish county (Johansson Krafve), the budding global market for environmentally labelled palm oil (d'Antone and Spencer), the markets implicated in Swedish consumers' efforts to engage in 'green' food practices (Kjellberg and Stigzelius), the introduction of market incentives in the Dutch education system (Dix), the European market for functional foods (Azimont and Araujo), the bioenergy market in Germany (Hauber and Ruppert-Winkel) and the efforts to design bottom-of-the-pyramid markets in the Sundarban islands (Chakrabarti and Mason).

Broadly in line with our three notions of concern discussed in the last section, these empirical market settings illustrate three facets of the term 'concerned markets': (i) Concerning as relating: organizing the direct transactions between market actors; (ii) Concerning as affecting: orienting market transaction so as to handle externalities for other actors, which do not take part directly in the market transactions, but nonetheless experience positive or negative consequences of these transactions; and (iii) Concerning as resolving controversies: making markets governable, that is to say, articulating economic and political regulation of markets.

Concerning in the Organizing of Transactions

The four chapters that address the first use of the term 'concerned' take up the market settings of subsistence, environment, food and bottom-of-the-pyramid (BoP). The first chapter under this heading, 'Credible qualifications: the case of functional foods' by Frank Azimont and Luis Araujo, addresses how product qualifications and the credibility of those qualifications are established in markets. The authors consider the emerging field of functional foods and the efforts in attempting to establish this as a product category. The standards required to establish health claims in functional foods bring this category closer to pharmaceuticals than food, but this also throws up a whole range of additional qualification and credibility issues. Standards and their implementation become a live issue for companies and regulators alike.

The chapter describes how one large food multinational attempted to develop a market for functional foods, in parallel with more conventional foods and cognate areas such as medical nutrition. The empirical analysis traces how this manufacturer addressed the development and marketing of functional foods and how it invested in creating an infrastructure to produce and use scientific evidence in its efforts to position itself in this market. These efforts, though, produced a clash of different orders of worth within the case company, which eventually led to a significant decrease in its commitment to the functional foods market. The chapter demonstrates just how complex and contested new qualification processes can be when they are not easily reconciled with existing scientific, business and marketing practices.

The second chapter with this theme is 'Designing better markets for people at the bottom of the pyramid: bottom-up market design', by Ronika Chakrabarti and Katy Mason. The authors problematize the issue of market design by questioning how market interventions are designed in Bottom of the Pyramid (BoP) markets. The starting point is that this market context turns market design from a top-down phenomenon to one in which the tension between shifting from the context of 'subsistence' to 'BoP markets' to 'markets as bundles of practices and connected systems' requires multiple stabilization efforts. The chapter presents findings from a two-year ethnographic study of the market-making efforts of villagers, NGOs, scientists and academics following a tsunami in the Sundarban islands, which removed the traditional income sources from inhabitants. In so doing, the authors explore the practices that enable people at the BoP to participate in markets and engage in a process of inquiry that brings benefits for their communities. By using an analysis tool based on Dewey's (1938) five-step inquiry process of situation-problem-solutions-reasoning-experiment, the chapter shows how multiple actors worked together to redesign a market 'bottom-up'.

The third chapter under this heading is 'Articulating matters of concern in markets: (en)tangling goods, market agencies and overflows' by Winfred Ikiring Onyas and Annmarie Ryan. In this chapter the authors highlight the process of articulating matters of concern in relation to how a market works in terms of how well it accounts for the multiple entanglements of the product that is subject to exchange. Specifically, as no market framing can be all-encompassing, the question becomes how a particular overflow, perceived by one group of actors, can be turned into a matter of concern which serves to direct the development of the market?

Based on an ethnographic study of an effort to reorganize exchanges in the up-stream Ugandan coffee market, the chapter analyses the multiple framings of coffee and how one group of market actors, the coffee farmers, seeks to articulate concerns about the way prices are set in this market. The authors' account particularly highlights how different actors respectively seek to render visible, handle and exploit disagreements concerning what entanglements/qualities to take into account when valuing a market object. Importantly, their analysis suggests that tracing how a matter of concern is articulated and responded to is a fruitful way of studying ongoing market shaping activities.

The fourth chapter, Hans Kjellberg and Ingrid Stigzelius's work about 'Doing green: environmental concerns and the realization of green values in everyday food practices', focuses on how individual consumers stabilize multiple, competing concerns in their day-to-day efforts to 'do green', that is realize environmental values, in relation to food. The chapter investigates how such attempts to 'do green' impact and are impacted on by practices related to the production, distribution and consumption of food. Three complementary case studies are used to describe and analyse explicit efforts to produce green values in different food-related practices. The cases encompass collective food production, online food retailing and efforts to educate consumers in 'green' cooking practices; three sites where consumers in various ways seek to 'do green'.

The authors' analysis shows how consumers are motivated by multiple concerns, traces how the tensions across such concerns are being balanced and how other actors attempt to influence consumers' attempts to realize green values by providing particular scripts. Finally, they highlight the central role of monitoring practices in assessing the extent to which you 'do green', underscoring the trade-off between convenient yet limited rules of thumb and more comprehensive but cumbersome monitoring procedures.

Concerning by Handling Externalities

There are two chapters which relate to this use of the term 'concerned' and these focus on the food and environment market settings. First, Simona d'Antone and Robert Spencer's chapter addresses 'Concerns and market-ization: the case of sustainable palm oil'. The authors examine the case of palm oil and the original attempts to organize palm oil markets through the Roundtable for Sustainable Palm Oil (RSPO) to investigate how it is possible to integrate the concerns of sustainable development in the construction of markets.

The RSPO initiative has grown into a large collective gathering of hundreds of actors engaged in the definition of the criteria for a more sustainable palm oil and has spawned labels and certification schemes enforcing these criteria. The Roundtable is devoted to facilitating the inscription of environmental concerns in the functioning of the market by creating a political space where a vast array of stakeholders can participate in the definition of the characteristics of goods entering in the market. As such, it replaces the blind logic of transactions and their aggregation by a process of formulating, making explicit and debatable, and negotiating concerns.

D'Antone and Spencer's analysis shows how there is nothing evident in the functioning of this system. On the one hand, it requires strong governance mechanisms in order to be efficient in the enforcement of the most adapted and desirable concerns. On the other hand, it contributes to transform the way in which actors calculate and frame their market actions. Thus, one of the consequences of the RSPO is increasing the multiplicity of market versions, including the emergence of other market spaces structured by actors, which do not consider the concerns supported by the RSPO legitimate or relevant. As a whole, this chapter suggests that the implementation of a hybrid forum enabling the integration of sustainability concerns in the market is in itself contested, and in fact leads to a deep transformation of the calculative spaces through which actors consider their participation in the market.

The second chapter here is 'Engaging diverging interests through pricing: the case of maize for bioenergy production in Germany' by Jürgen Hauber and Chantal Ruppert-Winkel. In this chapter Hauber and Ruppert-Winkel conceptualize the organization of markets in general and pricing practices in particular as a way to reconcile diverging interests, not just across a range of actors within one market but also across several overlapping markets. The authors address the efforts made in aligning the diverging interests of farmers in organizing the market exchange of corn as a substrate for the production of bioenergy in Germany. While on the one hand farmers as sellers of corn are interested in a mode of exchange that guarantees flexibility, on the other hand the buyers of corn are interested in a stable mode of exchange.

Farmers have two markets to choose from when selling their corn: the food market and the bioenergy market. Each of these two markets would allow farmers to realize one interest in particular while downplaying the other interest. The market actors use their position to influence pricing formulas in the bioenergy market that take reference from the corn food market to balance both interests. The prices for corn can be seen as a compromise that is enacted through the process of pricing, as conflicting interests are at least temporarily resolved through pricing practices.

Concerning by Making Markets Governable

The two chapters that address this third use of the term 'concerned' take up the market settings of education and health. The first chapter under this heading is 'Expressing concerns over the incentive as a public policy device' by Guus Dix. In this chapter Dix deals with an issue that is of primary importance for the understanding of marketization processes and the integration of public concerns in markets: the penetration of market mechanisms in public services. The empirical material centres on the introduction of monetary incentives in education, specifically a reform conducted at the end of the 2000s in the Netherlands. It questions to what extent an activity that is traditionally considered as external to the logics of the economy be redefined, transformed, improved or deteriorated with the infusion of market processes in its organization.

Dix shows that this reform gave rise to the public expression of a whole series of different meanings and values by three categories of actors: economists who, drawing on their scientific expertise, had conceptualized monetary incentives in the frame of principal–agent theory, and expressed the potential advantages and risks of the reform; political actors in the Dutch government in this period, who supported the reform in the name of a transformation of the organization but also of the culture of the public sector of education; and teachers' representatives and trade unions who opposed the reform, stressing its incompatibility with traditional values of education such as the spirit of team work and equality. As a whole, this chapter illustrates the process of interweaving market practices and the political concerns they engage through the dynamics of public controversy.

Linus Johansson Krafve's work, 'Marketization by the (rule)book: concern for market and public values in primary care', deals with how different values are enacted in the process of organizing a market through regulatory efforts. As part of market reform efforts, policy-makers often assign particular importance to free choice and competitive neutrality as means towards values such as efficiency and quality. This also applies to market reforms in the provision of public services such as health care. But are free choice and competitive neutrality only means towards such ends, or are they also ends in themselves?

The author attends to the practical work of regulating free choice and competitive neutrality in a primary care market in Sweden. By studying the work undertaken in one Swedish county council to formulate and subsequently revise a 'rulebook' for authorization of care centres, Johansson Krafve is able to gain detailed knowledge about the market regulatory process and the values enacted therein. The rulebook is suggested to frame free choice and competitive neutrality in the studied market and guide market action by establishing a concrete system for reimbursement. Interestingly, however, while this system of reimbursement is fundamentally revised, the values of free choice and competitive neutrality remain as central values. Besides raising important issues concerning the pliability of market devices, Johansson Krafve's chapter provides an insightful perspective on how particular values can be made to matter in markets.

Lastly, in the final chapter, Franck Cochoy offers a commentary and reflection on the idea of concerned markets. He sees the notion of 'concerned' markets as an alternative conceptualization of the interplay of the social and the economic to those of 'interested' markets, where the self-interest of *homo economicus* prevails, and 'contested' markets, where *homo moralis* fiercely resists market mechanisms. He returns to the value of reflexivity in markets: concern, across the triptych of relating, affecting and worrying that this book traces, ultimately signals that, as Cochoy puts it, 'ordinary actors are not just object-like agents equipped with nature-like interest', but that they can – and should! – be reflective of the potentially transformative power of their involvement in markets.

THERE ARE NO MARKETS WITHOUT CONCERNS

In sum, the empirical chapters and our earlier analysis suggest the bold conclusion that there are no markets without concerns. Each of the eight empirical chapters exemplifies an empirical market setting that is to a greater or lesser extent 'hot', where there is a need to organize and govern through taking into account multiple concerns. Importantly, however, the chapters also illustrate that market organization, design and governance is not (only) the business of 'macro actors', the State or some other all-powerful entity. Across the chapters, we see teachers, farmers, salespersons, scientists, consumers and even the destitute concern themselves with the ways those markets in which they are involved are organized.

Each of these 'hot' settings thus illustrates processes and practices that are recognizable to most of us and that are not necessarily confined to highly controversial markets. We would argue that, perhaps to different degrees, the clashes of concerns debated in the chapters can be seen even in the most mundane and ubiquitous markets. There are examples in the gradual move of more and more formerly uncontroversial foodstuffs into the 'concerned markets' corner, such as foods with high levels of fat or sugar, or the increasing need for clothes manufacturers to make supply chain issues regarding sustainability, animal welfare or worker conditions explicit. With the emergence of 'big data' available to market actors in a whole range of markets including those of 'the self' (such as social media), concerns have spread into the very fabric of our daily lives and further blurred the distinction between the social and the economic, the 'micro' and the 'macro', the 'matter of fact' and the 'matter of concern'. In other words, this is the era of the 'concerned market' as the norm, not the exception, and we are all concerned.

We would hope that future empirical research will take the notion of concern and the insights from the various chapters contained in this volume into the analysis of an even greater gamut of markets, including mundane or 'everyday' market sites. Such studies might address the role of various market actors such as regulators, politicians, citizens and the media (social and otherwise) to frame what concerns are made explicit and how; the role of certain types of market professionals in building different orders of worth into their products, services and market-framing activities (as highlighted for instance in Zwick and Cayla, 2011); or the role of regulators, politicians and other actors to make concerns count in markets via governance structures and hybrid forums.

To this last point, we would like to stress again that the proliferation of concern means that markets need to make space for concerns. We are, collectively, required to allow markets to become increasingly reflexive. While the ideal market may indeed be capable of handling its own overflows, the important distinction between the economists' notion of 'internalization of externalities' and our notion of concerns is that – as the chapters in this volume so aptly illustrate – we do not see 'the market' as a stable superstructure but instead as continually emergent. This emergence means that there is no inevitability in the way markets 'happen' but that each individual actor has a means of shaping the market by making their own concerns matter. In short, in any market groups can make themselves and their concerns count; not only as disruptions or disjunctures, but as opportunities for relating, for balancing, for finding compromises. Through making their concerns count, they can change the market, if only by creating a greater space for reflexivity. In our view, the resounding message to be drawn from the present volume is just that: concerns matter in markets, and it is our collective task to make them matter.

NOTES

1. Authors appear in alphabetical order.
2. On the relation between this beginning of the century pragmatist perspective and the analysis of political stakes in the contemporary period, as it is nowadays informed by Science and Technology Studies, see Marres (2007).
3. As an academic field, market studies could be said to be the ongoing outcome of the meeting between Science and Technology Studies, economic sociology and (critical) management studies. This would capture an important origin, but would also unduly reduce the multiple disciplinary backgrounds of researchers active in the field. Since 2010, we have been involved in organizing a biannual interdisciplinary workshop dedicated to market studies, through which we have had the benefit of exchanging ideas with political economists, economic historians, geographers, marketing and organization scholars, sociologists, philosophers, anthropologists, STS scholars, to mention a few.
4. We would count stakeholder theory (e.g. Donaldson and Preston, 1995; Hill and Jones, 1992), the dialectics of community and markets (Gudeman, 2008), and markets as socio-cognitive structures (Rosa et al., 1999) among these frameworks. Due to major differences in starting points, we have also excluded several economics approaches from our comparison, including institutional (Williamson, 1975, 1991) and evolutionary economics (Nelson and Winter, 1982), as well as more recent work on market design (Roth, 2009).

5. There is an obvious parallel here to Mol's (2002) work on how incoherent sources of knowledge can be handled through processes of privileging or calibrating (see also Sjögren, 2006).
6. Matters of concern are of course those matters that concerned markets deal with most often. This also demonstrates that concern does not have to be a purely ideological or value-driven issue; it can equally have a material basis. This is powerfully demonstrated in environmental markets, where for instance plastic bottles or shipwrecks act as visible and complex matters of concern and rallying points for those who are concerned (Hawkins, 2011; Gregson et al., 2013).
7. The chapters are the final selection from invited papers from the 2nd EIASM *Interdisciplinary Market Studies Workshop* held in Dublin in June 2012, which was organized by the editors. The theme of 'concerned markets' emerged out of the editors' efforts to select individual contributions from the workshop that fit well together while offering an interesting variation in terms of empirical sites of inquiry. We would like to thank the workshop participants as well as the reviewers of the chapters for their constructive comments and suggestions on the papers and evolving chapters.

REFERENCES

Araujo, Luis, John H. Finch and Hans Kjellberg (eds) (2010), *Reconnecting Marketing to Markets*, Oxford: Oxford University Press.

Araujo, Luis, Hans Kjellberg and Robert Spencer (2008), 'Market practices and forms: introduction to the special issue', *Marketing Theory*, **8**(1), 5–14.

Barry, Andrew (2002), 'The anti-political economy', *Economy and Society*, **31**(2), 268–84.

Beckert, Jens and Patrik Aspers (eds) (2011), *The Worth of Goods: Valuation and Pricing in the Economy*, Oxford: Oxford University Press.

Boltanski, Luc and Laurent Thévenot (2006[1991]), *On Justification. Economies of worth*, eds Paul J. DiMaggio et al., trans. Catherine Porter. Princeton Studies in Cultural Sociology. Princeton: Princeton University Press.

Çalişkan, Koray and Michel Callon (2009), 'Economization, part 1: shifting attention from the economy towards processes of economization', *Economy and Society*, **38**(3), 369–98.

Çalişkan, Koray and Michel Callon (2010), 'Economization, part 2: a research programme for the study of markets', *Economy and Society*, **39**(1), 1–32.

Callon, Michel (ed.) (1998a), *The Laws of the Markets*, Oxford: Blackwell Publishers and *The Sociological Review*.

Callon, Michel (1998b), 'An essay on framing and overflowing: economic externalities revisited by sociology', in Michel Callon (ed.), *The Laws of the Markets*, Oxford: Blackwell Publishers and *The Sociological Review*, pp. 244–69.

Callon, Michel (2007), 'An essay on the growing contribution of economic markets to the proliferation of the social', *Theory, Culture & Society*, **24**(7–8), 139–63.

Callon, Michel (2009), 'Civilizing markets: carbon trading between in vitro and in vivo experiments', *Accounting, Organizations and Society*, **34**, 535–48.

Callon, Michel and Fabian Muniesa (2005), 'Economic markets as calculative collective devices', *Organization Studies*, **26**(8), 1229–50.

Callon, Michel, Pierre Lascoumes and Yannick Barthe (2009), *Acting in an Uncertain World. An Essay on Technical Democracy*, Cambridge, MA: MIT Press.

Callon, Michel, Cécile Méadel and Vololona Rabeharisoa (2002), 'The economy of qualities', *Economy and Society*, **31**(2) 194–217.

Callon, Michel, Yuval Millo and Fabian Muniesa (eds) (2007), *Market Devices*, Sociological Review Monographs, Oxford: Blackwell Publishing and *The Sociological Review*.

Cochoy, Franck (ed.) (2012), *Du Lien Marchand: Comment le Marché fait Société*, Socio-Logics, Toulouse: Presses Universitaires du Mirail.

Dewey, John (1927), *The Public and its Problems*, New York: Henry Holt Publishers.

Dewey, John (1938), *Logic: The Theory of Inquiry*, New York: Henry Holt Publishers.

Donaldson, Thomas and Lee E. Preston (1995), 'The stakeholder theory of the corporation: Concepts, evidence, and implications', *The Academy of Management Review*, **20**(1) 65–91.

Fligstein, Neil (1996), 'Markets as politics: A political–cultural approach to market institutions', *American Sociological Review*, **61**(4), 656–73.

Fligstein, Neil (2001), *The Architecture of Markets. An Economic Sociology of Twenty-First-Century Capitalist Societies*, Princeton: Princeton University Press.

Geiger, Susi, Hans Kjellberg and Robert Spencer (2012), 'Shaping exchanges, building markets', *Consumption Markets & Culture*, **15**(2), 133–47.

Gregson, Nicky, Helen Watkins and Melania Calestani (2013), 'Political markets: recycling, economization and marketization', *Economy and Society*, **42**(1), 1–25.

Gudeman, Stephen (2008), *Economy's Tensions: The Dialectics of Community and Market*, New York: Berghahn Books.

Hawkins, Gay (2011), 'Packaging water: plastic bottles as market and public devices', *Economy and Society*, **40**(4), 534–52.

Hill, Charles W.L. and Thomas M. Jones (1992), 'Stakeholder-Agency Theory', *Journal of Management Studies*, **29**(2), 131–54.

Latour, Bruno (2004), 'Why has critique run out of steam? From matters of fact to matters of concern', *Critical Inquiry*, **30**(2), 225–48.

Latour, Bruno (2007), 'Turning around politics: A note on Gerard de Vries' paper', *Social Studies of Science*, pp. 811–20.

Marres, Noortje (2007), 'The issues deserve more credit: Pragmatist contributions to the study of public involvement in controversy', *Social Studies of Science*, **37**(5), 759–80.

Mol, Annemarie (2002), *The Body Multiple: Ontology in Medical Practice*, Durham: Duke University Press.

Nelson, Richard R. and Sidney G. Winter (1982), *An Evolutionary Theory of Economic Change*, Cambridge, MA: Harvard University Press.

Rosa, Jose Antonio, Joseph F. Porac, Jelena Runser-Spanjol and Michael S. Saxon (1999), 'Sociocognitive dynamics in a product market', *Journal of Marketing*, **63**(4), 64–77.

Roth, Alvin E. (2009), 'What have we learned from market design?', in Josh Lerner and Scott Stern (eds), *Innovation Policy and the Economy*, Chicago: University of Chicago Press, pp. 79–112.

Sjögren, Ebba (2006), *Reasonable Drugs. Making Decisions with Ambiguous Knowledge*, PhD thesis, Stockholm School of Economics.

Stark, David (2009), *The Sense of Dissonance. Accounts of Worth in Economic Life*, Princeton: Princeton University Press.

Williamson, Oliver E. (1975), *Markets and Hierarchies*, New York: Free Press.
Williamson, Oliver E. (1991), 'Economic institutions: Spontaneous and intentional governance', *Journal of Law, Economics, & Organization*, Vol. 7, 159–87.
Zwick, Detlev and Julien Cayla (eds) (2011), *Inside Marketing: Practices, Ideologies, Devices*, Oxford: Oxford University Press.

2. Expressing concerns over the incentive as a public policy device

Guus Dix

Monetary incentives have recently become a fashionable instrument in education. The overall level of education is expected to rise when teachers receive a bonus for increased student performance.[1] Israel was the first to experiment with performance-based pay for teaching personnel. In 2000, the Israeli government began to reward individuals and teams of the participating schools when they managed to accomplish a rise in student scores on matriculation exams. In the United States, several individual states similarly experimented with bonuses in primary and secondary education (Lavy, 2009). A nationwide program of performance pay for American teachers was established in 2006. The best performing among them would receive additional rewards drawn from the so-called Teacher Incentive Fund. Other countries such as Australia and the UK followed suit. In the Netherlands, the appreciation for and implementation of this particular policy measure came relatively late. A coalition of Liberals and Christian Democrats set 250 million euros aside in 2010 to spend on performance pay over a period of five years. In line with the Israeli approach, the Dutch government decided to begin with a series of experiments so as to ascertain what type of bonus would work best. Several schools participated in a pilot study just after the coalition agreement was signed. The research results of the pilot study were to help academic economists with the design of the actual experiments that all Dutch schools could participate in. However, the government resigned on the eve of the first round of experiments and performance pay was dropped soon afterwards. The money earmarked for it was used by a temporary coalition to meet EU requirements with regard to the budget deficit.

Even though performance pay failed to materialize on the scale envisaged, the route towards the incentivization of teachers makes for an interesting case study in the marketization of the public sector and the resistance it provokes. The term 'marketization' is an appropriate one for the policy measure discussed here. The appreciation for performance targets, monetary incentives and competition among politicians and economic experts fits a certain fashion for managerial practices 'derived' from the private sector. In many Western countries New Public Management (NPM) offered both novel directions for managing the public sector and a discourse to legitimize the proposed reforms (Abrahamson, 1996; Pollit, 2003; Pollit and Bouckaert, 2011). The overall justification for the use of monetary incentives as an instrument of public policy offered by NPM is that public service is neither efficient nor effective because there is not enough pressure to exert oneself and to deliver output. Private firms are said to perform well due to the fact that they face competition from other firms. A firm needs to keep ahead of its competitors and therefore to stimulate the performance of its employees. One of the ways to do so is to offer them additional rewards for increased performance. These 'powerful external incentives' for the firm and its members, however, are often absent or misdirected in the public sector (Dixit, 2002, p. 714). Yet the existing divide between 'market' and 'non-market' can be bridged, economists and management consultants say, by simulating the 'forces' supposed to be operating on market players via a specific set of devices (Ward, 2011). Public servants should be able to reach the level of productivity of individuals employed elsewhere on the condition that they are duly incentivized with the help of such market-style instruments of public policy.[2]

In this chapter I study the gradual transition of performance pay from policy proposal to political reality. I will do so by tracing the plurality of *concerns* that were expressed by different actors involved in the process by which the marketization of education gained epistemic and political momentum. To express concerns here denotes the act of publicly worrying about one concrete issue in an attempt to convince an audience either to follow a certain course of action or to abstain from it. In this way, the concerns expressed over the incentive as a public policy device fall into two distinct categories. On the one hand, actors are worried about the current state of education. They voice their concerns about the alleged bad performance of Dutch schools, teachers and students and say that the educational system will continue to deteriorate unless the government does something to stop it. The different concerns expressed are thus closely related to the advocacy of performance pay as a promising policy measure. On the other hand, the actors also articulate expected problems with regard to the measure itself. These concerns over performance pay are meant to question the appropriateness and effectiveness of introducing monetary incentives in education. Not all of the actors were equally effective in convincing the intended audience that the concerns expressed were justified. By tracing the succession of concerns it becomes possible to assess – be it tentatively – their (lack of) influence on the policy process.

As I am interested in the strategic dimension of expressing concerns, I study the attempts to legitimatize or delegitimize performance pay in publicly available written and spoken words of those actors actively engaged in the debate over its merits. The first group of documents analyzed comes from Dutch economic experts who work for The Netherlands Bureau for Economic Policy Analysis (CPB). These policy-oriented economists were the first to voice a set of concerns about the current state of the educational field. They pointed to the lack of inducements to perform which was due to the absence of competition between teachers and between schools. To counteract such weak incentives they proposed a set of policy measures to incentivize teaching personnel. From 2001 onward, CPB economists began to advocate the value of performance pay for Dutch education (CPB, 2001; Canton and Webbink, 2004; Koning et al., 2004; Vyrastekova et al., 2006; Van Elk et al., 2011a; 2011b). The first set of concerns thus had to do with alleged problems in education for which monetary incentives were deemed a solution. Yet the solution was not without concerns itself. The very same CPB economists who wrote favorably about performance pay also raised a number of doubts about the expected negative side-effects. As early as in the first published report on education they stated that 'the stimulation of free market processes in education has both favorable and unfavorable effects' and that the current state of empirical research 'provides no definitive answers as to the relative weight of these effects' (CPB, 2001, p. 127).

The articulation of concerns was not restricted to a narrow circle of economic experts. From 2006 onward, performance pay became an important topic for politicians. Several political parties made performance pay a plank in their platform for that year's elections. Political support for the measure grew in the years thereafter until it became part of the reform agenda in the 2010 coalition agreement. The large support for performance pay shows that the concerns over performance pay were subordinated to those over the state of contemporary education. The sources consulted to justify that claim include the economic assessments of electoral platforms (CPB, 2003; 2006; CPB and PBL, 2010), electoral platforms (CDA, 2010; D66, 2010, ChristenUnie, 2010; Groenlinks, 2010; PvdA, 2010; SGP, 2010; VVD, 2010); policy notes (Ministry of Education, 2011a; 2011b), legislative documents (*Regeling Experimenten Prestatiebeloning Onderwijs*), parliamentary protocols (Ministry of Education, 2012) and a promotional video message (*Experimenten prestatiebeloning van start*).

But if politicians were silent about the possible side-effects of introducing monetary incentives in education, teachers and their union representatives were certainly not. They expressed a new set of concerns about the measurement of performance and the rewards bound up with it. The doubts about the beneficial effects of performance pay were articulated in reports

(AOB, 2011b; Onderwijsraad, 2011), video messages and leaflets (AOB, 2011c; *Leerlingen en directeur; Prestatiebeloning onderwijs*) and (opinion) articles (AOB, 2011a; 2012a; 2012b; 2012c; 2012d; Besturenraad.nl, 2011; Dirks, 2010; Dresscher, 2010; 2011; Hoogenboom, 2011; Kersten, 2012; Sikkes, 2001a; 2001b; 2002; 2008; 2011; Telegraaf, 2012; Volkskrant, 2012).

MARKET DEVICES AND MARKET WORTH

Although these concerns might seem small and very much bound up with local circumstances, their specificity makes them an excellent starting point for addressing broader issues discussed in recent sociological studies of markets and marketization. First of all, my analysis of the concerns over the incentive as a public policy device is informed by the notion of *market devices* as developed by Callon and others. These market devices are 'the material and discursive assemblages that intervene in the construction of markets' (Callon et al., 2007, p. 2). For sure, markets are about individuals and groups that compete with one another, but they are equally furnished with a range of heterogeneous objects that mediate this competitive interaction: measuring instruments, trading zones, mathematical economic models, materializations of architectural design, protocols for trading and so forth (Garcia-Parpet, 2007; MacKenzie, 2007). The complex relation between economic science, market devices and actual markets of all sorts is discussed in much detail in the literature on the performativity of economics. Yet despite recent attention to the politics of performativity, there seems to be less attention for the politics of markets in general and the market-style devices used to govern public servants in particular (Cochoy et al., 2010, p. 141; Callon, 2010). For instance, the introduction to *Do Economists Make Markets?* opens with the political role played by economists in Bolivia, Peru and Russia and explicitly addresses the use of economics in a political context by saying that 'economics can be put into practice – and its proposals enforced – through specific political decisions and policies (from regulatory bodies to audit agencies)' (MacKenzie et al., 2007, p. 7). But little effort is shown in the subsequent chapters to trace the route by which economics ends up becoming political reality.[3]

Questions of politics should be given a more prominent place in the study of the instruments developed and used to judge the value of products and services, as Beckert and Aspers stress in their introduction to *The Worth of Goods*: 'it is crucial to integrate political sociology much more strongly into this perspective, emphasizing the power-laden political struggles leading to the use of specific judgment devices' (Beckert and Aspers, 2011, p. 23). I propose to extend the focus on the market devices that constitute and shape economic organizations and processes toward the market-infused policy devices with which government tries to transform the public sector. The introduction of performance pay in education is a suitable candidate for doing so. On the one hand, the wish to make the public sector more market-like was the explicit intent behind the planned incentivization of teachers. Even though performance pay is a material device that does not intervene directly on the market, it simulates market forces in a domain that is considered not competitive enough. The introduction of monetary incentives comes with its own set of material procedures of performance measurement and explicit expectations about the behavior of individuals and institutions. On the other hand, the controversy that came with the introduction of performance pay makes it possible to investigate the power-laden political struggle that led to its use. In the case of performance pay, economic experts articulated two sets of concerns. The concerns about the perceived problems in education dominated their analysis but economists were equally concerned about the possible side-effects of incentivizing teaching personnel. While there was little controversy within the political field, the policy measure in question became a contested one among the individuals who were explicitly targeted. Primary and secondary school teachers were quite outspoken on the matter. Many of them resented the coming reform and The General Union of Education (AOB) made the cancelation of this particular policy measure their main point of attention.

With the focus on the controversy about the value of performance pay we come to the second broader issue that is central to the present inquiry: that of the *worth* of education to those concerned. The three parties involved – economic experts, politicians and teachers – valued the issue of incentivization differently because they had a different outlook on what made (working in) education worthwhile. The concept of worth was developed in the work of Boltanski and Thévenot (2006) with the intention of keeping a number of questions together: what objects and objectives count as valuable to different people, what is it that brings esteem to them, and how do we calculate it? From the six orders of worth discerned by Boltanski and Thévenot, that of market order is especially insightful when it comes to the bond it creates between people:

> Such a bond is achieved through the arrangement of a marketplace in which individuals well disposed to one another but governed by their own personal interests enter into competition in order to acquire rare goods, in such a way that their wealth endows them with worth, since it is the expression of the unsatisfied desires of the others (2006, pp. 45–6).

The plea for performance pay clearly resonates with this depiction of the market bond. It is a device that redistributes worth among those who participate in the creation of educational value. In the competition for bonuses, those who manage to achieve their performance target will be rewarded and set as an example to those who have not (yet) managed to achieve theirs and whose desires are thus unsatisfied. In doing so, this particular market device simultaneously reconfigures the value of education itself. The emphasis on performance inherent in performance pay is inspired by the beneficial economic effects that are said to follow from enhanced educational achievements. The policy measure is thus a materialization of the political appraisal for the economic value generated by investments in education.

I consider the concept of *concern* as corollary to that of worth in that it is inherently value laden and is bound up with the evaluation of certain objects or objectives as worthwhile or worthless. In that sense, there is a significant difference in the appreciation for the introduction of such a market bond in education between economic experts and politicians on the one hand and educational practitioners on the other. Yet the notion of concern is not directly dependent on that of worth. I side with Stark's (2009, p. 13) consideration that the evaluative principles that play a role in the interaction between individuals should be specified anew for new cases studied. In the case of performance pay, the concerns expressed by the actors do not fit neatly in (one of) the different orders discerned by Boltanski and Thévenot. Indeed, some of the concerns are related to a notion of what is considered worthy. Others, however, are closely related to the epistemic valuation that things will turn out one way or the other should the government decide to follow a certain course of action or with the question whether the proper procedures have been followed.

ECONOMIC EXPERTS EXPRESS TWO SETS OF CONCERNS

The plan for incentivizing Dutch teachers came from The Netherlands Bureau for Economic Policy Analysis (CPB). The CPB has quite a long history as an institution operating at the interface of scientific inquiry and political advice. The latter is partly given on demand – by central government or political parties – and partly on its own initiative. When established in 1945, its main task was to analyze economic trends with the help of econometric models built by economist and Riksbank Memorial Prize winner Jan Tinbergen. These models were refined by CPB economists in the decades thereafter and remain the principal resource for their epistemological authority in matters of public policy (Maas, 2010). In recent years, a microeconomic focus of public sector performance was added to the macroeconomic account of both long- and short-term trends. The project on incentives for semi-public institutions – as an example of this partial shift in focus – brought the expertise of several researchers at the CPB together and culminated in a range of detailed studies on the 'organizational and incentive structures' of health care, police, science and education in the Netherlands (Koning et al., 2004). These studies brought a number of alleged structural problems to the fore with regard to the current 'direction' of incentives in the public sector. At the same time, each of them offered a range of solutions to realign the objectives of public servants with the objectives of central government.

With regard to the Dutch educational field, CPB economists wrote a number of reports to bring certain problems to the attention of Dutch politicians for which incentives were deemed a solution. The problems discerned and the solutions presented were articulated with the help of a sub-discipline of economic science known as principal–agent theory. In principal–agent theory there is a principal or planner with well-defined objectives who delegates certain tasks to others and there are agents who are interested in performing the task as designed and delegated by the principal. In the absence of constant surveillance by the principal, the agent has a more intimate knowledge of the ordinary course of events and his or her own role therein. With this surplus of knowledge he/she is in a position to neglect the objectives of the principal and pursue his/her own goals instead (Laffont and Martimort, 2002, pp. 28–9). The principal therefore devises an incentive scheme in order to induce agents to reveal the information they hide from the planner or to work harder for the planner than they would otherwise do. A well-designed incentive scheme allows the agents to maximize their own expected utility by pursuing the goals of the principal (Laffont and Maskin, 1983, pp. 31–32; Ledyard, 1987)[4].

At the turn of the new millennium the information-incentive problematic was firmly embedded in textbooks of microeconomic and public economics (cf. Pindyck and Rubinfeld, 2005, p. 613; Hindriks and Myles, 2006, pp. 251–98). Moreover, the economists who worked on the economics of incentives were lauded for their effort and research results and received the Riksbank Memorial Prize at around the same time (Nobel Prize, 1996, 2001 and 2007). The academic credentials of principal–agent theory were thus undisputed at the moment it became a key resource to articulate what went wrong in the public sector. The theoretical agnosticism as to the identity of the principal and that of the agent enabled Dutch economic experts to discern different (classes of) principals delegating tasks to different (classes of) agents in the educational field: 'In practice the subcontractor (agent) often has more information at his disposal than the originator (principal). The subcontractor can exploit this surplus of information to his own advantage and at the cost of the principal' (Canton and Webbink, 2004, p. 13).[5] To solve this 'practical' problem the originator – the State – has to redirect the behavior of the subcontractor – agents and institutions in the public sector – at the least possible expense. In the CPB reports on education this general problem was made more specific in three different relations where the asymmetrically dispersed information hampered the adequate functioning of the 'market' for educational goods (Koning et al., 2004, p. 83).

In the first instance, information asymmetry intrudes the relation between the management of the school and the 'operatives' on the work floor. As 'management (the principal) delegates the power to decide over the design of the educational process to teachers (the agents)' there is ample room for the latter to pursue their own goals (Canton and Webbink, 2004, p. 16). Individual teachers are able to do as they please because of the lack of direct access to their classroom. Even though the majority might not seize the informational opportunity, school managers cannot exclude the possibility of strategic behavior on the part of their teaching staff. Second, the relationship between the 'seller' and 'buyer' of education can equally be understood in principal–agent terms. The parents are then considered the contractors who hire school personnel to educate their children. For parents it is often quite difficult to assess the quality of the product on offer. What a specific school adds to the human capital of their offspring is not known to them nor is it clear how one school performs vis-à-vis other schools in the region. The lack of robust performance indicators enables schools to let things slide without facing the consequences of their (in)action. Finally, the relation between schools and the Ministry of Education can be described in terms of information asymmetry. Because 'central government (principal) delegates educational tasks to institutions (agents)' it creates opportunities for schools to slack off (Canton and Webbink, 2004, p. 14).

In all three cases, the expected lack of effort of schoolteachers and management is made possible by an insufficient knowledge of their performance. In line with the theory discussed above, CPB economists presented a range of incentive-infused solutions to solve the principal–agent problems discerned. The Ministry's informational disadvantage as to the performance of schools, for instance, could be remedied by a system of lump sum payment. Once schools are paid by the number of passes, they will begin to take care regarding the quality of the education offered. Especially in vocational training, too many students leave school prematurely and CPB economists therefore advise government to 'use stronger financial incentives for institutions or colleges to fight drop-out rates' (Canton and Webbink, 2004, p. 39). The financial incentive of paying by the piece should make it harder for a school to perform badly for a long period of time. Second, the relation between parents and schools can be improved by increasing the 'accountability' of the school. Parents are better able to choose the best school for their children with the help of publicly available rankings of school performance: 'This works as an additional incentive for schools to operate well, because parents are better informed about the ins and outs of the school: bad performances will be punished by a decreased number of pupils' (Canton and Webbink, 2004, p. 15). Headmasters have to take the effect of a lower ranking on parental behavior into account as it has now become possible to 'vote with one's feet' (Koning et al., 2004, p. 87). The fear of a significant decrease in students motivates them to increase the performance of their school. The third and final solution presented is a new system of monetary rewards for teachers as 'the principal–agent relation within the school between management and teaching staff might be a reason to consider performance pay' (Canton and Webbink, 2004, p. 17). Information asymmetry within the school would disappear when student performance was accurately measured and teachers held accountable for it. They now had to take responsibility for their students' results, and the best among them would be properly rewarded. Over time, CPB economists advocated the third solution most prominently. By piling up the available experimental evidence for its positive effects on student test scores, performance pay became the most promising measure for educational reform.

The principal–agent relations articulated all required one sort of incentive solution or another. Yet there were at least as many concerns with regard to the solutions presented as with regard to the problems discerned. The alleged overflow of the explicit purpose of the incentive as a public policy device was especially strong when it came to performance pay. Even though CPB economists considered it the most promising policy measure for improving education, they also brought a vast array of uncertainties and lacunae to the fore with regard to the existing experiments. The most prominent concerns over the robustness of the experimental relationship established were the following. First of all, the experiments gave rise to certain measurement problems. Although test scores seem clear indicators of performance, it proved difficult to measure the exact influence of individual teachers on student learning in a clear and consistent way. Such measurement problems were even more serious when it came to such competences as self-confidence and the ability to do things independently. Next to cognitive skills strictly speaking, these competences are considered important goals of education. But because they are hard to put in quantitative terms it is quite difficult to find out whether performance pay contributed to their enhancement or not. Moreover, as 'competition might even lead to exclusive attention for measurable (or measured) aspects of education' economists feared that working with rewards for specific targets would lead to the neglect of important aspects of a general education (CPB, 2001, pp. 129–30).

A second concern had to do with the correlation between the effort of a teacher and the test scores of his or her students. For even if the results of test scores were accurately measured and if the experimental results were positive, the correlation could be explained by something radically different from real improvement in learning. Two possibilities stand out here. On the one hand, performance pay might lead to a phenomenon dubbed 'teaching to the test' (Koning et al., 2004, p. 33). When teachers are rewarded for increasing the test scores of their students, they might focus primarily on the preparation for the test. When this is the case, the competence trained for is narrower than the competence actually sought. Gaming, on the other hand, was an even more extreme possibility. Teachers could deliberately manipulate the test scores by keeping certain students out of the test. Some of the experiments with performance pay paid no attention to the possibility of gaming or teaching to the test; in others there was evidence that such manipulation of the test scores indeed occurred. Several articles on American experiments with performance pay demonstrated that strategic behavior of teachers and managers was a very likely explanation for the experimental results (Van Elk et al., 2011b, p. 25).

Thirdly, it was uncertain whether the results found – if well measured and positive and not affected by manipulation – were incidental or structural. The often cited experiment in Israel was stopped after one year for political reasons and there was thus no clear way to assess the permanence of the results (Koning et al., 2004, p. 94). Fourthly, it was as yet unclear what incentives would do to the motivation of teachers. The more prominent role of extrinsic rewards might harm the intrinsic motivation teachers had to give their best (CPB, 2001, p. 130). And finally, there was a risk that performance pay would lead to an unwelcome dichotomy in education. If excellent teachers fled from badly performing schools to better performing ones, the educational field would be divided into a number of good schools with teachers who were better off in terms of bonuses and a number of bad schools with teachers who were worse off on these same terms (CPB, 2001, p. 130).

All in all, these five concerns bear witness to the fact that there were two well-established sets of concerns with regard to performance pay. On the one hand, there were concerns over the current state of education, and the introduction of monetary incentives for teachers was deemed a suitable policy measure to address them. On the other hand, there were concerns over the instability of the experimental results and the side-effects that could come from incentivizing teachers. It was still far from clear whether the advantages of performance pay really outweighed the disadvantages.

THE SKEWED RECEPTION OF CONCERNS IN THE POLITICAL FIELD

Though CPB economists played an important role in the debate over performance pay, they were certainly not the only ones to speak up on the matter. In this section the focus shifts from the sphere of economic expertise to that of politics. What happened to the concerns over education and monetary incentives when performance pay entered the political arena? The answer to this question comes in two stages. I will first trace the way in which political parties came to appreciate the use of incentives for teachers and then turn to the justification given by central government once it had become part of their reform agenda.

The initial point to notice is that there was no vibrant discussion in Parliament over the merits and drawbacks of performance pay at the moment CPB economists began to articulate its value. At the time of the elections in 2003 none of the political parties mentioned monetary incentives for primary and high school teachers as a way to enhance student performance. The first signs of political awareness with regard to the measure came three years later and political support for it grew steadily in the years thereafter. In 2006 five out of seven political parties made their positive attitude towards performance pay explicit; in 2010 seven out of nine parties were convinced as to its beneficial effects (CPB, 2006; CPB and PBL, 2010). The complete political center was favorable to the measure at the moment it became part of the 2010 coalition agreement.

The steady growth of political support for performance pay can be easily traced because of a particular political-epistemic ritual of Dutch politics. For nearly thirty years, the CPB offered parties the opportunity to assess the set of policy proposals with which they chose to enter the elections. The CPB was requested to do so in 1985 by the three biggest political parties at the time and over the years the practice became 'a veritable institution', to use its own words (CPB and PBL, 2010, p. 12). In the reports dubbed *Charted Choices*, CPB economists calculate the effects of different policy measures on government budgets, the income of Dutch citizens and the Gross National Product (GNP). Some months before every election, representatives of political parties begin to discuss their plans with CPB representatives. Given the economic effects bound up with a certain measure, politicians can decide whether they wish to take it on board or not. After the negotiations have been brought to a close, economic experts calculate the overall effect of the choices made on unemployment rates, budgetary deficits, future GNP levels and so on. The results of these calculations play an important role in the debates that take place in the weeks before the elections. Party leaders pick out specific parts of the economic assessment to attack their competitors and to bring the strengths of their own program to the fore.[6]

When it comes to the assessment of performance pay in subsequent editions of these *Charted Choices* we can say that the measure became more 'valuable' over time. In 2003 CPB economists stated there were too many unknowns with regard to educational policy measures and subsequently refrained from calculating the precise effects of performance pay (CPB, 2003, p. 9). Three years later they felt somewhat more secure. They now passed judgment on the economic value of different measures to enhance the output of education but did so only in a qualitative way. Performance pay was assigned to the highest class of 'promising policy measures' in a tripartite division of classes (CPB, 2006, p. 29). A model with which to estimate the economic effects of educational policies was established in 2010. With the help of this model it could be shown that performance pay was *the* most promising measure to increase economic productivity in the long run: its introduction would lead to a 1.5 per cent rise in the GNP level in 2070 (CPB and PBL, 2010, p. 16; Van Elk et al., 2011a, p. 64). The quantification of performance pay's economic effect was not unproblematic even if we leave the epistemological issues with such long-term predictions aside. In practice, it meant that the second of the two sets of concerns voiced in the previous section was lost from view. There was simply no place for experimental uncertainties and negative side-effects in the convergence of experimental results into a robust effect on future GNP levels.

The foregrounding of the alleged (quantifiable) economic benefits over the potential (unquantifiable) disadvantages left its mark on the disposition of politicians towards performance pay. In addition to the set of policy measures presented to the CPB for further analysis, political parties also explain their plans for the future in an electoral platform. The silence in these platforms over the introduction of performance-based bonuses in education is striking. The vast majority of the political parties told the CPB that performance pay was high on their list and gave a specification of the precise amount of money they were willing to spend on it. Yet only one political party acknowledged to be an 'advocate of differentiated pay' and said that 'a good teacher who proves himself to perform should earn more' (VVD, 2010, p. 16). Four other political parties were completely silent on the matter (Groenlinks, 2010; PvdA, 2010; D66, 2010; CDA, 2010). The platforms of the final two parties even went so far as to lament the fact that economic terms dominated the discussion over education. One of them stated that: 'Unfortunately, it has become more and more common to speak about education in economic terms. The emphasis is increasingly put on holding schools accountable for their own performances. We have to be careful with it' (SGP, 2010, p. 16). The other party insisted that '(higher) education is more than the engine of the economy' (ChristenUnie, 2010, p. 26). The path by which performance pay moved from promising policy measure to political reality thus matters for the concerns articulated by politicians – or the lack thereof. The subordination of the concerns over the incentive as an instrument of public policy in *Charted Choices* made it easy for political parties to embrace the measure in order to secure a more positive outcome in the calculations.

The coalition of Liberals and Christian Democrats that took office in 2010 made performance pay into a spearhead of their policy (*Vrijheid en verantwoordelijkheid*, 2010). In doing so, the Dutch government adopted the earlier asymmetrical attitude towards the concerns over (the lack of) incentives for teachers. Again, the worries over performance pay as an instrument of public policy did not resurface in prospects on the future of education in the Netherlands. What remained was the articulation of a set of concerns over the current state of education in two policy notes in which the policy plans were explained and justified (Ministry of Education, 2011a and 2011b). Though related to the concerns voiced by economic experts, the problems discerned by the Ministry of Education, Culture and Science are sufficiently distinct to merit their own discussion. Furthermore, the process of translating concerns is important in itself as teachers and union representatives respond to government plans and their justification and often not directly to the reports produced by economists. The first of these new concerns had to do with the position of Dutch students on the international Programme for International Student Assessment (PISA) rankings. These rankings showed that their performance slowly declined over the years, both in absolute terms and in comparison with students from other countries. In light of this general decline, the Government set itself the target to reclaim their former position. This goal was subsequently formulated in more specific terms. On the next PISA measurement in 2015 and 2018 student scores in mathematics, science and reading had to improve significantly. With regard to student performance in mathematics, for instance, each measurement should show a five-point increase in test scores (Ministry of Education, 2011b, p. 2).

This concern over the position of Dutch education in the global educational field was linked to a second concern over the professional culture of the teaching staff. The improvement in learning could only take place when teachers were willing to focus on the increase in output of education, and that is exactly where things went awry. Schools currently lacked a culture of 'achievement oriented working' and were not transparent as to the competences and professional development of individual teachers. Instead, teachers seemed to hold on to values of equality in their attitude towards their colleagues and pupils and there was a sense that this 'culture of equality in education devalues the individual qualities and the ambition of teams to do better than before' (Ministry of Education, 2011a, p. 9). The introduction of performance pay should help to break the culture of equality and guarantee that outstanding performances of teachers were 'identified and rewarded in order to allow for imitation' (Ministry of Education, 2011a, p. 9; Onderwijsraad, 2011). Performance pay would bring about a general focus of the teaching staff on the output of education. This in turn also affected the atmosphere in which excellent students could flourish, not only in the direct sense of teachers eager to increase their test scores but also in the establishment of an 'ambitious educational culture' (Ministry of Education, 2011b, p. 1). An atmosphere in which 'ambition' was no longer a dirty word was thought especially beneficial for the gifted students. In this way, monetary incentives for teachers could contribute to the explicit policy goal of challenging the segment of 'top-class students' currently left unchallenged (Ministry of Education, 2011b, pp. 3 and 7).

The third and final concern voiced in these two prospects had to do with the alleged lack of career opportunities in education. One of the background assumptions of the plan to incentivize teachers was the existence of a widespread idea among potential candidates that teaching was a lifelong job without possibilities for advancement once you were in. In order to make teaching more attractive as a vocation it was deemed inevitable that the ideal of personal and professional growth gained acceptance in the educational field. Performance pay seemed a suitable way to do so. Its introduction signaled to future teachers that the willingness to invest in oneself and one's students was both recognized and rewarded. With the identification of excellence and the rewards for quality, the cultural transformation would secure a sufficient number of people willing to join the teaching profession in the (near) future.

Over and against these well-elaborated concerns 'calling' for performance pay stood few explicit remarks on the negative externalities brought to the fore by economists. The main line of defense of the State Secretary of Education when confronted with worries coming from the field was to point to the experimental phase in the introduction of performance pay. Only the outcome of the experiments could put an end to the 'ill-informed discussion' on its advantages and disadvantages (Besturenraad.nl, 2011). In a video message that accompanied the opening of the registration period for the experiments, the State Secretary explained:

Some say: 'it works'; some say: 'it doesn't'. We want to get rid of that. Experience will have to show whether it works or not. The coalition will stay out of it for scientists have to come to their conclusions independently. Performance pay is no goal in itself; it is a means to increase the performance of the teachers and guarantee that our students receive a better education. I summon everyone who is into teaching: 'join us, start experimenting, get to work and discover this new way.' (*Experimenten prestatiebeloning van start*)

Indeed, no school was compelled to introduce performance pay for its teaching staff. After the pilot study was completed, schools could decide for themselves whether to participate in the experiments or not. Furthermore, some of the earlier concerns were addressed in the experiments designed by economists appointed for the task in hand. School governors could choose between six different experimental designs. The main differences between them had to do with the differentiation between individual rewards and team rewards. It was decided that 30 per cent of the budget went to experiments with individualized bonuses and 70 per cent to experiments with team bonuses. Furthermore, schools could decide whether they wanted to work with absolute standards of performance or with relative ones. In the former case, every teacher or team would receive the bonus if they reached a predetermined increase in student test scores; in the latter case only the best-performing teachers – say 25 per cent – would receive it. Next to these key experimental variables it was possible to add other indicators of performance such as the measurement of the social and emotional development of students or to include a questionnaire to find out what teachers thought about their relationships with their colleagues (*Regeling Experimenten Prestatiebeloning Onderwijs*).

The inclusion of an 'experimental phase' in the overall implementation of performance pay was thus meant to address any concern voiced beforehand. Despite the fact that some of the concerns were given a place as minor variables in the experiments, it was questionable whether the experimental project as a whole was really open enough to accommodate them. One of the principal economists of the research team that helped participating schools with their subscription was struck by the strong conviction on the part of government over performance pay's effectiveness. For the State Secretary, he noticed, the experiments were not meant to disclose *if* performance pay was an effective tool but *which type of bonus worked best* (Kersten, 2012). The ambiguous status of the experiments was corroborated by the post-experimental policy plans. For one, it was already decided beforehand that performance pay would become a permanent feature of Dutch education after the experimental phase was over. In one of the two policy notes we can read that 'the experiments will provide the principles for the structural introduction of performance pay' (Ministry of

Education, 2011a, p. 8). This particular attitude toward the experiments was also confirmed in the ambivalent explanation of its purpose. Before an audience of teachers, the State Secretary declared that government would give up on performance pay if the experimental results were negative, saying that 'if it really does not work, we will not continue' (Van der Mee, 2011, p. 20). While in response to questions from Parliament about the pilot studies he simultaneously declared that 'experiments really cannot fail'; the experiments with performance pay were just 'meant to establish which concrete incentive works and which not' (Ministry of Education, 2012).

THE COUNTERACTING CONCERNS OF TEACHERS AND UNION REPRESENTATIVES

The 'confirmative' role of the experiments in implementing perform-ance pay was not lost on the General Union of Education (AOB). In an ironic statement, the chairman of the union claimed the experiments were a great success already for they would lead to the consolidation of monetary incentives for teachers whatever the future experimental results (Dresscher, 2011). Instead of responding to the call to join in and discover its benefits, teachers and union representatives began to articulate a new set of concerns to counteract the stress on the beneficial effects of incen-tives. In this section I will focus on their response to government plans. What was the value of performance pay to the people who were to be incentivized?

The AOB had always been aware of the preference for performance pay of CPB economists. The editor-in-chief of the AOB magazine wrote several (critical) articles about CPB reports, academic research on bonuses and international experiences with the policy measure (Sikkes, 2001a; 2001b; 2002 and 2008). The union started actively to campaign against performance pay from the moment it became political reality. Union representatives and teachers brought several distinct and heterogeneous concerns to the fore in order to convince the Ministry to cancel the experi-ments. While some of these concerns resonate with the ones black boxed by the CPB, others call attention to entirely new issues.

The first concern was the sheer unpopularity of the plan among primary and secondary school teachers. The union found proof for this hostile atti-tude in a survey taken in 2011 of 3900 union members currently working in education. More than 70 per cent of the teachers who filled in the ques-tionnaire voiced a (strong) aversion to the introduction of performance pay in their sector. Moreover, an equal percentage of the respondents found the appointment of excellent teachers to motivate their colleagues either awkward or superfluous. Instead, they would rather see the worst teachers fired than the best teachers rewarded and heralded as a shining example to others (AOB, 2011b). A number of individual teachers and directors gave substance to their general negative disposition in the space left for comments. One of the teachers surveyed by the AOB wrote that 'performance pay is the deathblow to team spirit, solidarity and teaming up together; it [. . .] makes using one's elbows the prevailing standard' (AOB, 2011a). Other teachers shared this worry over the undermining of 'team spirit' and feared that 'teachers would become more selective' (AOB, 2012a, p.40). A director of a comprehensive school in Amsterdam told the press that she considered the introduction of performance pay both unnecessary and in opposition to what teachers value: 'We can already distinguish the quality of teachers with the help of salary scales. [. . .] And if I ask teachers what they consider most important, they say: "give me extra time to develop myself and my courses. That makes me happier than competing over an additional sum of money"' (*Leerlingen en directeur Open Schoolgemeenschap Bijlmer over prestatieloon*). These responses came from teachers for whom performance pay was not yet reality. Those who participated in the pilot study, however, voiced a similar hesitance over the benefits of performance pay. The chairman of the works council of the pilot school for vocational education made clear that he did not believe in the value of experimenting with bonuses:

> I think it does more harm than good. We have invested in a good team spirit, in colleagues who look after one another. It places strain on the willingness and the self-evidence to do someone a favor. Nobody really welcomes a performance bonus that is given to a small group only (Kersten, 2012).

The same goes for the teaching staff of a primary school in Amsterdam that figured prominently in the Ministry's promotional video. Several teachers spoke out on the matter and declared that individual bonuses were 'inappropriate' in education. They asked the school directors not to be rewarded in such a way. To accommodate these concerns, management decided to change the rules and allow teachers to spend the additional rewards on charitable institutions (Besturenraad.nl, 2011).

The perspective of employees on performance pay brings us to a second, procedural concern. The pilot study was a first step towards the implementation of performance pay. Yet the Ministry did not follow the normal procedures in the negotiations with the different schools concerned (AOB, 2012a; 2012b). A regular procedure with regard to changes in the pay system for teaching personnel would have included the explicit approval of employee representatives. The chairman of a board of representatives of a pilot study high school explained:

> This is an additional point: the regular procedures have not been followed.
> From the perspective of the board of governors there was no need for consent
> because it was a pilot study. The representative advisory board thinks oth-
> erwise: it is a matter of remunerating personnel, so we have the right to say
> something about it (AOB, 2012c).

This concern over teachers who were excluded from having a say subsequently led to a series of questions to the State Secretary of Education
in the Dutch Lower Chamber (Ministry of Education, 2012). Seizing the
opportunity, the union made a general appeal to the representative advisory boards of schools that intended to apply for funding. Via a leaflet
these boards were explicitly called upon to 'obstruct performance pay' and
were given several tips on how to do so (AOB, 2011c). The union also targeted individual board members by sending them additional information
about the right procedures with regard to changes in the wage structure
of school personnel (Hoogenboom, 2011; AOB, 2012c). The strategy was
quite effective: two out of three high schools that had initially agreed to
join the pilot study decided to withdraw after members from their representative advisory board objected. The sole remaining institution of senior
vocational education restricted its participation to one year in order to
keep the turmoil among teachers in check. In addition, the invitation to
join the first round of experiments met with a very low response. Only
40 out of a total number of 8000 schools applied for funding to carry out
experiments (Telegraaf, 2012; AOB, 2012d).

The unwillingness of the representative advisory boards to support their
schools when it came to participation in the experiment was not just due
to the lack of proper procedures followed or the sheer unpopularity of the
measure. The third major concern over the introduction of performance
pay weighed heavily on all those involved: the money earmarked for performance pay came with considerable cutbacks elsewhere. The investment
of millions of euros went hand in hand with a significant saving on special
education. Introducing additional rewards for one subset of teachers while
laying off another touched on a sore spot, as one of the union leaders made
clear:

> But for me, what is more important is the concurrent cutback on special
> education – and a considerable one at that: 300 million Euro will have to be
> saved; five to six thousand people will be fired. In times like these, you should
> not spend a hundred and forty million on such a dubious experiment. So: no
> bonus but jobs (*Prestatiebeloning onderwijs: schooldirecteuren zien er weinig in*).

The concern voiced here clearly resonated with the teaching personnel. In March 2012 the AOB managed to organize the largest strike in the
history of the union with the slogan 'no bonus but jobs' (Volkskrant, 2012).

The fourth and final concern articulated is bound up with performance pay's alleged effectiveness in increasing student test scores. Instead of reproducing the verdict of economic experts, the union challenged the 'fact' of its beneficial effects on the output of education. In an attempt to undermine the truth claims of CPB economists, the chairman of the AOB dismissed the evidence as flimsy: 'These are hopeful expectations from economists who advocate performance pay without sound evidence. Zijlstra [the State Secretary of Education GD] has declared himself a believer. When it comes to these kinds of experiments there is no use in believing because the results point in a different direction' (AOB, 2012b). The whole idea that science had sound proof for the effectiveness of incentives in education was considered as based on nothing but a myth (Dresscher, 2010). To substantiate the claim that individual or team bonuses did not increase educational output, other prominent union representatives mobilized as many available counterexamples as possible. The chief editor of the AOB magazine drew support from experiences with the measure in the very same countries the CPB claimed as its ally. In recent years, he said, there were quite a number of fraudulent schools in America who received large sums of money for fake increases in test scores. In other cases, the introduction of bonuses just led to chaos and discontent because of the lack of clarity over the rules. Furthermore, not all economists were convinced as to the promising nature of performance pay. Next to the scientific experts in favor of the measure, there were others who claimed the evidence over performance pay was unconvincing (Sikkes, 2011).

Some of the concerns brought forward by practitioners were immediately dismissed by the State Secretary of Education. When asked to explain the choice for performance pay, he countered by saying that fear of competition and the elimination of team spirit were out of place: 'I have heard that it can lead to quarrels in the canteen, but do not consider it a sound argument. Differences in performance should be rewarded, in education too' (Van der Mee, 2011, p. 20). In the same interview he made clear that there was no relationship between the budget cut and the investment in incentives, saying that 'you cannot contrast the two. What have the budget cuts on special education and performance pay to do with each other?' (Van der Mee, 2011, p. 20).

EXPRESSING CONCERNS OVER THE INCENTIVE AS A PUBLIC POLICY DEVICE

In the previous sections the evaluation of performance pay was brought to the fore by way of the concerns that accompanied its rise and demise.

Dutch CPB economists were the first to discuss the measure and their feelings were initially mixed. Clearly, the concerns over the existing lack of incentives for teachers and schools dominated in their reports on education. But even if economic experts were generally in favor of performance pay, they did acknowledge the vast array of problems that its introduction could bring about. We saw above how the concerns brought to the fore by the economists were dealt with in the political field. Political parties proved susceptible to the first set of concerns but were largely silent with regard to the second set. The coalition that took office in 2010 adopted this asymmetric disposition and was convinced that incentivizing teachers was necessary to enhance the performance of Dutch students. The teachers and union representatives, finally, were overtly hostile to the introduction of performance pay. Their main strategy was to articulate a number of concerns voiced that were not addressed before. In this final section I will extrapolate from the concerns over performance pay to the added value of the above analysis for current debates on markets and marketization.

First of all, I sought to extend the discussion over market devices towards market-infused instruments of public policy and the political struggle that leads to the use of such devices. The analysis of the heterogeneous concerns expressed by different parties involved in the debate over its merits makes it possible to assess which concerns were able to affect the actual design and implementation of the measure. There are two different relationships that call for further explication when we consider the power of concerns to convince the government to introduce or withdraw performance pay. The relationship between economic experts and political actors is the first one to study in order to assess the 'strength' of these concerns to influence the process of marketizing the public sector. We saw that the economists who brought two sets of concerns to the fore also pushed one of them to the background. There was no place for the second set of considerations discussed above when quantifying the long-term effect of performance pay on the Dutch economy. The emergence of performance pay as a promising policy measure was thus shown to depend on the political-epistemic work of policy-oriented economists. The use of a particular theoretical framework of principals and agents, the calculation of the economic effect of incentivizing teachers and the economic assessment of the electoral platforms together provided political leverage for the measure in question. The vast majority of political parties proved susceptible to the positive economic effect thus construed. Some parties were still concerned about the economization of education but not to such an extent as to refrain from taking the policy measure aboard. When performance pay became part of the coalition agreement in 2010, the main concerns were equally related to the current state of primary and secondary education and not to the measure itself. The subordination of the second set of concerns and the value placed on the first in the economic assessment of the election programs increased the interest in the measure and aided in the acceptance of performance pay in the political field.

The relationship between teachers and union representatives on the one hand and central government on the other is equally interesting in terms of the political struggle over incentivizing teachers. When the experiments with performance had become reality, what room was there to make amendments or even to negotiate its abolition? The reaction of the State Secretary of Education to the concerns expressed by practitioners shows that the government was not particularly receptive to them. He dismissed some of these concerns as simply unsound or irrelevant and maintained that only experimental evidence could reveal what kind of incentives worked best. That these concerns did not immediately convince the State Secretary to cancel the experiments, however, does not mean that they were completely ineffective. The members of employee representative boards of the pilot study schools did prove susceptible to the plea of the union to object when they were asked for employee approval. The low response to the call to apply for funding, moreover, indicates that school boards were not very much inclined to assist in the development of knowledge about incentives in education. Because the plan to incentivize teachers disappeared from the political agenda for different reasons, it is difficult to assess whether the effect of these counteracting concerns was strong enough to put a stop to the eventual establishment of performance pay in education.

The susceptibility to the concerns expressed leads to a second broader theme addressed at the beginning of this chapter. I have zoomed in on the ways in which different (sets of) actors – economic experts, politicians, teachers and union leaders – express different (sets of) concerns about the introduction of monetary incentives for teaching personnel. On a more abstract level the elaboration on concerns tells us something about the worth of education for those concerned and in the reconfiguration of its value. First of all, the introduction of wage incentives recasts the worth of working as a teacher. The value of education now becomes predominantly determined by the performance of students as defined by the net gain in their test scores. The relationship established between increased test scores and increased pay, moreover, means that teachers are to get used to competition and to esteem based on output previously unknown in their field of work. Indeed, CPB economists acknowledged they had 'a certain a priori appreciation for competition' (CPB, 2001, p. 128), while politicians equally thought that competition over bonuses guaranteed that excellent teachers were properly rewarded and could be an example for others. However, the new articulation of worth was immediately contested as the concerns of both practitioners and their union representatives reveal. They set out to express their negative disposition toward performance pay by emphasizing the moral characteristics thought essential to their professional culture. Team spirit and professional development were considered incompatible with the selection of excellent teachers by way of a competition over bonuses.

Second, the introduction of performance pay not only entailed a transformation in the (e)valuation of teachers, but also a reconfiguration of the value of education itself. In the CPB reports the value of educational achievements was expressed in terms of the expected economic benefits. The justification for performance pay in the policy notes, moreover, shows that the gifted students should be given priority. A challenging educational climate fostered by performance pay was considered especially beneficial for the best and the brightest. The simultaneity of an investment in performance pay and a budget cut on special education, noted by practitioners, corroborates the economic value attached to education. The long-term economic effects of investing in students with a handicap, chronic disease or mental disorder are probably less than those of investing in gifted students who are the future pillars of the knowledge economy. The introduction of performance pay is therefore bound up with a bifurcation in those who are considered more worthy of investment and those who are considered less worthy.

NOTES

1. The bonus is the most visible incentive to induce individuals to enhance their performance. But besides monetary inducements there are equally important but less visible aspects of governing by way of incentives such as the fostering of 'transparency'; the use of 'indicators' of quality and performance; the creation of competition over scarce resources; and the establishment of procedures of 'accountability'.
2. If we take a look at the use of incentives as an instrument in private enterprises, however, it immediately becomes clear that they are not uncontested there. In the recent financial crisis, for instance, the place of monetary incentives in organizations was heavily debated for their reputed role in favoring the short-term benefits of mortgagers and financial institutions over the long-term tenability of the economic system (Seager and Wearden, 2008; Taleb, 2011). In Switzerland, the controversy became political and even led to legal restrictions on the use of bonuses (Shotter and Barker, 2013).
3. An exception could be made for the analysis of auctions. Yet Guala (2007) only ends his chapter on the FCC auctions with some general remarks on the politics of auctions, leaving the political process by which economics becomes embraced by policymakers unaddressed. Mirowski and Nik-Khah (2007) come closest in analyzing the politics of the dispersion of market devices. A similar exception should be made for the study of the emergence of the Norwegian market for fish quota by Holm and Nielsen (2007).
4. For a full account of the emergence of principal–agent theory out of an earlier debate over the role of information in socialist and capitalist economies, see Dix (2014, pp. 99–134).

5. The articulation of current weaknesses in education as instantiations of a general problematic of information asymmetry is particularly strong in the CPB report written by Canton and Webbink (2004). References to that report thus dominate this section. The other CPB reports are more important when it comes to the articulation of the value of performance pay as the most promising policy measures to enhance educational output.
6. The Dutch Labor Party (PvdA), for instance, was proud of its title 'champion of education' during the 2010 election campaign. The title was bestowed on the PvdA on the basis of CPB's *Charted Choices* and therefore partly indebted to the promise to invest in performance pay (Dirks, 2010).

REFERENCES

Source Material

AOB (2011a), 'Onderwijspersoneel wijst prestatiebeloning af', available at: http:// www.aob.nl/default.aspx?id=220andarticle=48073andq=andm=.
AOB (2011b), 'Enquete-uitslagen Prestatiebeloning', available at: http://www.aob. nl/ kixtart/modules/absolutenm/articlefiles/48073-Enqu%C3%AAte.pdf.
AOB (2011c), 'Actiekrant 3. Geen bonus, maar banen!', leaflet sent with *Onderwijsblad* 15:15.
AOB (2012a), 'Geen instemming gevraag bij proef prestatiebeloning', available at: http://www.aob.nl/default.aspx?id=287andarticle=48615andq=andm=.
AOB (2012b), 'Deel pilots aan de slag zonder instemming medezeggenschapsraad', available at: http://www.aob.nl/default.aspx?id=287andarticle=48613andq= andm=.
AOB (2012c), 'Medezeggenschapsraden aarzelen over experimenten prestatiebeloning', available at: http://www.aob.nl/default.aspx?id=287andarticle= 48869andq=andm=.
AOB (2012d), 'Veertig aanmeldingen voor proef prestatiebeloning', available at: http://www.aob.nl/default.aspx?id=287andarticle=48842andq=andm=.
Besturenraad.nl (2011), 'Prestatiebeloning op z'n Amsterdams: het team centraal', available at http://www.besturenraad.nl/content/prestatiebeloning-op-z%E2% 80%99n-amsterdams-het-team-centraal.
Canton, Eric and Dinand Webbink (2004), 'Prestatieprikkels in het Nederlandse onderwijs: wat kunnen we leren van recente buitenlandse ervaringen?', CPB Report No. 49, available at: http://www.cpb.nl/sites/default/files/publicaties/ download/ prestatieprikkels-het-nederlandse-onderwijs-wat-kunnen-we-leren-van-recente-buitenlandse.pdf.
CDA (2010), 'Slagvaardig en samen. Verkiezingsprogramma 2010–2015', available at: www.cda.nl/Upload/2010_docs/Verkiezingsprogram2010/CDA_VKPnieuw. pdf.
ChristenUnie (2010), 'Vooruitzien. Christelijk-Sociaal Perspectief. Verkiezingsprogramma ChristenUnie 2010–2014', available at: http://www. christenunie.nl/l/library/download/WhAF0ucVKzwFhGbUzEfr_a_nt0P-DixRD3P/ChristenUnie+Verkiezingsprogramma+Tweede+Kamer+2010.pdf.
CPB (2001), 'Centraal Economisch Plan', available at: http://www.cpb.nl/publica-tie /centraal-economisch-plan-cep-2001.
CPB (2003), 'Keuzes in kaart 2003–2006. Economische effecten van acht

verkiezingsprogramma's', Bijzondere publicatie 39, available at: http://www.cpb. nl/publicatie/keuzes-kaart-2003–2006-economische-effecten-van-acht-verkie zingsprogrammas.

CPB (2006), 'Keuzes in kaart 2008–2011. Economische effecten van acht verkiezingsprogramma's', Bijzondere publicatie 65, available at: http://www. cpb.nl/publicatie/keuzes-kaart-2008–2011-economische-effecten-van-achtverkiezingsprogrammas.

CPB and PBL (2010), 'Keuzes in kaart 2011–2015. Effecten van negen verkiezings programma's op economie en milieu', Bijzondere publicatie 85, available at: http://www.cpb.nl/publicatie/ verkiezingsprogrammas-doorgerekend-keuzeskaart-2011–2015.

D66 (2010), 'Verkiezingsprogramma Tweede Kamer 2010', available at: www.d66. nl/d66nl/item /verkiezingsprogramma_tweede_kamer.

Dirks, Bart (2010), 'Bezuinigsmonster lijkt onderwijs ongemoeid te laten', *Volkskrant*, 3 June.

Dresscher, Walter (2010), 'Mythen en misverstanden rond prestatiebeloning', *Onderwijsblad* 14:11.

Dresscher, Walter (2011), 'Prestatiebeloning moet en zal er komen', *Onderwijsblad* 15: 4.

Elk, Roel van, Debby Lanser and Sander van Veldhuizen (2011a), 'Onderwijsbeleid in Nederland. De kwantificering van effecten', CPB Achtergronddocument, available at: http://www.cpb.nl/publicatie/onderwijsbeleid-nederland.

Elk, Roel van, Frans Bauke van der Meer, Marc van der Steeg and Dinand Webbink (2011b), 'Zicht op Effectiviteit van Beleid', CPB Achtergronddocument, available at: http://www.beleidsevaluatie.info/wp-content/uploads/2011/06/cpbachtergronddoument-zicht-op-effectiviteit-van-beleid.pdf.

'Experimenten prestatiebeloning van start' Available at: http://www.youtube.com/ watch?feature=player_embeddedandv=tZLA8ldOo_c#!

Groenlinks (2010), 'Klaar voor de toekomst. Verkiezingsprogramma 2010', available at: http://tweedekamer.groenlinks.nl/files/Verkiezingsprogramma GroenLinks2010.pdf.

Hoogenboom, B. (2011), 'Geen bonus maar banen', *Onderwijsblad* 15:15.

Kersten, Arno (2012), 'Het is en blijft voor een deel tasten in het duister. Onderzoeker Robert Dur over experimenten prestatiebeloning', *Onderwijsblad* 16:2.

Koning, Pierre, Eric Canton, Maarten Cornet, Marc Pomp, Martijn van der Ven, Richard Venniker, Ben Vollaard and Dinand Webbink (2004), 'Centrale doelen, decentrale uitvoering; do's en dont's van prestatieprikkels voor semi-publieke instellingen', CPB Document no. 45, available at: http://www.cpb.nl /sites/ default/files/publicaties/download/doc45.pdf.

'Leerlingen en directeur Open Schoolgemeenschap Bijlmer over prestatieloon', video available at: http://nos.nl/video/314298-leerlingen-en-directeur-openschoolgemeenschap-bijlmer-over-prestatieloon.html.

Mee, Gaby van der (2011), 'De heilige overtuigingen van Halbe Zijlstra', *Onderwijsblad* 15:15.

Ministry of Education, Culture and Science (2011a), 'Actieplan Leraar 2020 – een krachtig beroep!', available at: http://www.rijksoverheid.nl/documenten-enpublicaties/kamerstukken/2011/05/23/actieplan-leraar-2020.html.

Ministry of Education, Culture and Science (2011b), 'Actieplan Beter Presteren: opbrengstgericht en ambitious. Het beste uit leerlingen halen', available at:

http://www.rijksoverheid.nl/documenten-en-publicaties/kamerstukken/2011/05/ 23/actieplan-vo-beter-presteren.html.

Ministry of Education, Culture and Science (2012), 'Vragen van het lid Jasper van Dijk (SP)', 17 February 2010, ref. 378363.

Onderwijsraad (2011), 'Excellente leraren als inspirerend voorbeeld', available at: http://www.onderwijsraad.nl/publicaties/2011/excellente-leraren-als-inspirerend-voorbeeld/item3479.

'Prestatiebeloning onderwijs: schooldirecteuren zien er weinig in', video available at: https://www.youtube.com/watch?v=W1QGg3ZUyW8.

PvdA (2010), 'Iedereen telt mee. De kracht van Nederland, PvdA Verkiezingsprogramma 2010', available at: www.pvda.nl/publicatie/bibliotheek/ publicaties/2010%5B3%5D/Verkiezingsprogramma+2010.html.

'Regeling Experimenten Prestatiebeloning Onderwijs', available at: http://www. rijksoverheid.nl/documenten-en-publicaties/regelingen/2011/11/17/   regeling-experimenten-prestatiebeloning-onderwijs.html.

SGP (2010), 'Daad bij het Woord: de SGP stáát ervoor! – Verkiezingsprogramma 2010–2014, available at: www.sgp.nl/Media/download/19720/ Verkiezings programma%20SGP%202010–2014.pdf.

Sikkes, Robert (2001a), 'CPB wil meer marktwerking in het onderwijs', *Onderwijsblad* 5:8.

Sikkes, Robert (2001b), 'Liberale maakbaarheid', *Onderwijsblad* 5:8.

Sikkes, Robert (2002), 'Prestatiebeloning werkt niet, bonus wel', *Onderwijsblad* 6:1.

Sikkes, Robert (2008), 'Presteren en belonen', *Onderwijsblad* 12:11.

Sikkes, Robert (2011), 'Prestatieprikkels onderwijs vragen om *Dutch approach*', available at: http://www.aob.nl/doc/prestatiebeloning.pdf.

Telegraaf (2012), '40 scholen willen prestatiebeloning uittesten', available at: www. telegraaf.nl/binnenland/20035458/__Scholen_testen_prestatie__.html.

Volkskrant (2012), 'Lerarenprotest heeft geen invloed op standpunt coalitie', 6 March, available at: http://www.volkskrant.nl/vk/nl/5288/Onderwijs/article/ detail/   3220340/2012/03/06/Lerarenprotest-heeft-geen-invloed-op-standpunt-coalitie.dhtml.

'Vrijheid en verantwoordelijkheid. Regeerakkoord VVD–CDA' (2010), available at: http://www.rijksoverheid.nl/documenten-en-publicaties/rapporten /2010/ 09/30/regeerakkoord-vvd-cda.html.

VVD (2010), 'Orde op zaken. VVD Verkiezingsprogramma 2010–2014', available at: www.vvd.nl/actueel/925/orde-op-zaken-vvd-verkiezingsprogramm a-2010–2014.

Vyrastekova, Jana, Sander Onderstal and Pierre Koning (2006), 'Team incentives in public organisations. An experimental study', available at: http://www.cpb.nl/ publicatie/team-incentives-public-organisations-experimental-study.

References

Abrahamson, Eric (1996), 'Technical and aesthetic fashion', in Barbara Czarniawska and Guje Sevón (eds), *Translating Organizational Change*, Berlin: De Gruyter, pp. 117–37.

Beckert, Jens and Patrick Aspers (2011), 'Value in markets', in Jens Beckert and Patrick Aspers (eds), *The Worth of Goods. Valuation and Pricing in the Economy*, Oxford, UK: Oxford University Press, pp. 3–38.

Boltanski, Luc and Laurent Thévenot (2006), *On Justification. Economies of Worth*, Princeton, NJ: Princeton University Press.

Callon, Michel (2010), 'Performativity, misfires and politics', *Journal of Cultural Economy*, 3 (2), 163–96.

Callon, Michel, Yuval Millo and Fabian Muniesa (2007), 'An introduction to market devices', in Michel Callon, Yuval Milo and Fabian Muniesa (eds), *Market Devices*, Oxford, UK: Blackwell Publishing, pp. 1–12.

Cochoy, Franck, Martin Giraudeau and Liz McFall (2010), 'Performativity, economics and politics', *Journal of Cultural Economy*, 3 (2), 139–46.

Dix, Guus (2014), *Governing by carrot and stick. A genealogy of the incentive*, unpublished PhD thesis.

Dixit, Avinash K. (2002), 'Incentives and organizations in the public sector. An interpretative review', *The Journal of Human Resources*, 37 (4), 696–727.

Garcia-Parpet, Marie-France (2007), 'The social construction of a perfect market: the strawberry auction at Fontaines-en-Sologne', in Donald MacKenzie, Fabian Muniesa and Lucia Siu (eds), *Do Economists Make Markets? On the Performativity of Economics*, Princeton, NJ: Princeton University Press, pp. 20–53.

Guala, Francesco (2007), 'How to do things with experimental economics', in Donald MacKenzie, Fabian Muniesa and Lucia Siu (eds), *Do Economists Make Markets? On the Performativity of Economics*, Princeton, NJ: Princeton University Press, pp. 128–62.

Hindriks, Jean and Gareth D. Myles (2006), *Intermediate Public Economics*, Cambridge, MA: MIT Press.

Holm, Petter and Kåre N. Nielsen (2007), 'Framing fish, making markets: the construction of Individual Transferable Quotas (ITQs)', in Michel Callon, Yuval Milo and Fabian Muniesa (eds), *Market Devices*, Oxford, UK: Blackwell Publishing, pp. 173–95.

Laffont, Jean Jacques and David Martimort (2002), *The Theory of Incentives: The Principal–agent Model*, Princeton, NJ: Princeton University Press.

Laffont, Jean Jacques and Eric Maskin (1983), 'The theory of incentives: An overview', in Werner Hildenbrand (ed.), *Advances in Economic Theory*, Cambridge, UK: Cambridge University Press, pp. 31–94.

Lavy, Victor (2009), 'Performance pay and teachers' effort, productivity, and grading ethics', *American Economic Review*, 99 (5), 1979–2011.

Ledyard, John O. (1987), 'Incentive compatibility', in James Eatwell, Murray Milgate and Peter Newman (eds), *The New Palgrave: A Dictionary of Economics*, London, UK: Macmillan Press, pp. 739–944.

Maas, Harro (2010), 'Rekenmeesters, heelmeesters en vogelaars. De vinger aan de pols van de economie', *Krisis: Tijdschrift Voor Actuele Filosofie*, 3, 6–25.

MacKenzie, Donald (2007), 'Is economics performative? Option theory and the construction of derivatives markets', in Donald MacKenzie, Fabian Muniesa and Lucia Siu (eds), *Do Economists Make Markets? On the Performativity of Economics*, Princeton, NJ: Princeton University Press, pp. 20–53.

MacKenzie, Donald, Fabian Muniesa and Lucia Siu (2007), 'Introduction', in Donald MacKenzie, Fabian Muniesa and Lucia Siu (eds), *Do Economists Make Markets? On the Performativity of Economics*, Princeton, NJ: Princeton University Press, pp. 1–19.

Mirowski, Philip and Edward Nik-Khah (2007), 'Markets made flesh: Performativity, and a problem in science studies, augmented with consideration of the FCC auctions', in Donald MacKenzie, Fabian Muniesa and Lucia Siu (eds), *Do Economists Make Markets? On the Performativity of Economics*, Princeton, NJ: Princeton University Press, pp. 190–225.

Nobel Prize (1996), 'The Sveriges Riksbank Prize in Economic Sciences in Memory of Alfred Nobel 1996', available at: http://www.nobelprize.org/nobel_prizes/ economics /laureates/1996/.

Nobel Prize (2001), 'The Sveriges Riksbank Prize in Economic Sciences in Memory of Alfred Nobel 2001', available at: http://www.nobelprize.org/nobel_prizes/ economics /laureates/2001/.

Nobel Prize (2007), 'The Sveriges Riksbank Prize in Economic Sciences in Memory of Alfred Nobel 2007', available at: http://www.nobelprize.org/ nobel_prizes/ economics/laureates/2007/.

Pindyck, Robert S. and Daniel Rubinfeld (2005), *Microeconomics*, New Jersey: Pearson Education.

Pollit, Christopher (2003), *The Essential Public Manager*, Maidenhead, UK: Open University Press.

Pollit, Christopher and Geert Bouckaert (2011), *Public Management Reform: A Comparative Analysis*, Oxford: Oxford University Press.

Seager, A. and G. Wearden (2008), 'Bank of England chief launches attack on City bonus culture', *The Guardian*, 30 April.

Shotter, J. and A. Barker (2013), 'Swiss vote for corporate pay curbs', *Financial Times*, 3 March, available at: http://www.ft.com/intl/cms/s/0/ca90f1b4–83ff-11e2-b700–00144feabdc0.html#axzz2Ow8wXJvD

Stark, David (2009), *The Sense of Dissonance: Accounts of Worth in Economic Life*, Princeton, NJ: Princeton University Press.

Taleb, Nassim N. (2011), 'End bonuses for bankers', *The New York Times*, 7 November.

Ward, Steven C. (2011), 'Commentary', *Journal of Cultural Economy*, **4** (2), 205–15.

3. Marketization by the (rule)book: concern for market and public values in primary care

Linus Johansson Krafve

INTRODUCTION

Health care provides a fruitful setting for learning about concerns over values. Provision of health care is often thought of as a cornerstone in welfare societies. It is truly a matter of concern, as it regularly resides at the center of political rhetoric, public debate and reform agendas. There are many actors who want to have a say in what constitutes proper conduct in health care, what is financially viable and which health caring activities are worth pursuing before others. Practical considerations of the economics of health care, managerial challenges, along with questions of quality in treatment are never far away. Health care is thus thoroughly saturated with values of very different kinds.

Values also matter a great deal in how health care is organized in practice. This chapter builds on a case study of the making of a primary care market in a Swedish county council. More precisely, I have studied how public officials at a Swedish county council HQ design a 'market device' (Callon et al., 2007) for the primary care market: a rulebook for authorization of care centers.[1] This rulebook is revised and issued by the county council each year. It consists of nearly 50 pages of guidelines, prices, justifications and more, stipulating the rules for market conduct in the primary care market. It is supposed to regulate the market by codifying the criteria for being granted permission to open a care center in the county. I treat this rulebook as a setting in which concerns over values come to the fore in a very concrete sense.

The aim of the chapter is to describe how values are enacted by the rulebook. The analytical strategy is to make a detailed reading of the rulebook, and to supplement this reading with some data of how the rulebook is written and revised. The chapter deals with the following questions: what values are at stake in the primary care market, and how are these manifested in the rulebook? Since I regard the rulebook as a practical expression of values and their interrelation, I also ask: how are different values made to matter in relation to one another in the rulebook?

By 'enactment of value' I refer to activities that perform values and make them appear as states of the world. Valuation is here understood as the practices – involving metrics, rules, doings and sayings – that enact particular values or versions of value (cf. Helgesson and Muniesa, 2013).[2] Consequently, the chapter discusses how values are enacted and manifested by the rulebook, rather than assuming they are determined in the marketization reform per se. By doing so, it interrogates the grandiose concept of 'market reform' – and the forces, ideals and effects associated with it – by treating it as an ongoing experimental practice manifested in the making of a particular device. The values that come to the fore are not treated as clear or fixed, but as emerging from being tinkered with. The choice of approach is based on a recognition of the contingency, heterogeneity and multiplicity (e.g. Kjellberg and Helgesson, 2006; 2007) of values that characterize the primary care market under study. The practice-orientation turns these values and valuations into empirical objects of study, and acknowledges that values are not entities for abstract space only, but grappled with in concrete situations available for observation.

The rulebook is not a unique site, but represents a market situation in which new and old value concerns are raised and a new device is employed to secure them. Therefore, a careful analysis of the rulebook is a stepping-stone towards a more general argument about the potential for markets to produce a multitude of values. By approaching the rulebook from a pragmatic perspective, I interrogate taken-for-granted assumptions about what markets can and cannot do, what values they will promote and what values they will suppress. My close scrutiny of the rulebook illustrates how tinkering with markets entails the handling of value conflicts, which are not necessarily resolved, but moved and altered, in the process of regulating the market.

The chapter is structured as follows. First, I present a background to the studied case, relating it to quasi-market theory. This provides a theoretical backdrop and deepens the interest with public and market values in relation to the case of the rulebook. Second, I outline and justify the chosen analytical approach and present the central analytical concepts. Third, I provide a note on methodology and data collection. Fourth, I present my analysis of the rulebook case, together with a discussion of the findings. Finally, the concluding section summarizes the argument and relates the findings to the broader theme of the chapter.

BACKGROUND: THE PROMISES OF QUASI-MARKETS IN WELFARE SERVICES

One of the most pressing debates in welfare states is how to organize welfare service provision. These discussions often revolve around what values and qualities will be safeguarded and how. The values of empowerment and promotion of the capacity of patients to choose are not new in such policy discussions, but in recent decades they have been increasingly associated with the working of health care markets. Whereas, in the past, public organizing, financing and provision of health care was seen as an answer to market failures, market elements have more recently been presented as a solution to public sector failures of aligning health care to the needs and wishes of individual patients (Zuiderent-Jerak et al., 2010).

Sweden is a striking case in this respect. In the years following WW2, the Swedish welfare state expanded enormously. The Social Democratic universalistic welfare model, 'the people's home', was widely considered to be a unique realization of the value of 'social egalitarianism' (Esping-Andersen, 1990). Over the past 20 years, however, 'choice' as policy content and quality indicator has 'revolutionized' (Blomqvist, 2004) Swedish welfare policy, and according to *The Economist* (2 February, 2013), Sweden is best in class when it comes to choice in welfare services. But the change didn't happen overnight. Nordgren (2010) investigated the genealogy of this development in Swedish policy discourse and found that increased discursive couplings between themes such as money, capitation and customer choice gave rise to the so-called 'voucher' concept in welfare policy. Today, the voucher is invoked as a prominent governance technique in Swedish welfare policy.

Vouchers, Patient Choice and Competition

In textbook economics and neo-classical doctrine, markets function through the mechanism whereby supply meets demand. The value of a product is equal to its price, which is determined in the interaction between buyers and sellers in the market (so-called exchange value). Competition between providers of goods and the exercising of free choice by buyers secures a dynamic mechanism to lower the prices and increase quality. Above all, markets promise to solve the distribution of goods and services in an efficient manner. As such, 'market' is an organizational form that could be enrolled to decide the value and distribution of goods in a polity (Friedman, 2009[1962]). Conversely, the idea of 'market failure' counterbalances the sturdiest promises of market advocacy. Health care specifically – as memorably claimed by economist Kenneth Arrow – is often portrayed as a sector burdened with too much uncertainty and lack of information for supply and demand, price and quality to be coordinated spontaneously. Markets in health care are therefore said to force 'interventions' to reach 'optimal states' (Arrow, 1963).

In economics, there are thus ideas that markets could do well as an organizing principle, but that there may be a need for 'intervention'. There are entire academic fields devoted to finding the best ways to design such market interventions, of which health economics has been at the forefront (Ashmore et al., 1989). How to improve health care through marketization of public services has been occupying health economists and others for decades. It is, however, no straightforward task to do market reform in practice. The challenges have proved to be immense. The practical and theoretical problems of health care markets have therefore continued to gain attention. One of the most influential notions in this context has been the 'voucher' as advanced by quasi-market theory (e.g. Le Grand, 2007; Le Grand and Bartlett, 1993). Quasi-market theory is a telling example of how market interventions could be designed. It offers proponents of marketization a promising way in which markets could be designed to realize their full potential (in terms of the market values of efficiency, choice and competition), while also adhering to the 'special case' of health care (that is, public values such as equity, fairness, adequacy of treatment, etc.). Applied to primary care, the idea of quasi-markets can be summarized in the following way.

Quasi-markets combine the principle of free choice of care provider with competitive neutrality between such providers. Each patient is given a voucher and is allowed to choose any one among the competing providers. When a patient uses the voucher to contract a care provider (which amounts to the patient being 'listed' by the provider), the provider is entitled to a certain payment from the county council. The voucher comes with many different rules for reimbursement to care providers. There are set prices determined beforehand, for example, depending on the service provided or on the need of the patient. Public as well as private actors compete for the right to produce the care service, but the public sector pays for it and has the overall responsibility for the service being produced. The competitive mechanism is thus to be based on patient preference on one hand, and equal rules to reimbursement to care providers on the other (Le Grand, 2007; Le Grand and Bartlett, 1993).[3]

Quasi-market theory invokes very specific ideas about 'competition' and how competition ought to be 'neutral'. Le Grand (2007) writes that competition is: 'the presence in the public service of a number of providers, each of which, for one reason or another, are motivated to attract users of the particular service' (Le Grand, 2007, p. 41). 'Competitive neutrality' means that all providers are to play by the same rules; that no actors enjoy 'unfair' competitive advantages over their competitors. The aim is a 'level playing field', where all providers adhere to the 'same-for-all' market rules. A foundational idea in this is that motivation matters. And motivational structures could be modeled with market interventions. This lies at the heart of Le Grand's idea that: 'models that rely significantly upon user choice coupled with provider competition generally offer a better structure of incentives to providers' than other systems (Le Grand, 2007, p. 39).

Le Grand advances the idea that mixed forms of policy instruments should be employed to design 'robust incentive structures' for providers. This is where the rulebook finds its justification as a policy instrument: the precise design of policy instruments, in the form of schemes with rules, financial reimbursement and incentivizing ambitions, has become a major concern to academics, policy-makers and medical professionals.[4] Previous research on the organization of the voucher system in primary care in Sweden has revolved around how the 'reimbursement systems' of different county councils function, and how they should be designed as 'incentive schemes' (for example Anell, 2010). This research utilizes, among other things, Le Grandian quasi-market theory to highlight the importance of 'informed choices' and increased competition.[5]

According to the literature referenced above, foremost quasi-market theory, values such as 'free choice' and 'competition' are hot topics in market reform. The challenge is to design the right type of 'interventions', 'incentives' and 'reimbursement schemes' for voucher markets. Le Grand (2007) emphasizes that choice and competition are means to realize policy aims, not ends in themselves, as means and ends are discrete categories. The structure of quasi-market theory is complex, in that it crosses the borders between market and public values; *market* organization is advanced as a solution that safeguards *public* values such as accessibility and quality of care. It advances the idea that certain means (choice, competition and the voucher mechanism) will realize certain values (such as quality, accountability and equitability), all brought together in the voucher.

The technicalities involved in designing voucher and reimbursement schemes seem to offer room for a multitude of different values, meeting in new ways. However, exactly how this works in practice is the source of much debate. The literature review leaves room for several pressing questions: exactly how will choice and competition be secured? What types of 'incentives' are enacted? A close reading of a device like the rulebook is one way of addressing such questions about values meeting in new ways.

Above all, there is a need to look into the assumptions and practices that make the primary care market appear as a state of the world, instead of assuming that the values at stake are already settled in the reform as such. By doing this, the chapter takes an alternative position vis-à-vis quasi-market theory: it adopts an agnostic view regarding the rulebook, and poses critical questions about the values that are said to prevail in the market. Going into the rulebook without a prefixed notion of values will allow new aspects of value to surface in the analysis. This is where the ideas of enactment of values and valuation play their role.

CONCEPTUALIZING THE ENACTMENT OF VALUES

The notion of 'enactment of value' rests on the idea that values and representations of values are brought into being and maintained in practical productive processes, outside of which they have no existence (cf. Asdal, 2008; Law, 2004; Mol, 2002). In short, that value is the result of practice, not the other way around. This ontological stance is vital to the analytical approach, given my ambition to describe how the rulebook enacts values, rather than assume that such values are determined beforehand.

When taking value to be determined by practical action, it makes sense to start from valuation (as a verb) (Kjellberg et al., 2013; Muniesa, 2012). To study value as valuation brings attention to the metrics, rules and other concrete measures that enact particular values or versions of value (Helgesson and Muniesa, 2013). Values are not defined apart from these practical measures, but *because* of them. In practice, this means that I take seriously the claims made concerning values as they are written in and performed by the rulebook. This allows me to investigate the rulebook as a device that renders the market and related values as matters-of-fact, while paying attention to the details that make them appear as such. My starting point, then, is the performance of value by the rulebook, rather than preset standards as to what counts as value.

I take the rulebook to enact particular versions of value, while also representing a reified form of theories and abstract ideas of value found in quasi-market theory. The rulebook could therefore be seen as a 'market device'. The performativity literature has convincingly demonstrated how market devices can impact on real markets by enacting and shaping conventions and configurations concerning how markets are supposed to work (see Callon, 1998; MacKenzie et al., 2007; Muniesa et al., 2007). This literature also highlights that devices are shaped and saturated with theories of markets. Interest has foremost been targeted to the materiality of such devices (Callon et al., 2007), but also to their discursive disposition and effects (Roscoe, 2013). These devices are also involved in making value judgments and political choices in a very fundamental sense (Roscoe, 2015; Zuiderent-Jerak et al., 2015).

Applied to this case, the performative gaze makes the rulebook appear as a market device that expresses the voucher idea as outlined by quasi-market theory. From this follows an interest in how the rulebook performs in the primary care market and its associated values in practice. This interest targets how the rulebook qualifies and configures market objects, subjects and relations, while rendering things and services commensurable and valuable (cf. Callon et al., 2007). In practice, this means that I trace how the rulebook expresses what actors and objects are important to the function of the market. This allows me to see how market forces are enacted, and how market mechanisms are tied to the voucher, to choice and to competition. It furthermore provides opportunity to scrutinize the technicalities and details of pricing and prioritizing and how these in turn enact value.

Devices play a crucial role in the framing of markets. Framing denotes an active process whereby the specific rules of the market are established. The result from framing (verb) efforts is a market frame (noun), which is the reified form of the theories and justifications that underpin the ideas of how the market is supposed to work (Callon, 1998). I use the framing term – with the particular flavor of enactment, valuation and market device – as a heuristic to think through the case of the rulebook and what it does in terms of values. Seen from this perspective, the rulebook becomes a market device that frames the market. In doing so, it performs valuations and enacts specific values as partaking in that market. This heuristic serves to shed light on and bring the performance of the rulebook in focus.[6]

The terminology speaks directly to the pressing themes of agency, subjectivities and values in markets (cf. Kjellberg and Helgesson, 2010 and the current volume). It helps to unpack concerns for public and market values in a very practical sense, as they appear in the rulebook, seen as a market device. The merit of this analytical approach is that it does not 'fix' the case too much, but allows it to develop in unforeseen ways. It cherishes complexity and allows the rulebook to be manifold in terms of values and valuation.

Given these conceptual starting points we can now refine the research questions posed at the outset of the chapter. The first research question – what values are at stake in the market, and how are they manifested in the rulebook? – can now be theoretically ingrained and rephrased as: what valuations are enacted in the rulebook, and how? The term 'enactment' emphasizes that values, as they appear in the rulebook, are to be taken seriously. 'Valuation' denotes the activities of enacting values. The second research question – how are different values made to matter in relation to one another in the rulebook? – grapples with the relation between values. Another term for this is framing, and how it establishes market relations and forces. The developed question thus becomes: how is the market frame enacted by the rulebook? What relations (between market subjects and market objects) are deemed important, and how are they enacted?

METHOD AND DATA COLLECTION

The data used for the study consist primarily of different versions of the rulebook. The bulk of the argument is built around a detailed reading of these. In addition, I have conducted fieldwork and interviews at the HQ of the studied county council. The interviews were recorded and transcribed. Field notes were made in connection to observations at county council HQ, at meetings in some other locations and during visits to care centers. Discussions were also held with the informants in connection with interviews and observations. The general research strategy was guided by an ethnographical methodology (Hammersley and Atkinson, 2007) in that research questions were open and a wide range of data was collected.

My guiding interest was towards the concrete activities pursued to get the primary care market in place. The main research strategy was to 'shadow' (Czarniawska, 2007) purchaser officials at the county council HQ, as their job descriptions included working with the care choice system. As exploration progressed, it was evident that their attention was mostly oriented towards designing the rulebook. At first, this struck me as a very peculiar practice. However, through the course of the study, it became quite clear that the rulebook played a decisive role for the involved actors as part of their efforts to organize the primary care market. I witnessed how officials, medical professionals, economists and others devoted much time and effort to the rulebook. Among other things, it seemed to constantly provoke articulations of valuation and judgment. The rulebook designers amassed many of these judgments; some caused distress, some provoked revision, while others were ignored. Therefore, I treat the rulebook as a key device for enacting values and getting a primary care market in place.

There are two important challenges with respect to this methodology and data collection. The first has to do with the difference between data types. At first glance, the data sources appear to be distinctly different: the rulebook as a text, the interviews and the field notes allow me to see different things. However, in the spirit of the analytical strategy, I treat *all* data sources as practical manifestations, in that they all perform work in getting the market in place.[7] This allows me to appreciate how the rulebook performs the market, and foremost, how it enacts values.[8]

The second challenge has to do with the timing of data collection. In descriptive accounts of processes in the making, the time of data collection could have profound effects. As I entered the county council, the rulebook had been in effect for some time. There is a risk here; retrospection might entail *post hoc* rationalization of the process. Real-time ethnographical data is preferred (Hoholm and Araujo, 2011), especially when processes are 'messy' or controversial (Law, 2004). Real-time data allows sensitivity towards uncertainties and contingencies, while it provides the opportunity to witness decisive moments first-hand. It furthermore allows controversies, tensions, issues and alternative choice paths to be witnessed and recorded, as they appear unmediated through time and rationalizing practices (Hoholm and Araujo, 2011). However, in the performative gaze of devices as texts, materials speak and perform continually. Related to the point above about work to get the market in place, I treat the rulebook as an ongoing practice. Reading the rulebook as a market device can thus provide insight into how it enacts values and performs the market.

ANALYSIS: MARKETIZATION BY THE (RULE)BOOK

Organizing, financing and performing health care is by far the biggest task for Swedish county councils. The county council organization is based on the purchaser/provider split, which seeks to imitate the procurement procedure that takes place in business. The split calls for clear-cut roles and contractual management, in which the purchaser concentrates on specifying requirements to be placed on the service, and the providers sell the service demanded (Siverbo, 2004). The politically assigned County Council Assembly works to set the strategic plan and the budget for the county council, to which all other county council businesses are obliged to adhere. The County Council Executive Committee leads and coordinates the affairs of the county council. It consists of politicians from the political parties, which are represented in accordance with their relative size in the Assembly. The Healthcare Committee, finally, is a political body assigned to ensure that the health care needs of the population in the county are met. The idea is that the Healthcare Committee assigns providers of care and manages contracts with suppliers. The Healthcare Committee is responsible for the purchasing function, while the County Council Executive Committee is the principal for the health care provision units operated by the county. The work to design the rulebook is carried out by many different professionals at the administrative office (serving both purchasing and provider functions), for example statisticians, economists and medical specialists. The Health Care Committee takes the final decision to accept a rulebook.

The history of the rulebook in the studied county council starts in 2006, when the Health Care Committee assigned a task force to assess requirements and make an inventory of 'opportunities for development' in primary care. In practice, this meant that the group conducted a round of interviews and focus group sessions with medical professionals at primary care centers in the county. The county council also set up a couple of grand discussion meetings for medical professionals and other personnel in the county. Between these meetings, working groups consisting of primary care personnel and staff from the administrative office were assigned to solve different problems and issues that surfaced from the grand meetings and the inventory. Apart from the inventory, the grand meetings and the working groups, the county council had recently performed a public procurement of a care center. And for that purpose, a specification document of the service being procured had been put together. This specification was eventually to become the first draft of the 'authorization document' for the care choice system, called the 'rulebook'.

However, policy-making in the national government came to interfere with the ongoing process. As the county council was about to launch their authorization document, the national government released two white papers with the intention to issue legislation to force all county councils to arrange for 'care choice systems' in their primary care. The Swedish Government at the time was not satisfied with the extent to which patient choice had spurred competition in primary care (Regeringskansliet, 2008). From now on, there were other conditions to be met than the traditional procurement legislation. In the new legislation, *all* tenderers – whether they be owned and run by the county councils or private enterprises – that fulfill the contract specifications would be eligible to set up their service to compete and attract patients on an equal footing with all other providers. That is, all providers are thus under the same agreement and must adhere to the same contract; in this case the rulebook.

The coming legislation forced county councils to revise their primary health care according to the principles of 'free choice' and 'competitive neutrality'. In the end, however, the political majority in the studied county council concluded that the new legislation only made market principles appear more fully-fledged in the reform attempts, and that the rulebook would be a suitable device for pursuing those aims. The political decisions taken by the 2008 Health Care Committee in the county emphasized that a broad political majority (with the exception of one party) supported the reform agenda. In December 2008 the Health Care Committee decided upon the suggested rulebook and conditions for the care choice system. The care choice system was subsequently launched on 1 September 2009.

Taking a Look at the Rulebook: what Values are at Stake?

The 2013 rulebook begins with a declaration:

[The care choice system] aims to strengthen citizens' status as patients by free choice of care center and an individually balanced voucher that follows the individual's choice. Citizen choice shall be secured by objective and easily accessible information, available to all. The aim of [the care choice system] is increased quality and accessibility in primary care through competition where care centers are free to develop within the framework of the mission to best meet patients' needs.

For patients/citizens the selected care center will create security and be perceived as the natural first choice when in need of care. The care center will provide advice and assistance to citizens on how they can maintain and improve their health. Contact with the care center is characterized by great flexibility.

Citizens will be well received and able to influence their treatment. To create a sense of security, patients/citizens must feel assured that assessment, treatment and advice is safe and of good quality, that the care center maintains high continuity and takes responsibility for patients' care pathways, which comprises information on options of treatment, care guarantees, etc. Primary care practices will be characterized by cohesive care processes, which require deepened and broadened cooperation between care providers with different organizational affiliation and other concerned societal parties.

[The care choice system] means that primary care financed by the county council is operated by authorized care centers, public as well as private. For the supplier to provide care in [the care choice system] it has to be approved by the county council, that is, be authorized as a care center. The authorization provides basic quality assurance and levels the playing field while allowing for a multitude of suppliers. The authorization requires that the care center undertake the mission as formulated in [the rulebook]. Pertinent priorities in the care choice system are health promotion and disease prevention, cohesive care processes and that special consideration is paid to the needs of underprivileged patients.

This passage sums up the ambitions of the care choice system rather well. The list of values enacted by the text is comprehensive: free choice, competition, quality, accessibility, security, flexibility, influence, safety, continuity, responsibility, cohesiveness, cooperation, health promotion, disease prevention and consideration for the underprivileged. Primary care clearly is a site where many values come to the fore, and this list provides a first glimpse of the value landscape that the rulebook models.

The rhetoric and spirit of patient choice and competition between care providers prevail up front in the declaration. It is rather straightforward to discern that the voucher brought forth in the rulebook emanates from quasi-market theory: 'an individually balanced voucher that follows the individual's choice.' Overall, the rulebook resonates well with quasi-market theory, in that it frames free choice and competition as drivers and mechanisms (i.e. expressed as 'means') for the market, while values such as quality and accessibility are regarded as targets (expressed as 'ends') (cf. Le Grand, 2007).

However, 'choice' is placed in a rather ambivalent position, as it is put forth both as an abstract value and as a practical mechanism for competition. It is a value, as the rulebook states that the care choice system 'aims to strengthen citizens' status as patients by free choice of care center'. 'Choice' cannot be dismissed only as a means, given how the rulebook brings it to the fore. It is furthermore a very particular form of choice, albeit one that follows quasi-market theory. The underlying intention is that patients should choose one care center and remain with it over time, and not choose a new one every time she/he is in need of care. The patient is enacted as capable of making informed choices, that is, choices based on readily available and objective information.

'Competition' also has dual character. It is a value, as it is expressed as a bottom-line rationale for the care choice system. And it is also a means, as the declaration frames the economic agency of care providers and enacts care providers as market actors who pursue economic interests by competing for patients. 'Competitive neutrality' means all eligible care providers have the same right to open care centers and compete for patients in accordance with the specifications and regulations of the rulebook. The rules for running care centers should be exactly the same for all providers, and are supposed to 'level the playing field', regardless of ownership. By controlling the behavior of all care providers in this way, the rulebook frames primary care as a competitively 'fair' market.

By relating the values of free choice and competitive neutrality in the above manner, the rulebook enacts a particular version of 'market force', which resembles the 'invisible hand' that Le Grand (2007) asks for. Furthermore, the rulebook frames the market as a mechanism for realizing ambitions of high quality and accessibility. The road is paved towards these goals by the principles of 'free choice' and 'competitive neutrality', as spelled out above. In this sense, the (market) values of free choice and competition are enacted as both abstract values (or goods in their own right) and as very practical matters linked to concrete activities. While the activities of free choice and competition are exercised, the values of quality and accessibility will be strived towards.

The rulebook could be viewed as an outright application of quasi-market theory; at the very least, the voucher modeled by the rulebook is expected to function in accordance with quasi-market theory. But what does this voucher look like? What are the specific features of the voucher that secure this function? One answer is found in the reimbursement scheme.

Relations of Value: Reimbursement Schemes in the Making

By enacting a market model building on free choice and competitive neutrality, the rulebook could be said to reify quasi-market theory. It has picked up the key notions of choice and competition, and it has related these notions via a voucher. The rulebook, while being a device for reifying quasi-market theory, also models a 'reimbursement scheme'. The term 'reimbursement scheme' comes from the quasi-market literature, which usually views financial reimbursement in the light of 'incentives' (e.g. Anell, 2010; Le Grand, 2007). The reimbursement scheme is particularly interesting as it points to the connection between different values and different standards for pricing. It highlights how enactment of value is also a matter of calculative valuation practices. It is therefore interesting to note that there has been a shift in reimbursement schemes in the current rulebook.

From Capitation . . .

From the start of the care choice system and up until 2013, the rulebook made clear that the main rationale for reimbursement was 'capitation', that is to reimburse on the basis of enlisted patients at each care center.[9] The payment is fixed in relation to the age and gender of each patient and does not depend on treatment or other caring activities. The rulebook for 2013 states that the county council has deliberately chosen to use capitation as the main rationale for reimbursement: 'Reimbursement for listed persons is a balanced individual-based compensation to promote comprehensiveness and responsibility' (LiÖ, 2012). Here, the principle of capitation is claimed to be conducive to the values of comprehensiveness and responsibility. Capitation is enacted as suitable when the intention is to provide caregivers with an incentive to take a broader and holistic responsibility for patients' welfare. It is intended to promote long-term relationships with patients (not least in that it is a way to stabilize revenue for care centers).

In addition to capitation, the 2013 rulebook distinguished three other types of reimbursements. First, there was 'Basic' reimbursement, purporting to provide care centers with a basic reimbursement, depending on the unique conditions for each care center (mostly determined by the location of the care center). Second, there was 'Variable' reimbursement, purporting to provide incentives to improve performance in particular areas. Third, there was 'Special' reimbursement, purporting to reimburse care centers for activities they conducted that were not captured by the other reimbursement categories in the scheme, including patient fees.

Table 3.1 *The different types of reimbursements included in the 2013 reimbursement system*

Basic	Variable	Capitation	Special
Base Dependent on number of listed patients. If more than one care center in a community, no payment.	*Coverage* Payment for each patient up to coverage of 56% of listed patients.	*Listed patients* Individual weights on age.	Patient fees Government grants
Socio-economic Areas with lowest 10% of disposable income receive payment per listed patient.	*'Infidelity' visits* Payment for visits from unlisted patients. Deduction if listed patients go to other caregiver.		Development grants Asylum seekers
Geography For patients over the age of 75 living 11–25 or >25 km from care center.	*Pay-per-performance* Variable, but 2011: • Availability • Multimodal treatment • Diagnosis registration • Health promotion	*Medicine* Individual weights according to age and gender on both common drugs and focus drugs.	Patients from other county councils and foreign citizens Interpreters
	Treatment pressure DDD (defined daily dose): minimum level and comparison to LiÖ average.		Education and internship Communicable disease control

Source: Adaption and table by author.

Table 3.1 depicts a condensed model of the reimbursement system from 2013. It shows some of the different principles and activities related to each type of reimbursement.

The reimbursement scheme speaks in a very fundamental sense to enactment of particular versions of value. The table highlights that payment to care centers follows a multitude of different rationales and that payment depends on very different principles. This could be seen in the light of the value landscape enacted in the starting paragraphs of the rulebook. The different items in the scheme embody several different values, and are used as proxies, reflecting different beliefs about what is valuable in primary care.

There is both a representational and an incentivizing aspect to this. In terms of the former, the informants told me that it's vital that the reimbursement scheme captures and appropriately accounts for the work performed by care centers. Here, then, the reimbursement scheme is enacted as a device ensuring that care centers are paid according to their actual performance. The challenge is to model the scheme exactly right, to be 'just' and 'fair' in relation to the work performed. But despite the efforts to achieve this, I witnessed contestations about the justness of certain reimbursements on countless occasions in the field, examples ranging from chronically ill to newborns and mentally ill (cf. Johansson Krafve, 2011). Many of these disputes originated in the reimbursement system being 'unfair' in relation to the work performed at a care center, and above all, in it not being fair to all care centers at once.

In terms of incentivizing properties, the reimbursement scheme could be seen to enact such ambitions. That is, the scheme is intended to steer behavior in a certain direction. This is most clearly articulated in the 'Variable' reimbursement category: 'The variable reimbursement aims to create incentives to improve the work in prioritized areas' (LiÖ, 2012). This category is employed particularly for those values that are prioritized as policy aims at specific points in time. The rulebook for 2013 emphasizes, for example, availability and health promotion as such prioritized areas.

But the scheme also shows that capitation is laden with incentivizing ambitions in a more fundamental sense. It incentivizes certain types of engagement with patients. On one hand, there might be a risk of under-provision of care, as frequent patient visits will not render more payment. On the other hand, capitation fosters longer engagements, rather than temporary relations, between patients and care center. Capitation means care centers bear the costs of their listed patients; hence they have an interest in controlling the overall situation of patients. In this way, the scheme also fills the principle of 'free choice' with a certain value and meaning. As patients and care centers are not able to influence price, choice is put center stage as a competitive mechanism. It strengthens the enactment of free choice as a matter of choosing a care center. The two aspects of the reimbursement scheme – its representational and incentivizing ideals – could thus be seen in relation to different values. Capitation as a reimbursement principle foremost embodies a political will, expressed as comprehensiveness and responsibility and long-standing relations between caregiver and patient.

. . . to ACG

For the 2014 rulebook, a quite substantial shift occurred in the reimburse-ment scheme: A decision was made to abolish capitation and instead use a Diagnosis Related Groups (DRG) model of reimbursement.[10] (The other items in the scheme remain largely the same, albeit proportionally smaller than before.) In short, DRG means to reimburse care centers according to the individual diagnosis profiles of their listed population of patients. Specifically, in Swedish implementations of DRG models, a particular module called Adjusted Clinical Groups (ACG) is often used.[11] For ACG to work as intended, all care centers are expected to register diagnoses accurately, and reimbursement will follow duly. In the new rulebook, about 88 per cent of all reimbursement would follow from ACG, while 'the combination of diagnoses provides a weight that determines the level of reimbursement' to each care center (LiÖ, 2013).

Here is an excerpt from the 2014 rulebook explaining how ACG is a weight granted to individual patients, and that this weight determines reimbursement:

> From 2014 begins the transition from a system of reimbursement based pri-marily on age and gender to ACG-based reimbursement (Adjusted Clinical Groups). . . The reimbursement consists of the following basic elements:
>
> - Compensation for the listed individuals based on residents' health care needs (ACG)
> - Compensation for citizens' care needs based on socio-economic factors under the Care Need Index (CNI)
> - . . .
>
> [. . .]
> The reimbursement for listed individuals based on ACG is a remuneration that aims to promote comprehensiveness and responsibility, based on citizens' care needs. [. . .] ACG is based on the diagnosis put on patients, during visits or indi-rect contact that replaces a visit, during the period for compensation. The com-bination of diagnoses gives a weight that determines the level of compensation.

It is worth noting that the expected values to be fulfilled by ACG – 'comprehensiveness and responsibility' – are exactly the same as for capi-tation. This is something of a paradox, since the difference between the two reimbursement principles is generally emphasized.

The rulebook continues to explain the next acronym, 'CNI':

> A strong link exists between low socioeconomic status and poor health, there-fore reimbursement is based on socioeconomic considerations. Patients with socioeconomic problems may require a greater effort of care, regardless of

diagnosis. As the basis for reimbursement based on socioeconomic conditions in the listed population, CNI (Care Need Index) is used. CNI is individualized and based on seven different variables with different weights:

- Age over 65 and living alone   6.15
- Born in a foreign country (Southern and Eastern Europe
  but not the EU, Asia, Africa and South America)   5.72
- Unemployed or in labor market policy measure, age 16–64   5.13
- Single parent with children aged 17 or younger   4.19
- Person 1 year or older who moved into the area   4.19
- Low-skilled, age 25–64   3.97
- Age younger than 5 years   3.23

Much like ACG, CNI is an indexed score for each patient. The difference is that ACG builds on registered diagnosis, and CNI rests on checking the different variables of each listed patient against a national database.[12] On average, CNI accounts for about 7 per cent of total revenue to care centers, but this figure differs significantly between care centers.

ACG and CNI appeal more to a representational ideal than does capitation. They have been mobilized to better account for patients as *individuals*; ACG is designed to account for diagnosis patterns of individuals, while CNI utilizes the socioeconomic status of individuals as an indicator of expected need of care. In this way, the reimbursement scheme could be said to better represent the prospect and probability of patients being ill according to a number of established criteria. The ACG and CNI indices enact the status of citizens according to their expected effect on the workload of a care center. Citizens' status is made commensurable according to a single metric, neatly defined beforehand in the scheme. The value (in terms of the reimbursement received) of particular patients is determined by their diagnoses and socioeconomic 'attributes'.

DISCUSSION: FRAMING THE MARKET, ENACTING VERSIONS OF VALUE

The rulebook represents an ambitious attempt to assemble all regulation for primary care providers in the county within one document. It enacts the care choice system as a market that realizes certain values. In this market frame, free choice of care provider and competitive neutrality between providers are supposed to secure the function of the market. Importantly, the values of free choice and competitive neutrality are also very practical matters. Not least because other values – I have brought to the fore a few: quality of care, accessibility, comprehensiveness, responsibility – are supposed to be realized by carefully modeling free choice and competitive neutrality as market mechanisms.

The 'voucher' is a construction contained within the rulebook, and is operationalized through the mechanism of the reimbursement scheme. This scheme is fairly complex as it is designed to represent many different activities and values performed in primary care. Because reimbursement follows patients, the rulebook frames the economic agency of care providers and enacts care providers as market actors who pursue economic interests by attracting patients.

The rulebook also enacts a compilation of rules of what services to offer and how to behave in certain caring situations. Caring situations and actions are thus not absent from the rulebook. On the contrary, there are many incentivizing underpinnings related to such situations and actions, not least framed in monetary terms via the reimbursement scheme. To put this in terms of market framing terminology, the rulebook qualifies the service, while also putting into words and numbers the objects, subjects and relations of importance to the market situation.

In qualifying the service and enacting the market frame, the rulebook serves as a device that simultaneously constructs both market demand and market supply (cf. Callon et al., 2002). Regarding supply, the rulebook states what should be done and how, what service should be provided and by whom. There are several elements to this. First, there is free patient choice and competitive neutrality. The free choice rule states what type of market it is and what type of choices patients are able to make. The competitive neutrality rule states what actions care centers are allowed to pursue in this market. Second, there is the reimbursement scheme, which regulates the total amount that the county council will spend on primary care, as well as how these funds will be allocated to care centers.

The rulebook constitutes a planning resource for care centers. Since prices (compensation levels) are set beforehand, the scheme enacts transparency concerning revenue. But it doesn't set the volume of service to be provided. Rather, it enacts the wills and expectations of care centers and patients, in the form of incentives and choice respectively. The latter is expressed as choice and pricing of patients' 'attributes', the former through the structure of the voucher and the incentives built into the reimbursement scheme. The rulebook thus enacts the market 'force' of this particular market, whereby other values could be realized. What is furthermore adding complexity to the market force enacted by the rulebook is that it doesn't target patients, it targets care providers. Choice is enacted as a value by the rulebook. But in order for it to be realized, competing care providers must be present in the market. Without competing providers, patients have no choices to make.

Reflections on Quasi-market Theory and its Instantiation in the Rulebook

The rulebook is susceptible to critique usually targeted at quasi-market theory and its preoccupation with free choice and competition, but also makes it possible to recast some of this critique. Some critical literature (e.g. Greener, 2003; Mol, 2008) suggests that patient activities in (good) care involve much more than making 'informed choices' in particular situations, like the choice of care center. In an ideal type 'logic of choice', free patient choice is considered to be valuable in itself, as a way to empower patients. Hence, it is highly normative. But apart from free choices, the 'logic of choice' doesn't determine what constitutes good care. This question is passed along to the choosing individuals; free choice is a way for individuals to promote their respective assessment of value. In the 'logic of care', patients are active participants in care situations. Value judgments are integral to caring situations, in that values are determined by practical considerations and actions. In the 'logic of care', that which is valuable is embedded in the practices that establish what is best for patients. In the 'logic of choice' autonomy is exercised as a way of empowering patients, but this is of little help in deciding what is good treatment. While both logics share the vision of empowering patients, the 'logic of care' suggests that care is unsuitable for marketization in the form of patients acting as customers (Mol, 2008).

Mol (2008) criticizes the ideal-type 'logic of choice' promoted by quasi-market theory, but does not pay much attention to the concrete activities that model and change it in practice. In terms of values, it is important to note that the different logics enact different versions of values, but each also entails different practices to secure these values. For example, the rulebook makes clear that the value of 'choice' is a practical matter. The rulebook puts great effort in defining caring situations in relation to choice, whether it is exercised or not. Mol claims that choice cannot determine good care. However, the analysis of the rulebook illustrates that 'choice' is not separate from questions of good care. The rulebook is a powerful device to enact the 'logic' of primary care as entailing elements of both 'choice' and 'care'. It secures patient choice, at the same time as it provides a detailed account of rules of conduct in caring situations. Both of these elements must be in place for authorization of care centers.

Building on Mol's critique, Grit and de Bont (2010) look into the difference between capitation (reimbursement of the average patient) and DRG-models (individualized solutions, such as client-based budgets) in long-term care. Their argument is that the use of devices such as 'tailor-made' financial instruments (like ACG, which ties reimbursement to the diagnosis profile of individual patients) transforms patients' 'needs' into 'economic demand'. This transformation builds on a priori specifications of the provided service. Economic transactions are only performed when there is mutual agreement concerning the quality of the service and the payment. But specification of care beforehand can be very problematic. The risk is that care providers only perform what has been settled in a contract – no more, no less. The system is thus not responsive to the contingency of care.

Their point is that the difficulty of predicting in advance what the actual need is causes an inflexibility that threatens the care situation. It is not possible to determine beforehand the best care for an individual patient; this is the result of a daily process of searching for what is best. The act of care giving needs some latitude. Therefore, tailor-made finance is actually less flexible to the needs of individual patients than is capitation. Capitation allows for some adjustments to be made through shuffling budgets in the organization and for patient 'needs' to be negotiated gradually. Therefore, the risk with reimbursement based on DRG is that care becomes care as performed by the financial instrument (Grit and de Bont, 2010).

Translated to the case study reported above, ACG and CNI could be seen as such specifications and financial instruments. By establishing the indices and scores beforehand, the needs of patients are defined in terms of their diagnoses and socioeconomic attributes, valued according to weights in the reimbursement scheme. The rulebook enacts patients as their diagnoses and socioeconomic statuses; as parts of the reimbursement scheme, patients *are* their diagnoses and socioeconomic statuses, which is a numerical value. ACG and CNI could thus be seen as devices that enact the value of representation, standing in opposition to the political will of promoting comprehensibility and responsibility in caring situations. Political will is eliminated from the scene. There is no room for values (in the sense of what is desirable) when the evaluative mechanism builds so strongly on representation.

CONCLUSION

The aim of this chapter was to describe how values are enacted by the rulebook in the primary care market under study. What values are at stake in this market, and how are they manifested in the rulebook? How are different values made to matter in relation to one another in the rulebook? By employing the framing terminology – with particular emphasis on enactment, valuation and market devices – I have sought to shed light on the rulebook and what it does in terms of values. The rulebook as a market device frames the primary care market, while embodying and acting as a proxy for a multitude of different values. In doing this, it could be seen as a device that enacts particular versions of value, many of which are 'public' in character. In the declaration of the care choice system in the rulebook, values such as care quality and accessibility are emphasized. In the analysis of the reimbursement system, several more values become important, such as comprehensibility and responsibility, albeit in different ways for the capitation and the ACG/CNI schemes, respectively. Overall, the values of 'free choice' and 'competitive neutrality' are emphasized as the *modus operandi* of the market, and seen as means towards the realization of other values. But free choice and competitive neutrality are not only means; they are also advanced as important ends in themselves. In this respect, the rulebook reifies quasi-market theory.

But the rulebook does more than reify. It is fundamental for the marketization reform as it performs the market and makes it manifest *as* a market. It establishes relations between patients, care centers and the goods provided in the market for primary care. Further, the rulebook is also something very practical and a site for experimentation. When the rulebook is altered, as in the case of the reimbursement scheme, the problem that is to be solved and the values to be realized are also changed, developed and altered. This transformative process is at the same time complex and subtle, as evident in the movement from capitation to ACG. The two reimbursement schemes both claim to adhere to and strengthen the values of comprehensibility and responsibility, but they differ in their representational and incentivizing ideals and effects. Capitation embodies a stronger incentivizing political will, while ACG primarily aims to represent patient needs according to their individual diagnosis profile.

There is also a lesson for the performativity literature here; performativity is not only a matter of *economics* shaping the (primary care) market. On the one hand, the market values in the studied case – foremost free choice and competitive neutrality – are placed center stage by the rulebook. It enacts them as forces, or means, that dictate the production of other values. On the other hand, when regarded in practice, there is a certain plasticity to both market and public values. A look at the handling of free choice and competitive neutrality in this particular case illustrates that there are many possible market designs. The shift from capitation to ACG represents a shift in the enactment of agency of patients, of political will and of representational and incentivizing ideals. In this way, the study points to the possibilities for formatting new and unexpected positions from which to enact market and public values in designing market devices.

The rulebook is very much in the making and its content changes over time. The market for primary health care under study is not the only market site where the market frame and devices are ambivalent and in experimental flux. The argument made by, for example, Callon (2009) and Zuiderent-Jerak et al. (2015) is that 'good' market devices are the ones that are constantly renegotiated and capable of taking care of their own overflows. Market processes are too unpredictable for an 'implementation logic' (Zuiderent-Jerak et al., 2015) of values to prevail. Values are not static and could not be implemented as such. Market development is better viewed as an experimental process, where values are shaped in the practice of grappling and tinkering with market devices, and where constant re-evaluation is fed back to the experiment and (re-)design of these devices. The task would be to experimentally compose rather than implement values in the market. The design activities are therefore of strategic importance and ought to be organized after careful consideration. The values of the welfare state are at stake in the details of such practices.

ACKNOWLEDGEMENTS

A previous version of this chapter was presented at the 2nd Interdisciplinary Market Studies Workshop and at the ValueS seminar at my home department; thank you all for useful comments. A warm thanks to the editors and anonymous reviewers for detailed and constructive critique of previous drafts of the chapter. I also wish to thank my supervisors C-F. Helgesson, Teun Zuiderent-Jerak and Steve Woolgar, who all provided creative input to the process of writing the chapter.

NOTES

1. In Swedish primary care, a care center consists of several clinics in the same or adjacent buildings, sometimes sharing the same staff. It comprises a doctor's office and district nurses, and most often other professionals, such as child care specialists and counselors.
2. Traditionally, 'value' has been theorized either as an ethical/social problem or as an economic problem ('Parson's pact', as explained by Stark, 2000). Here, values are treated in a way that cuts across this divide. The route taken differs from Durkheimian and Parsonian sociology, which treats values as social facts explaining outcomes of social phenomena. First, value is taken to denote principles of higher good or desirable states of the world, such as freedom or justice. though not in an ethical sense, but as outcome of valuation, that is, practical activities that render such states valuable. Second, value concerns the (relative or absolute) worth of things. This means that value could have a calculative and numerical quality to it, in that things can be judged and ordered as being of more or less value, but also encompasses the idea that things are sometimes considered qualitatively different (for example the difference in classical economy between use-value, exchange value and labor value, e.g. Marx, 1990[1867]). The bottom line argument is that values don't explain, but are the object of inquiry in

a very concrete sense. In this respect, the chapter speaks explicitly to recent discussions within valuation studies (e.g. Dussauge et al., 2015; Kjellberg et al., 2013; Lamont, 2012; Muniesa, 2012).

3. In the types of markets of concern to Le Grand, choice is not 'free' in the definitive sense, but conditioned in particular ways (though this doesn't stop policy rhetoric from referring to 'free' choices). In this study, choice refers to the right of the individual patient to choose a care provider among a range of authorized competitors, as opposed to public authorities choosing a provider for the patients.

4. Quasi-market theory has had a decisive influence on health care marketization reform. Here, an isomorphic tendency is discernible, in which the preconditions, terminology, conclusions and tone of research and policy-making become increasingly aligned regarding health care markets. (For example, both Julian le Grand and Alain Enthoven have been very influential in advising governments and developing the British NHS.) This is also evident in Sweden, where there are strong policy convergences in health care markets in general (Blomqvist, 2002), and in vouchers in particular (Nordgren, 2010).

5. This is not only a Swedish concern. In the international literature, economic theories of agency are drawn strongly upon: 'Methods of payment constitute a form of incentive contract, linking the individual physician with the larger organization [. . .] As such, the analysis and interpretation of physician payment falls within the larger economic literature on contracts and financial incentives, known as agency theory' (Robinson, 2001). If involved market agents are constituted in certain ways, careful design of policy instrumentation could align the will of the policy-maker with that of the contractors. This, in turn, will ensure that the contractors work to secure whatever values the policy-maker has set up.

6. Elsewhere, I have investigated the framing-overflowing dynamic of the market under scrutiny in depth (Johansson Krafve, 2011).

7. However, I have intervened and staged the interviews outside the studied practice. I treat data from the interviews as representations and illustrations of the (discursive) practice involved in establishing the primary care market. The talk in interviews has centered on this practice, and I have asked informants to explain or elaborate on the matters in their own words.

8. I treat all data as 'text'. This strategy is not novel, but previous studies have highlighted the agency of texts and how they perform in organizational settings (e.g. Cooren, 2004; Smith, 2001).

9. Capitation makes up the bulk of reimbursement. The budget for 2013 allotted approximately $\approx$ 4 billion SEK to care centers. Capitation for listed patients was 1113 SEK (weight 1.0). Capitation for medication was 1439 SEK (weight 1.0). These reimbursements are weighted against age and gender of the patient according to a set scheme.

10. This model has strong theoretical underpinnings from health economics (Van de ven and Ellis, 2000). The idea is to 'risk adjust' reimbursement to avoid adverse selection of patients (which is suggested to be a risk coupled with capitation). Capitation is not considered to be fair, as listed patients could differ considerably across care centers. DRG is said to pertain even more strongly to the principle that rules must be 'competitively neutral'. However, a number of challenges have also been identified, such as 'creative up-coding'.

11. ACG is a particular product developed at Johns Hopkins (http://acg.jhsph. org/) and marketed in Sweden by Ensolution (http://www.ensolution.se/pages. aspx?r_id=24552).

12. For 2014, ACG renders 648.58 SEK/patient (weight 1.0) and CNI renders 106.96 SEK/patient (weight 1.0). In calculating revenue from ACG and CNI, the basic reimbursement is multiplied with a scored weight. In calculating ACG, patient records are read for diagnosis registration. In calculating CNI, Statistics Sweden (www.scb.se) runs listed patients against their records of socioeconomic data.

REFERENCES

Anell, A. (2010), 'Choice and privatisation in Swedish primary care', *Health Economics, Policy and Law*, FirstView, 1–21.

Arrow, K.J. (1963), 'Uncertainty and the welfare economics of medical care', *American Economic Review*, 53 (5), 941–73.

Asdal, K. (2008), 'Enacting things through numbers: Taking nature into account/ ing', *Geoforum*, 39 (1), 123–32.

Ashmore, M., M. Mulkay and T.J. Pinch (1989), *Health and Efficiency: A Sociology of Health Economics*, Milton Keynes: Open University Press.

Blomqvist, P. (2002), *Ideas and Policy Convergence: Health Care Reforms in the Netherlands and Sweden in the 1990s*, doctoral dissertation, Columbia University.

Blomqvist, P. (2004), 'The choice revolution: Privatization of Swedish welfare services in the 1990s', *Social Policy and Administration*, 38 (2), 139–55.

Callon, M. (1998), *The Laws of the Markets*, Oxford: Blackwell Publishers and *The Sociological Review*.

Callon, M. (2009), 'Civilizing markets: Carbon trading between in vitro and in vivo experiments', *Accounting, Organizations and Society*, 34, 535–48.

Callon, M., C. Méadel and V. Rabehariosa (2002), 'The economy of qualities', *Economy and Society*, 31, 194–217.

Callon, M., Y. Millo and F. Muniesa (2007), *Market Devices*, Sociological Review Monographs, Oxford: Blackwell Publishing and *The Sociological Review*.

Cooren, F. (2004), 'Textual agency: How texts do things in organizational settings', *Organization*, 11 (3), 373–93.

Czarniawska, B. (2007), *Shadowing and Other Techniques for doing Fieldwork in Modern Societies*, Copenhagen: Copenhagen Business School Press.

Dussauge, I., C-F. Helgesson and F. Lee (2015), *Value Practices in the Life Sciences*, Oxford: Oxford University Press.

The Economist (2013), 'The Nordic countries: The next supermodel. Politicians from both right and left could learn from the Nordic countries', 2 February.

Esping-Andersen, G. (1990), *The Three Worlds of Welfare Capitalism*, Princeton, NJ: Princeton University Press.

Friedman, M. (2009 [1962]), *Capitalism and Freedom*, Chicago, IL: University of Chicago Press.

Greener, I. (2003), 'Patient choice in the NHS: The view from economic sociology', *Social Theory & Health*, 1, 72–89.

Grit, K. and A. de Bont (2010), 'Tailor-made finance versus tailor-made service: Can the state improve consumer choice in healthcare by reforming the financial structure?', *Journal of Medical Ethics*, 36 (2), 79–83.

Hammersley, M. and P. Atkinson (2007), *Ethnography: Principles in Practice*, London: Routledge.

Helgesson, C-F. and F. Muniesa (2013), 'For what it's worth: An introduction to valuation studies', *Valuation Studies*, 1 (1), 1–10.

Hoholm, T. and L. Araujo (2011), 'Studying innovation processes in real-time: The promises and challenges of ethnography', *Industrial Marketing Management*, 40 (6), 933–9.

Johansson Krafve, L. (2011), 'To design free choice and competitive neutrality: The construction of a market in primary care', *Scandinavian Journal of Public Administration*, 15 (4), 45–66.

Kjellberg, H. and C-F. Helgesson (2006), 'Multiple versions of markets: Multiplicity and performativity in market practice', *Industrial Marketing Management*, 35 (7), 839–55.

Kjellberg, H. and C-F. Helgesson (2007), 'On the nature of markets and their practices', *Marketing Theory*, 7 (2), 137–62.

Kjellberg, H. and C-F. Helgesson (2010), 'Political marketing: Multiple values, performativities and modes of engaging', *Journal of Cultural Economy*, 3 (2), 279–97.

Kjellberg, H., A. Mallard, D-L. Arjaliès, P. Aspers, S. Beljean, A. Bidet, A. Corsín, E. Didier, M. Fourcade, S. Geiger, K. Hoeyer, M. Lamont, D. MacKenzie, B. Maurer, J. Mouritsen, E. Sjögren, K. Tryggestad, F. Vatin and S. Woolgar (2013), 'Valuation studies? Our collective two cents', *Valuation Studies*, 1 (1), 11–30.

Landstinget i Östergötland (LiÖ) (2012), *Regelbok för auktorisation 2013*, Linköping: Landstinget i Östergötland (LiÖ).

Landstinget i Östergötland (LiÖ) (2013), *Protokoll Hälso- och sjukvårdsnämnden 9 April 2013*, Linköping: Landstinget i Östergötland.

Lamont, M. (2012), 'Toward a comparative sociology of valuation and evaluation', *Sociology*, 38 (1), 201.

Law, J. (2004), *After Method: Mess in Social Science Research*, New York: Routledge.

Le Grand, J. (2007), *The Other Invisible Hand: Delivering Public Services Through Choice and Competition*, Princeton, NJ: Princeton University Press.

Le Grand, J. and W. Bartlett (1993), *Quasi-Markets and Social Policy*, Basingstoke: Macmillan.

MacKenzie, D., F. Muniesa and L. Siu (2007), *Do Economists Make Markets? On the Performativity of Economics*, Princeton, NJ: Princeton University Press.

Marx, K. (1990[1867]), *Capital: A Critique of Political Economy (Vol 1)*, London: Penguin Classics.

Mol, A. (2002), *The Body Multiple: Ontology in Medical Practice*, Durham, NC: Duke University Press.

Mol, A. (2008), *The Logic of Care: Health and the Problem of Patient Choice*, London: Routledge.

Muniesa, F. (2012), 'A flank movement in the understanding of valuation', *The Sociological Review*, 59 (2), 24–38.

Muniesa, F., Y. Millo and M. Callon (2007), 'An introduction to market devices', in M. Callon, Y. Millo and F. Muniesa (eds), *Market Devices*, Oxford: Blackwell.

Nordgren, L. (2010), 'The healthcare voucher: Emergence, formation and dissemination', *Financial Accountability & Management*, 26 (4), 443–64.

Regeringskansliet (2008), Proposition 2008/09:74 Vårdval i primärvården, Stockholm: Fritzes Offentliga Publikationer.

Robinson, J.C. (2001), 'Theory and practice in the design of physician payment incentives', *The Miliband Quarterly*, 79, 149–77.

Roscoe, P.J. (2013), 'On the possibility of organ markets and the performativity of economics', *Journal of Cultural Economy*, 6 (4), 386–401.

Roscoe, P. (2015), 'A moral economy of transplantation: Competing regimes of value in the allocation of transplant organs', in I. Dussauge, C-F. Helgesson and F. Lee (eds), *Value Practices in The Life Sciences*, Oxford: Oxford University Press.

Siverbo, S. (2004), 'The purchaser–provider split in principle and practice: Experiences from Sweden', *Financial Accountability & Management*, 20 (4), 401–20.

Smith, D.E. (2001), 'Texts and the ontology of organizations and institutions', *Studies in Cultures, Organizations and Societies*, 7 (2), 159–98.

Stark, D. (2000), 'For a sociology of worth', *International Affairs*, 1100, 3355.

Van de Ven, W.P.M.M. and R.P. Ellis (2000), 'Risk adjustment in competitive health plan markets', in J.C. Anthony and P.N. Joseph (eds), *Handbook of Health Economics*, Philadelphia: Elsevier.

Zuiderent-Jerak, T., K. Grit and T. van der Grinten (2010), *Markets and Public Values in Healthcare*, Rotterdam: Department of Health Policy and Management.

Zuiderent-Jerak, T., K. Grit and T. van der Grinten (2015), 'Critical composition of public values: On the enactment and disarticulation of what counts in health-care markets', in I. Dussauge C-F. Helgesson and F. Lee (eds), *Value Practices in the Life Sciences*, Oxford: Oxford University Press.

4. Concerns and marketization: the case of sustainable palm oil

Simona D'Antone and Robert Spencer

INTRODUCTION

> Well first of all, tell me: Is there some society you know that doesn't run on greed? [. . .] What is greed? Of course, none of us are greedy, it's only the other fellow who's greedy. The world runs on individuals pursuing their separate interests. (Friedman, 1979)

This chapter investigates the integration of concerns into contemporary markets and the influence of this integration on the way markets organize. Our considerations relate to two main aspects: first, the interplay between markets and values; and second, the processes of marketization, or the emergence, development and shaping of a market.

In terms of the first aspect, a well-worn philosophical and sociological debate speculates as to whether markets improve society, tend to corrupt it or are influenced, in turn, by the social order in which they develop (Hirschman, 1982). The discussion seems to find an answer with the realist turn in social studies which no longer considers markets and order of values as two separate realities, but rather defines markets as intensely 'moralized and moralizing entities' (Fourcade and Healy, 2007, p. 286). This idea is consistent with Latour (2004) calling for recognition of the idea that facts cannot be disentangled from the concerns animating and constructing the social realm. There are many examples of markets intertwining values and economic value, for example biotechnologies and genetics, nanotechnologies, sustainable and environmental productions and energies.

What is problematic is that what was previously considered as an externality – because of its link to the once-considered distinct sphere of ethics – is now integrated into market framings (Callon, 1998). As a consequence, it is both difficult to submit to economic valuation what was previously regarded as 'non-marketable' (Fourcade, 2011), and markets are assigned a new political role which was previously taken on by public policy (Cochoy, 2008).

In this chapter we analyse one example of this kind of market. In so doing, we focus first on the ways in which concerns intervene in the processes of market shaping, emergence and design. We then look at how these mechanisms enable the marketization of values (a broad set of reference principles that lie in a variety of social spheres, cf. Kjellberg et al., 2013) and associated concerns.

Our point of departure is a constructivist performative perspective which considers that markets are not stable and given states but are ongoing, changing processes resulting from the continuous performing of agents. This generates influences and adjustments among three main dimensions: norms, representations and exchanges (Kjellberg and Helgesson, 2006). A central concept in the performativity perspective is the notion of 'translation'. Recognizing the contiguity between the world of ideas and the world of actions, the performativity of markets considers how *ideas* about markets shape real-world markets and, inversely, how *material reality and practices* influence ideas about markets (Kjellberg and Helgesson, 2006).

The case reported here focuses on the sustainable palm oil market as an example of marketization. Concerns about the 'unsustainability' of the palm oil industry have become increasingly vocal over the last fifteen years. This has encouraged key market players and other influential organizations to take a stand. Palm oil is one of the vegetable oils that demonstrate the highest production, trading and growth levels across the planet (FAO, 2002). It is common in food and consumer uses (soaps, detergents, cosmetics, pharmaceuticals, biscuits, crisps and many other household and industrial products). Palm oil is mostly cultivated in tropical areas in Asia, Africa and Latin America, with the cultivated area doubling every ten years since 1980 (*Oil World*, www.oilworld.biz).

Indonesia and Malaysia are the leader producers and exporters (almost 90 per cent of world exports). China, Europe and India represent almost 50 per cent of the importing countries and are among the main consumer countries (AOCS, 2012). Palm oil dominates the vegetable oil market because it is highly competitively priced when compared with the main substitute (soybean oil), and because of its versatility.

One matter for concern relates to the fact that the demand for palm oil is expected to continue to rise both for food uses and in the biofuel sector (Sheil et al., 2009). The governments of the main producing countries planning to increase their production (Wong, 2010; Teoh, 2010) and new countries are being targeted to establish further oil palm cultivations (*The Ecologist*, 2011). As a consequence, the intensive oil palm plantations will expand in tropical regions to the detriment of rainforests and peatlands, leading to the loss of critical habitats for many species and to increases in pollution.

Plantations often also have a negative societal effect, for example in annihilating local human communities, provoking social injustice including child and slave labour, and unsafe working conditions. Another cause for concern relates to recently raised nutritional and health issues regarding palm oil, as some claim that it causes cardiovascular disease.

Given this scenario, over the last decade many non-profit organizations (e.g. Friends of the Earth International (FOEI); Greenpeace; Rainforest Action Network (RAN); The Forest Trust (TFT); and World Wildlife Fund (WWF)) have been sensitizing public awareness on the issue, directing their campaigns to the main stakeholders, suggesting possible solutions and ways to act and proposing measures. Answering the cry for a more sustainable production of palm oil, in 2004 the Roundtable on Sustainable Palm Oil (RSPO) was formed, with the objective of promoting the growth and use of sustainable palm oil products through credible global standards and commitments by stakeholders. The Roundtable includes stakeholders from seven sectors of the palm oil industry, including palm oil producers; palm oil processors or traders; consumer goods manufacturers; retailers; banks and investors; environmental or nature conservation NGOs; and social/societal or developmental NGOs.

Since its foundation the Roundtable has become the reference for the settlement of a sustainable palm oil market through its RSPO oil certifications and the Green Palm certificate trading programme. However, discordant views and methods to translate concerns into a sustainable version of the palm oil market have emerged, which has resulted in multiple efforts and alternative markets of various designs.

In the following sections we will analyse the process of emergence of multiple versions of the palm oil market as a result of the consideration of some or all of the different concerns mentioned above and their inclusion in and transformation of the market. Our aim, using as analytical underpinning the notions of market(ing) practices, translation and the associated notion of market multiplicity – specifically here the *emergence* of multiple versions of market (Kjellberg and Helgesson, 2006) – is to provide an improved understanding of two critical issues: specifically, what are the modalities – types of translations – adopted to transform concerns into ideas of market, norms or exchange practices? How, at the same time, do concerns themselves evolve and change through their participation in the market-shaping process? The data presented and analysed here includes many written sources (company reports, press articles, government reports, NGOs' minutes and reports and so on), nethnographic material (online forums, blogs and online video debates) along with data from qualitative open-ended interviews with respondents in NGOs (WWF and Max Havelaar) and companies (Sodexo and L'Occitane). A total of seven face-to-face interviews were performed in all, along with two round-table sessions involving companies and NGOs.

In the next section we will expand on the theoretical background and present the main concepts mobilized in our analysis. Subsequently the palm oil case will be presented, followed by a discussion in the final section on the main findings and conclusions.

THEORETICAL BACKGROUND

Callon (1998) points out that the unceasing work of market construction is linked to a peculiar aspect of contemporary markets, whereby it becomes increasingly difficult to identify a neat distinction between what pertains to markets and what pertains to the world of values (Callon, 1998). He argues that in the economic tradition markets have been depicted as closed structures, clearly identifiable and separated from the rest of the world. In this setting any negative/positive effect that they produce outside their boundaries is identified as 'externalities' or 'overflows' and, ideally, avoided through more effective market (re)framing (for example pollution internalized through carbon tax).

However, today's overflows in markets are not just accidents, but the rule. Framing activities are continuous efforts to extrapolate entities from their original values-context and frame them in the market context. Callon contends that contemporary markets are typically characterized by 'hot' situations whereby all the aspects needed to frame markets – identify overflows, their sources and measure them – require ongoing shaping. In other words, markets seem to be in a constant state of flux (Nenonen et al., 2013), dominated by controversies, with attempts to stabilize them being extremely costly and often ineffective.

Moreover, interest has developed of late around the theme of marketization, the study of how markets emerge and organize. This is seen as a process of ongoing socio-technical enactments (Geiger et al., 2012) resulting from the unceasing work of configuration and reconfiguration taking place via the assemblage of different marketing practices and expertise (Araujo and Kjellberg, 2010). Adopting this constructivist performative view of markets, Rinallo and Golfetto (2006), for example, examine the context of the clothing industry and explore the market-shaping activities implemented in a leading trade fair in Paris. Through strong representational activities and collective action the exhibitors are able to define and impose new trends and place themselves at the very core of a network, imposing direction on the entire market and delineating innovation trajectories. Similarly, Kjellberg (2010) examines the

interfacing between competing efforts in ongoing market design practices involving the airline SAS and the Swedish Competition Authority,
with particular focus on the interrelation between ideas and principles
concerning markets and marketing on the one hand, and market(ing)
practice on the other.

Kjellberg and Helgesson (2006, p. 843) suggest three kinds of practices
participating in the construction of markets: (i) exchange: the concrete
activities involved in consummating individual economic exchanges of
goods; (ii) normalizing: activities that contribute to establishing normative
objectives for actors, that is how a market and/or its actors should be (re)
shaped according to some (group of) actor(s); and (iii) representational:
activities that represent economic exchanges as markets, that is that depict
markets and/or how they work (Kjellberg and Helgesson, 2006, p. 843).
The way markets organize and evolve from this perspective depends on
the extent to which these three types of practice are mutually (mis-)aligned
and on the ways multiple versions of each kind of practice interact and
influence each other.

Examining in depth the way values influence market design, different contributions adopting a constructivist approach have specifically
focused on how market forms are shaped to take environmental issues
into account. Reijonen and Tryggestad (2012), for instance, investigate
the 'greening' of markets by examining how product qualities are constructed in the market through the juxtaposition of different competing
versions. In order to design for the 'greening' of markets the authors
advocate the importance of socio-technical market arrangements 'sustaining' the new version of the product and the ability of the product
itself to take different matters of concern into account. Similarly, other
studies have focused on the integration of greening concerns into markets
through the analysis of the organization of carbon markets (Callon, 2009;
MacKenzie, 2009).

An example of market organizing, with a focus on values, is discussed
by Holt (2012) when examining how the bottled water market developed
in the US. Holt, specifically, uses the notion of 'ideological lock-in' and
demonstrates how this is integrated into specific market institutions and
consumer practices. These market ideologies in fact correspond to concerns that at a certain point have been integrated into the market (for
example 'we need to be hydrated'; 'tap water is not safe'; and 'soft drinks
favour obesity'). Ideological lock-in is seen to be dynamic and, influenced
in unexpected ways through *cultural code inflation*, becomes institutionally
'sticky'. For Holt this stickiness involves three mechanisms: naturalization
of the market ideology in cultural discourse; the habituation of everyday
consumption practices that embody the ideology; and the materialization

of the ideology in backstage market institutions that structure the market according to ideological assumptions. These three dimensions demonstrate close links with the representation, exchange and normalization practices proposed by Kjellberg and Helgesson (2006).

Cochoy (2008) links values with characteristics and roles of actors. He points out that apparently 'private' interests in the market become intrinsically political; what defines the private and the public in a market is the primary link with public life. Entities are not essentially public or private, rather they are states that can be embodied in any actor. In this way, for instance, Google is more public than a town library, since despite being a private company it offers a service that is worldwide and constantly available. Consequently Google's role as knowledge provider and related concerns are more interlinked with society and the common good than a state-funded library.

Taking this one step further, de la Bellacasa (2011) distinguishes 'interests' from 'concerns'. *Interests* refer to individualistic stances, whereas *concerns* involve moving 'the notion of "interest" towards more affectively charged connotations', and calling upon 'our ability to respect each other's issues, [. . .] to build a common world [. . .], implying the respect of others' positions.' The discussion on interests and concerns is extended to consider the notion of 'care'. Care is related to 'concerns' since both are interpreted as affective states.

> Care, however, has stronger affective and ethical connotations. The difference between 'I am concerned' and 'I care' lies in the fact that the former denotes worry and thoughtfulness about an issue as well as the fact of belonging to those 'affected' by it, whilst the latter implies a strong sense of attachment and commitment. Moreover, the quality of care is more easily translated into a verb: to care. One can feel concerned, but 'to care' more strongly directs us to a notion of material doing' (de la Bellacasa, 2011: 89–90).

THE PALM OIL MARKET: RESEARCH TO DATE

Previous research on the palm oil market has developed in two main directions. The first deals with the opportunity costs of preserving the forests against palm oil cultivation (e.g. Morel and Morel, 2012; Martin Persson, 2012; Nantha and Tisdell, 2009), while the second examines market-based multi-stakeholders' governances' legitimization (e.g. von Geibler, 2012; Nikoloyuk et al., 2010; Schouten and Glasbergen, 2011). These studies show that the palm oil market is an example of a 'hot' situation (Callon, 1998), with many representations and tools competing, and stability being difficult to achieve.

For example, Boons and Mendoza (2010) stress the composite nature of the sustainability definition for the specific palm oil chain, showing how the prevailing meaning is often buyer-driven. Moreover, Nantha and Tisdell (2009) contrast supply-side and 'payment for biodiversity' approaches to tackle the environmental issues linked to the palm oil industry. They suggest that while the first solution can only act as a temporary measure, the latter can be financially competitive with palm-oil cultivation.[1]

This chapter contributes to two main strands of literature. First, we adopt a market-wide and constructivist performative approach to studies on sustainable development and specifically palm oil issues. Secondly, we relate to the constructivist market studies literature by focusing not only on how concerns are constructed under the influence of markets but also on how these matters in turn influence the way markets become configured. While most studies have focused on markets emerging from scratch (Callon, 2009; MacKenzie, 2009; Reijonen and Tryggestad, 2012), we provide an example of a concerned market which progressively evolves from former configurations. Moreover, in contrast with Reijonen and Tryggestad (2012), we deal with a case of 'sustainabilization' of the market which demonstrates more complexity than the simple 'greening' transformation, and produces multiple market versions.

The three main underpinnings for analytical purposes here are, as discussed earlier, market(ing) practices – the concrete activities that constitute markets; translation; and market multiplicity, with as empirical setting the palm oil market. Specifically, and with reference to the notion of translation (Callon, 1986; Kjellberg and Helgesson, 2006), we analyse the spreading of sustainable concerns in the palm oil market. The concept of translation is used to denote a basic social process by which something – such as a token, rule, product, technique, truth or idea – spreads across time and space.

A translation can involve the following (Kjellberg and Helgesson, 2006):

1. Transformations in terms of 'materialization', from more abstract to more concrete practices (and back), 'the translations that abstract or concretize [. . .] taking place orthogonally in relation to the three interlinked categories of market practice' (p. 845). For instance this is the case of a conceptualization of sustainability being concretized in principles and valuation criteria for marketers.
2. Transformations 'in scale', from micro to macro contexts (and the opposite), such that '[. . .] any perceived difference in scale is an outcome of translations [. . .] thus a perceived difference in scale

between paying in cash at the gas station (exchange practice) and analysing the structure of the petroleum industry (representational practice) is an outcome of local translations' (p. 844). This is also the case of local concerns for biodiversity in tropical forests which expand across the world and involve any kind of forest.

3. Translation in terms of 'nature of practices': shifting across the three types of normative, representative and exchange practices, so that 'the term translation is used to characterize the interrelation of market practices [. . .] within the same broad category, or [. . .] spanning the three categories' (p. 843). For example, measures of deforestation versus carbon emissions competing to become part of the representation of the unsustainable palm oil market, thus influencing the content of norms (created to protect the forest or reduce carbon emissions) and consequently differently orientating exchanging practices.

Law (1997) argues that translation is an activity of diffusion and transformation, meaning that at the same time it displaces representations and entities and mutates them. From this point of view the notion of translation seems to fit with our aim of mapping how values are integrated in the market, consequently affecting its structuring dynamics. To help track these dynamics, then, we observe among other things the unfolding of conflicting values in market designs. We use the notions of market(ing) practices and translation as tools to track the plastic nature of values, the way they spread and shape markets on the one hand, while at the same time being themselves subject to being shaped by the market.

PALM OIL AND THE PALM OIL MARKETS

Four main market versions can be seen to emerge over time. Each of these involves different assemblages of representative, normative and exchange practices for a sustainable palm oil market. As a result, they trace diverse trajectories for building a sustainable palm oil market.

The first version is the RSPO market, mainly driven by an environmental motivation. The second version is the POIG (Palm Oil Innovation Group market initiative), an 'advanced' and stricter version of the RSPO attempt. There are also two additional configurations, both of which are more radical. Hence the third version is 'total elimination' of palm oil, and the fourth, we term the 'fair palm oil market'. This last version advocates the temporary setting aside of environmental issues in favour of the social issues of poorer producing countries.

These four configurations represent the most easily identifiable ones in a realm that displays many other 'grey' representations. All four market versions identified embody and portray on the one hand different representations of the market; and at the same time different sets of organized efforts and practices by various actors in attempts to reshape and reconstruct the market. We now discuss each configuration in turn.

Version 1: the RSPO Market

The development of the RSPO market version began in 1998, with the emergence of the RSPO organization described below, when WWF and Migros, the biggest retailer chain in Switzerland, started collaborating on a responsible purchasing project in support of more sustainable palm oil cultivation. At the time specific criteria to certify sustainable production of any kind of oil, including palm oil, did not exist. Moreover, according to WWF, no NGO alone was able to provide specific indications and advice to the industry concerning the best way to cultivate palm trees sustainably. WWF saw the Swiss collaboration with Migros as a first test toward the implementation of a global standard for sustainable purchasing of palm oil.

Collaborations with companies 'to help them change the way they do business' represent one main activity implemented by WWF to protect the environment. WWF's Market Transformation Initiative 'centres its activities around commodity industries such as timber bio-energy, pulp and paper, cotton, palm oil, beef and dairy, sugarcane, wild-caught tuna and whitefish because these activities, representing a vital economic resource for many developing countries, risk to explode, with no consideration for the environment' (www.WWF.com). At the very core of the philosophy is the concern for forest protection. This concern is translated into the development of measures to identify high conservation value (HCV)[2] forests and into ranked calculations of the most dangerous threats to their survival.

The choice of focusing on the palm oil market stems from it being identified as one of the most environmentally high-risk activities. As declared by the WWF France programme leader for forest conversion issues (palm oil and soya):

> even if the population's needs are taken into account in the representation of an HVC area, the main concern for WWF is environmental not social. This maybe leaves WWF open to criticisms from a social perspective, but this relates to the mission of our organisation. Other associations deal with these social problems as priority.

At the end of 2000 Migros and WWF jointly established another translation of the initial concerns for the forests into a list of seven criteria for sustainable palm oil production, and then asked the two Migros palm oil suppliers to join the initiative. After negotiations a model of supply contract was agreed upon and subsequently adopted to regulate exchange practices with other palm oil suppliers. The agreement envisaged a smaller price increase in return for a fixed quota of purchasing share granted to suppliers in return for an initial partial fulfilment of the criteria, with full respect of criteria to be obtained within three years.

In 2001, in response to WWF's statement regarding not having sufficient resources to complete the project alone, Migros agreed to include Proforest, an Oxford-based NGO, as independent sustainability assessor. Two other NGOs then joined forces with WWF with the objective of joint diffusion through integrated campaigns of representations concerning the main issues linked to deforestation: Greenpeace and Friends of the Earth (Hamprecht and Corsten, 2007).

Between 2002 and 2005, a number of actors joined in a group that was finally formally established as the RSPO in 2004. In September 2002 a preparatory meeting was organized by Reinier de Man, an independent consultant engaged by WWF, to avoid the impression that the event appeared to be staged by Migros and WWF alone. Various European retailers (Sainsbury's, Marks & Spencer, Safeway, Migros), manufacturers (Unilever), processors (Karlshamns, Anglia Oils/Aarhus, FEDIOL), bankers (Rabobank, ABN AMRO) and others attended the event.

The result was the first exchange in order to develop a common representation of the meaning of sustainability in the palm oil domain, and to define ways the nascent organization could potentially exert an influence on palm oil production and exchange practices in the market. The debate addressed organizational issues of the RSPO so as to favour inclusion of different interests, establishing clear goals and membership issues. It was agreed that palm oil producers should become full members of the roundtable, and that the palm oil roundtable should not become an activity driven by European interests alone.

The question as to whether the focus of concern should be exclusively on palm oil or on all vegetable oils was also raised. The NGOs and companies converged on the idea that it was best to start with just one and transfer the experiences gained later. It was also discussed whether to address at the same time the problems of management of existing plantations and that of forest conversion, and whether to include only deforestation or also a wider list of concerns, such as the compatibility of action envisaged with the economic development of local populations in producer countries.

The consensus was that sustainability for palm oil has to simultaneously include environmental, social and economic concerns and that the roundtable could not be opposed to new plantations, but could help in choosing where they would be best situated. These decisions were consistent with WWF's focus of attention on HVC forests. They also fitted with WWF's mode of action based on the creation of stakeholder participation with a view to confronting and converging interests, and the establishment of voluntary systems setting norms and standards for a sustainable production at affordable costs.[3]

After the preparatory roundtable, the first official international roundtable took place in August 2003 in Kuala Lumpur. It was the first step toward wider international stakeholder participation, including governmental bodies, palm oil producers and traders, further NGOs, retailers and manufacturers and banks.

The RSPO was formally established in 2004 and registered in Zurich in 2005. A first draft of criteria for normalizing sustainable palm oil production was posted online and reviewed on the basis of the comments (more than 800) received by participants. The final version of the 'Principles and Criteria for Sustainable Palm Oil Production' (P&C) was adopted by the RSPO in November 2005 and first reviewed in 2007 after a pilot period of two years, and more recently in 2013.[4] According to the head of environmental and ethical projects at Migros, although interests evolved to include new perspectives, the RSPO's standards are consistent with the criteria initially developed by WWF, Migros and Proforest.

In 2012 the RSPO had 617 ordinary members representing the interests of seven sectors of the palm oil industry. Various tools and procedures have been designed and implemented by the RSPO in favour of the business transforming process for a sustainable palm oil market.

The P&C document gives the RSPO organization's representation of what sustainable palm oil is. Principles and criteria constituting this representation are at the core of the evaluations performed via the RSPO Certification System. Two types of Certification process are carried out via the RSPO. The first is the producers' certification, which checks in respect of RSPO P&C via accredited certifying agencies. The second is a dual system comprising a supply chain certification (SCC), drawn up by the RSPO, and a traceability process,[5] monitored by UTZ Kapeh, a non-profit certification programme for agricultural products launched in 2002.

The Supply Chain Certification (SCC) requires that all actors in the supply chain respect a set of technical and administrative requirements. UTZ traces the flows of individual batches of sustainable palm oil from one actor to the next in the supply chain, with three different levels of traceability. That is, the lower level allows for mixing RSPO and non-RSPO certified palm oil; the intermediate level only permits usage of certified oil even if its source is not identifiable; finally the highest level certifies traceability of oil from various identified sources.

A tool developed by RSPO to bridge the gap between the palm oil supply chain and end-users/consumers is the Green Palm programme. This defines 'Green Palm certificate' exchange practices between producers and manufacturers. RSPO certified producers are awarded one Green Palm certificate for each tonne of sustainable palm oil they produce. These certificates can be sold to manufacturers and retailers who can then display the logo on packaging and communication to demonstrate to consumers that they have supported the sustainable production of palm oil, even if they did not directly purchase RSPO certified oil.

With the same aim of keeping consumers informed and favouring growth in demand for responsible palm oil, a RSPO Trademark has been registered since 2011 in more than sixty countries worldwide. Two versions of the RSPO trademark have been developed, respectively named 'certified' and 'mixed'. The first identifies those products actually containing certified sustainable palm oil; the second identifies products that have contributed to the production of certified sustainable palm oil without exclusively containing sustainable palm oil.

The ultimate aim of RSPO, enacted via the set of norms, standards, measures and signs described above, is 'to transform markets to make sustainable palm oil the norm'. The objectives that guide the progress of the programme promote improvement of the sustainable palm oil market (production, procurement, finance and use) and the related update of international standards. Monitoring the economic, environmental and social impacts of this market and committing all stakeholders throughout the supply chain are at the heart of the sustainable palm oil effort.

WWF is at the same time discouraging the funding of unsustainable palm oil production by means of a Palm Oil Financing Handbook and by encouraging companies to use certified palm oil via the publication of the Palm Oil Buyers' Scorecard. Based on four main principles – essentially related to being a member of the RSPO network, and the usage of certified palm oil[6] – national evaluations of companies are published every two years on the WWF websites and re-broadcast via the mass media. The same evaluation criteria are applied transversally by all the national sections of WWF.

In early 2013 WWF also published an assessment of RSPO Palm Oil Producers, in response to a similar Scorecard published by Greenpeace at the end of 2012. In the same year WWF took part in the review of the RSPO P&C, as required by the ISEAL (International Social and Environmental Accreditation and Labelling), in order to update and tighten its rules. However, despite emphasizing the importance of managing HCV areas, WWF was not able to have all targeted objectives approved, such as planting on peatlands and use of dangerous pesticides not being clearly banned.

WWF accepts these results as the outcome of the compromise with the different interests present in the market:

> WWF did not achieve all of its goals. Although significant clarifications and improvements to the P&C were achieved WWF accepts that the final outcome is a compromise, because the P&C review was a consensus-driven, multi-stakeholder standard setting process. The RSPO aims to transform the industry as a whole. The P&Cs therefore need to retain widespread support from all RSPO members and not act as a niche standard that only a few companies can achieve (WWF Website, 2013).

Version 2: the POIG Market

Because of the compromises made with certain actors in the market the RSPO approach has been criticized and a second version of the sustainable palm oil market has emerged, the so-called POIG (Palm Oil Innovation Group) market initiative.

A first step in this sense was in May 2010, Nestlé's collaboration with TFT (The Forest Trust) to develop a responsible sourcing approach and guidelines complementary to its membership to RSPO. TFT is a non-profit organization founded in 1999, which acts primarily for the protection of forests taking a specific angle of attack which is 'the change of products' stories', that is breaking a product down into main components and raw materials, and working towards a production process that has the weakest impact on the surrounding environment and people. With considerable experience in many groups of products in the field, TFT helps companies in developing and implementing credible action plans, from mapping risks and setting up traceability systems to providing technical and legal assistance and support in communication.

Starting from collaboration with Nestlé, the initiative now includes palm oil producers (Agropalma, GAR, NBPOL, Daabon Organic), social NGOs (Forest People Program) and environmental NGOs (namely RAN, Greenpeace and also WWF). The word 'innovative' included in the POIG title signifies the willingness of this group to look for new solutions that are alternative and more effective when compared with the RSPO system. Indeed, POIG promotes itself as an *enhanced* version of the RSPO solution declaring the intention 'to push the boundaries of current requirements of the Roundtable on Sustainable Palm Oil (RSPO)' (POIG Statement).

Many aspects in the RSPO approach are criticized, such as the neglect of the primary preoccupation for forests which has been translated into 'a responsible land conversion' issue; the resulting exclusion of smallholders' interests from the certification programmes; the segregation oil model (separating responsible from irresponsible oil) which involves expensive practices not adapted to a liquid product such as palm oil; the inadequate reward to growers for their efforts.

The last two aspects make a complete adhesion to the RSPO model economically uninteresting for RSPO company members. They prefer to apply for less demanding mechanisms such as the 'book and claim' Green Palm programme. This slows down the scaling up of the RSPO and the achievement of a full market transformation. Moreover, the reference to the HCV areas is considered a limited translation of environmental concerns into a representation which only includes a restricted part of forests needing protection. This is clearly expressed by the founder of TFT in this extract from a passionate online debate with the WWF's US Senior Vice President, Market Transformation:

> Got to disagree with you Jason. . . You say that every credible certification WWF supports has strong anti-deforestation criteria. Not so RSPO [Roundtable on Sustainable Palm Oil]. Deforestation of secondary yet still important forests is perfectly acceptable and is happily done by companies celebrated under the RSPO standard which only obliges protection of primary and HCVF areas. Likewise, the RSPO standard doesn't preclude the clearance of peatlands. [. . .] few know because no one goes out to look or understand exactly how the industry works. TFT does and we're horrified. This is collusion at its worst.

These criticisms are particularly consistent with Greenpeace's position, another NGO which considers the RSPO proposal as an 'imperfect solution' and which is active in stopping the advancement of oil palm cultivated lands into forest areas through numerous campaigns. In contrast with WWF, Greenpeace is more focused on producers' interests and social concerns. They show particular support for small-scale farming initiatives. In line with these concerns, Greenpeace published a Scorecard in October 2012, evaluating palm oil producers based on their own criteria. The aim was to shift the attention toward the sustainability of producers including those in the RSPO, thus bringing to the fore the unsustainable practices of major producers.

In a similar manner to WWF, Greenpeace also helps companies to get a thorough representation and develop a clear position on the palm oil issue. This is clearly demonstrated by an extract from an interview conducted by the authors with the Sustainable Development Director at L'Occitane:

> We evaluated different options regarding palm oil, trying to avoid *false good ideas* which simply displace the problem or decrease product quality. We adopted a position toward the RSPO also taking into account the discussions that we had with some representatives of Greenpeace who pointed out to us the main controversial aspects of the RSPO programme. In 2009, when we

approached the RSPO, we pointed out the inconsistencies of the label previously discussed with Greenpeace and finally obtained firmer guarantees by the RSPO on palm oil lot traceability.

An alternative measure has been proposed by the POIG group in order to map which lands should be included in protecting actions first: the HCS (High Carbon Stock). This classifies lands into six different classes (stratification) according to their natural carbon stores, distinguishing forests from degraded lands with very little vegetation, and suggesting that agricultural activities should develop in these latter areas with low carbon stock. Another main point is that, instead of investing in complex downstream logistical traceability practices in order to distinguish sustainable from unsustainable oils, POIG definitively eliminates these latter from the flux and submits to traceability checks only actors validated upstream in the supply chain (processors, mills, growers). Simplifying the process translates as greater efficiency and frees up resources to support direct 'transformation in the field' in plantations and for smallholders. Moreover, the approach defines itself as being 'open source' because easily reproducible and not relying on one single organization's interest but on universal and impartial values such as 'traceability' and 'no deforestation'. The main strengths of the approach are thus its ambition, economic viability and quick scalability, and inclusiveness.

Version 3: the Palm Oil-Free Market

A parallel form of market has emerged that we can group under the 'palm oil-free movement' label. It includes a set of non-profit organizations, manufacturing companies and activist consumers which support the view of 'side-stepping' the palm oil solution and finding other alternatives. Among the NGOs, those advocating this position are particularly concerned about the protection of animals' interests (e.g. Borneo Orangutan Survival (BOS), Sumatran Orang-utan Society (SOS), Centre for Orang-utan Protection and so forth) and advocate boycotting practices by consumers, and the providing of lists of 'palm oil-free' products.[7]

In line with this orientation some companies are explicitly communicating on their non-use of palm oil. This spans different sectors such as food manufacturers (e.g. Cadbury's confectionery), retailers (e.g. Système U in France) and cosmetics (e.g. Lush). When it is not easy to completely eliminate palm oil from their product design, some of these actors – Cadbury's or Système U for example – adopt RSPO certified palm oil for the product in question.

The 'palm oil-free' position has also been adopted by some informed consumers who act independently to avoid palm oil consumption: they engage to inform other consumers, put pressure on companies while asking for a detailed list of ingredients – especially when palm oil presence is disguised under different derivatives' names – providing 'black lists' and palm oil-free lists of products.

Some of these consumers also link to the fact that palm oil is also bad for health. In France, in this respect, a bill was put to Parliament to impose a 300 per cent tax increase on palm oil due to the fact that its consumption generates high health care expenses. Although the standard was not approved, the so-called 'Nutella amendment' has generated high visibility for the theme, due in part to the dramatic response by Ferrero, the group producing Nutella, who placed full-spread adverts in French newspapers in defence of its use of palm oil.

A more consumer-focused campaign of this kind is the one successfully developed in Norway by the Rainforest Foundation Norway and Green Living, resulting in palm oil consumption reductions of 64 per cent in 2012. The campaign included a web-based palm oil consumer guide to inform customers faced with the problem of multiple palm oil names in the ingredients lists on product labels. European legislation[8] also requires that vegetable oil names be detailed on ingredients labels, with the explicit objective of informing consumers so that they can identify these oils, and especially palm oil.

Version 4: the Fair Palm Oil Market (Business as Usual)

Eliminating palm oil from production chains is a position that strongly affects producer populations' interests. In some cases the palm oil-free claims have thus turned into legal action against the companies claiming to avoid this substance. The French retailer Système U, for instance, was denounced by smallholders, members of the Ivorian Association of Oil Palm Producers (AIPH), for broadcasting a TV advert which indiscriminately tagged any kind of palm oil cultivation as unsustainable and as destroying forests. Ivorian producers complained because the advert sent out a generic negative message about the whole industry, with corresponding negative impact for producers such as AIPH members, who are in fact engaged in sustainable practices.

Other similar practices are emerging which attempt to design another version of the sustainable palm oil market which takes into account producers' social conditions. Farmers from other countries have complained about the anti-palm oil trend and about the sustainability-driven pressures on growers to achieve certification. Indonesian growers, for instance, have already pulled out of the RSPO, while the Malaysian Palm Oil Association (MPOA), according to some sources, is looking at leaving the RSPO by the end of 2013. The main issue at stake for these actors resides in the incompatible friction between environmental concerns and socio-economic interests in developing countries. Since the RSPO's outset, for instance, Malaysian actors have strongly underlined the role palm oil plays in dealing with poverty:

> Poverty threatens the survival of the poorest. To appeal to them to join in saving the planet is pointless unless we link it to their own survival. Simply to tell those at the margin of existence not to cut down the forest or not to have many children when they see both as necessary to their survival is to be not only insensitive to their predicament but also downright provocative. (RSPO, 2003)

The World Growth (TWG), a US-based international NGO, defends the interests of these producing populations. Its activities target the support of economic development in less fortunate countries (that is promoting conditions that favour transparency and equality for free trade) as a prerequisite for their substantial engagement in environmental policies. The World Growth strongly attacks WWF and other environmental NGOs, such as Greenpeace, accusing them of trying to control markets by means of voluntary certification systems and public campaigns. These systems, then, instead of simply adopting market-driven solutions to prevent environmental disaster, are considered by The World Growth as, to all intents and purposes, actually dictating norms and standards to consumers and producers and putting pressure on governments to regulate markets in compliance with their representations.

According to TWG the goal of these environmental NGOs is to justify trade barriers which 'restrict entry to the European market of products that are cheaper than goods produced in the EU. This is Green Protectionism. Legal experts consider most of these measures to breach WTO rules. Similar measures have been adopted in the US and are under consideration in Australia' (TWG, 2011). In the specific case of palm oil, TWG sees the RSPO as a mechanism born in collaboration with Dutch interests with the support of three other European-based and one Malaysian company, because the Netherlands is a key player for the European supply of palm oil, with Rotterdam being a central hub controlling almost 80 per cent of imports.

TWG further claims that RSPO certifications result in distorted market exchange practices, where Dutch first movers gained competitive advantage. At the same time retailers and processors were, according to TWG, committed to pay a premium for the product, without any corresponding demand existing but where the cost was forced onto the producers, who were obliged to adopt 'voluntary' certification standards. TWG contends that the threefold representation of sustainability – including people, profit and planet – does not necessarily apply to all countries. Malaysia, for instance, 'still preserves widespread forest cover – about 60% of the total land area is still forested – but requires some regulated land clearing in order to develop strong industrial and agricultural sectors, in the same way Western countries have managed their forest resources to achieve economic development' (TWG, 2011).

Indeed, certain cases of environmental sensitivity may look suspect when they appear, or are made to appear, to hide protectionist interests and behaviour. TWG take the example of:

> French biscuit manufacturer St Michel, recently implementing a 'zero palm oil' commitment, following actions in France that have seen intensified lobbying against the palm oil industry. St Michel has said that it is replacing all palm oil with locally sourced butter and rapeseed oil, in a statement that points to the protectionist nature of the campaign (TWG newsletter, May 2013).

DISCUSSION

The four versions presented above provide a narrative describing the main dynamics at play in the palm oil market(s) from the inception of sustainability concerns to the present day. They identify the various versions/ ideal-types of the market which have emerged. The versions illustrate the interplay between market, concerns and interests. This reveals a dual, reciprocal perspective: on the one hand how market organization and dynamics change concerns, and on the other how concerns change the market.

How do Concerns Change Market Organization?

Values and concerns, and the multiplication of market versions: chains of translations of practices
Integrating concerns into the market triggers and stimulates a multiplication of market versions. In the case of the palm oil 'original' version of the market we can observe a 'concern-free' situation. A progressive integration of concerns, via an agglomeration and mutualization of different actors' interests, results in the initial market version – with its own strong 'ideological lock-in' (Holt, 2012) – being dispersed, and the emergence of multiple representations and market versions, and the formulating of new normative framings (Kjellberg and Helgesson, 2007, p. 153). These different versions of the sustainable palm oil market are, in fact, the result of multiple chains of translations of representations into norms, in view of bringing about a corresponding change in exchange practices (see Table 4.1).

Table 4.1 Examples of chains of translation in the four versions of the sustainable palm oil market: a summary

	RSPO	POIG	Palm oil free market	Fair palm oil market
Measurable target objects translate concerns into market representations and are diffused in the market	Environmental concern is translated specifically as the protection of forests, translated into HCV areas, with the palm oil market as specific target. These representations are diffused through integrated awareness-raising campaigns	Quantitative measurements and new representation of threatened forests (HCS) are used to justify a claimed need for adjusting the RSPO representation of what a sustainable palm oil market should be	Concern for the forest is mainly translated into the concern for wildlife through different campaigns in favour of the protection of wildlife, along with a concern for health (i.e. obesity)	Poverty, transparency and free-trade translate concerns linked to the socio-economic conditions of producing-countries in denouncing campaigns
Representations translated into norms	P&C (Principles and Criteria) for sustainable production translate representations into norms	New norms translate the new vision of market proposed, eliminating any possibility of producing and transporting unsustainable palm oil	Normative principles such as the 'Nutella amendment' or the lists of 'good products to buy' convey market representations	WTO rules are evoked as a guarantee of fair palm oil market development
Examples of tools and devices transforming norms and representations into practices	Green Palm Certificates and RSPO Trademark, along with face-to-face consulting work with companies, aim at transforming norms and representations into market practices	A novel supply system is implemented by first movers (e.g. Nestlé) to promote changes in exchange practices	Web-based consumer guides and companies' 'zero palm oil' labels habilitate consumers toward practices of palm oil avoidance	Legal procedures are designed and implemented to enforce WTO principles in matters of fair trade

| Examples of Measures / Measurement practices to legitimize representations | Measures such as the RSPO certifications and SCC for producers, and Palm Oil Buyers' Scorecards for manufacturers, provide concrete exchange practice back up to the communication carried out on the need to change the market in line with the new representation | Measures of results obtained through new practices used as elements for further promoting and supporting the new version of market proposed | Data on Norwegian palm oil consumption reductions (64% in 2012) legitimize the settlement of further activities | Societal data (poverty levels, unemployment statistics etc.) are used to illustrate the need for consideration of developing countries in palm oil production and processing |

Interests, concerns and the dynamics of multiple market versions

The identified versions of the market are interrelated and in constant evolution. Some of them coexist, stemming from a previous given market version, with progressive shift over time. The RSPO and the POIG market versions constitute two distinct versions of a market, demonstrating differing forms and degrees of 'sustainability', but both are grounded on the compatibility between sustainability and market growth.

The other two market versions compete and represent the simultaneous evolution of the market through dissimilar and conflicting possibilities and concerns. In the third version, a 'business as usual' approach is promoted since the 'green' preoccupations primarily addressed by RSPO and POIG contrast with the needs of poor populations. In the fourth, total elimination of the palm oil market is envisaged as the only way to stop the threat against the environment and wildlife, and any attempt to 'sustainabilize' the market is viewed with suspicion.

Whether as the internal evolution of a specific market form or as the diversification of positions in the market, the multiplication of market versions seems to be peculiar to the interplay between values and markets. The more concerns are integrated into the market, the greater the different solutions that appear, stimulating in turn new thought on the issues at stake, and thus the emergence of new forms of market. In this respect, 'values are the engine of change'.

A specific mechanism driving this circular 'concerns–markets–concerns' process is the definition itself of the limits of the concern and its relation with specific interests. Concerns are influenced by, and intersect with, interests in the market. The protection of forests intersects, for each of the market versions proposed, with the (Western) manufacturers' interests, with the (Eastern) producers' interests, the retailers' interests, the NGOs' interests and the consumers' interests.

Indeed, the notion of concern is intricately interwoven with that of interest; interests of some being seen as the concerns of others and vice versa. Thus each market version sees its own position as addressing 'real' concerns, in contrast with the interests that it sees underpinning other market versions. A crucial issue at stake thus becomes the definition of boundaries between what is 'common good' (concerns) and how this intertwines with the 'individual/particular' (interests).

When integrating collective concerns into markets – traditionally the place *par excellence* of individual interests – markets are assigned the role of defining the boundary between what is a general concern and what is a particular interest. For example, the RSPO defines sustainability as being three-dimensional: people, planet and profit. However, in assigning a priority to the planet, this market version considers the right to preserve a healthy environment (that is forests and biodiversity for present and future generations) as being collective, and thus as a priority. It confines the subject of economic growth more to a lesser role of specific interest.

Yet the interests/concerns demarcation line is subject to permanent (re) definition and is materialized through different market(ing) practices. The RSPO P&C, for instance, promotes the message that environmental issues are a concern that needs to involve palm oil producers and manufacturers. Similarly, consumers' lists relate the concern for the environment and wildlife to everyday purchasing activities, and the need for consumers to consider such concerns when purchasing. Buyers' and Manufacturers' Scorecards are devices defining measurements of which concerns should be taken into account (environmental, social, or both) and serving to shape the market.

Thus new forms or versions of market emerge in attempts to adjust the perceived distortions provoked by other market attempts and provide a 'better' solution in defence of the common good. Other market versions criticize the actions and functioning of the RSPO as being restricted to the protection of the interests of a few. POIG, for instance, claims that the RSPO does not defend smallholders' interests, claiming, in this way, that economic development should also be considered and thus defended in the same way as the environmental priority, that is taking into account the *others' interests* (and thus concerns) of under-privileged populations, and not just major producers.

In the same vein TWG and other producer associations argue that the RSPO and POIG represent Western interests, against the concerns regarding developing countries. Supposed environmental and wildlife concerns, in their opinion, are thus in fact particular interests, benefiting a minority, at the expense of developing economies. At the same time the participants in the 'palm oil-free' version of the market express doubts that any industry-driven solution – be it the RSPO, the POIG or producer associations – addresses concerns, rather they defend particular interests. Struggling to address previously unaddressed issues and impose its own view of what represents concerns and interests, each new market version tries to enlarge its base, to embrace new sets of interests, and enrol and include new actors, and thus to translate into concerns.

In fact the process of integrating many different voices in the same market space results in these different demarcations colliding, entangling, or coexisting, making equilibrium within and between market versions difficult to attain. In the end no one single legitimate collective concern seems to be represented, either within or between market versions. Indeed the contrary occurs in the case of palm oil, with several competing or coexistent market versions emerging. Revisiting the notions of interests and concerns, an inclusion of the notion of care into the discussion can help to explain the dynamics observed here.

De la Bellacasa (2011) sees concerns as collective yet still partial since they belong to those who are 'affected' or 'concerned' by the issues at stake. Concerns are thus less related to a notion of 'material doing' (de la Bellacasa, 2011, p. 90), and there are always 'neglected things' in the definition of concern. This contrasts with the notion of care that actively embraces those neglected. In the palm oil case here, one would say that in fact all the new representations of the market are related to specific 'concerned entities'. A common universal concern, care, does not exist. Each representation – WWF, for example, with focus on environmental rather than social issues – leaves 'neglected things' (de la Bellacasa, 2011, p. 94). In the words of Mr Deveze (WWF France, Program Leader for forestry conversion issues): 'This maybe leaves WWF open to criticism from a social perspective, but this relates to the mission of our organization'. This stance is not total or definitive, however, as witnessed by ongoing discussions between WWF and Max Havelaar with a view to linking social/societal concerns (Max Havelaar) with environmental concerns (WWF), thus integrating multiple concerns and tending towards a 'caring' market solution.

Matters of care, then, go beyond concerns. They adopt a longer-term perspective whilst integrating a multi-concern approach. Common, in fact, to all the different market versions, and which most 'take care of' – to a greater or lesser degree – is that of market economics and growth. This can be considered to represent the 'ideological lock-in' which makes it difficult for valid alternatives to the original market to emerge. At the heart of all new sustainable palm oil market versions observed – RSPO, POIG and Fair Palm Oil – this same fundamental ideological lock-in persists, albeit translated slightly differently through representations, norms and exchange practices. Even the *palm oil-free* version, in fact, embraces this ideology, but applied to the entire oil market as opposed to just palm oil, dropping the latter in favour of a portfolio of oils and switching to other types of oil (the market must grow, and if this is not possible through palm oil it will use other oils).

How does Market Change Concerns? Simplification, Agglomeration and Transformation Processes

Relative to the way market changes concerns, other forms of translation can be seen to complement the three proposed by Kjellberg and Helgesson (2006) discussed earlier and better understand the forces at play. These forms relate to the processes of simplification, agglomeration and transformation of concerns via their translation across different areas of the market.

Simplification of concerns

Simplification relates to the limitation of the near infinite possible relationships of the concern with entities/issues entangled in the context where it finds its origins (for example environment 'reduced' into forests, in turn reduced into HVC forests). The birth of the sustainable palm oil market(s) was initially driven by a specific green concern: forest protection. It was, indeed, with the aim of protecting the rainforests from deforestation that WWF initially launched a sensitizing campaign in Europe in 1997 and that subsequent attempts from POIG emerged. WWF thus acts as initiator and catalyst of a process involving translations of concerns for forests into market regulations, standards and new market practices.

Through the first series of roundtables a clear and precise position is adopted: focus on HVC forests and restrict the focus to palm oil. A first translation then – one of simplification – is operated. Ideally the preoccupations include all forests and all types of oils that are employed in industrial production, but the movement cannot encompass the complexity of this full set of concerns, and calls for focus. This simplification of the problem via focus allows reduction of the potential complexity to a set of relations with distinct and well-defined entities. In the case presented here, the selection of these entities thus excludes a multitude of actors such as producers of other types of oil, certain geographical areas, many other crops (e.g. soya oil) and derived products, and focuses on the protection of certain species (orang-utans), whilst limiting measurements of sustainability to a delimited calculative space (Callon and Latour, 1997; Callon and Muniesa, 2005). As suggested by Callon (1987), simplification is possible through the juxtaposition of the delimited contexts – of palm oil and HVC forests – to a wider network of other oils and other forests accompanied by their own related set of relations.

Agglomeration of concerns

Agglomeration relates to the accumulation/gathering of concerns of different kinds with a view to expanding the base of 'supporters' of a given market version (for example from environmental to societal preoccupations). The creation of the RSPO focused public attention on the theme of sustainable production of palm oil, provoking a resonance effect, and attracting interest from many actors who wanted to take part in its development. The organization gradually enlarged its base to include members from various origins. Newly integrated concerns progressively agglomerate, involving new actors and entities, and become broader and more complex. The initial environmentally focused preoccupation subsequently spread to a broader perspective with emphasis now not only on environmental, but also social and economic issues, attracting actors from diverse origins, demonstrating diverse interests. The POIG market version subsequently aimed at ensuring an effective and concrete engagement, and at backing its credibility by integrating specific new actors, smallholders and their sets of concerns.

Transformation of concerns
Transformation or translation by 'genetic mutation' (Law, 1997) refers to a process of addition of new preoccupations which are not simply cumulated with previous ones but partially replace them, reformulating the composition of the concern with a change in its core object. This is accompanied by a corresponding shifting of debate such as happens, for example, in the DNA recombining process, where two different genotypes are not simply juxtaposed but intimately recombined. For example health preoccupations are not simply juxtaposed to environmental ones, but change the nature of the concern itself (collective, because it deals with physical danger for human beings, and which encompasses the environmental aspect, also a threat for human survival/wellbeing). The example of the 'Nutella amendment', and the consumers supporting it, provides an interesting illustration of this. In the Nutella case Government proposals, as well as the public debate and consumers' claims, set aside environmental concerns to highlight the impact of palm oil consumption on health.

Through simplifications, agglomerations and transformations, then, many entities are continuously displaced, mobilized and gathered together into more or less common and bounded market spaces. The ways and devices in or via which these entities are presented and represented also help to explain the way concerns are constructed. Forests are translated into specific HVC areas, which are represented through maps and numbers showing how these zones have been eroded over time; orang-utans are transformed into numbers accounting for the current population and its progressive decline; pollution is translated into numbers representing quantities of carbon emissions and insecticides used; the palm oil menace is translated into statistics on the increasing demand for the product and graphs of forecast volumes; sustainable palm oil and the many and varied practices needed to obtain or produce it are translated into logos; actors of various kinds are represented through a set of companies' and organizations' members of the RSPO who choose in turn their representatives inside the RSPO via elections and roundtable regulations.

In a context of translation of interests and concerns, the notion of 'betrayal' is important. It is in particular starting from this notion that we question whether concerns – collective and inclusive by nature – remain such when translated into local portions of the network (market versions). Many examples in the case illustrate that when concerns are simplified and transformed, this brings them closer to a specific position where each version of the market sets out to defend a slightly different concern that is closer to its interests (producers focusing on market growth, WWF on forests, consumers and government on health). In other words concerns exist and are shared and collectively constructed, and what remain of them at a particular level are simple interests in the parochial agonistic sense. This is consistent with Stengers (1993) stating that interests can have two souls. On the one hand they play a dividing role, protecting partial positions; on the other they provide connecting points to other interests contributing towards higher-level preoccupations (concerns and ultimately care).

What constitutes concerns, then, in a civilized market is not the result of a process of comparison and aggregation of interests across a market. Rather it is the result of an agreement about what is common to various visions and versions of markets. The extent to which this agreement can be made depends on the degree of overlap or conflict between these market versions. This complements Latour's view and comments regarding the term '*res publica*'. '*Res*' reflects the notion of concern, as it represents 'the issue that brings people together because it divides them' (Latour, 2005, p. 13). But the concern, which gathers people together to discuss, is also at the same time collective ('*publica*'). It is the result of the debate, more than something that preceded it.

These reflections on the relation between the whole and its parts as discussed here, between concerns and constituent interests in a market setting, merit further attention in studies on the emergence of the civilized market.

Finally, the dynamics discussed above between market versions, interests and concerns demonstrate more complexity and ambiguity than appears at first sight, due to the apparently fickle nature of underlying interests and motivations of actors involved. In some cases what may be considered apparent 'schizophrenia' can be observed, with certain companies claiming simultaneously to adhere to a palm oil-free vision of the market, yet still belonging to the RSPO and – when necessary for production purposes – purchasing RSPO certified sustainable palm oil, thus supporting in apparent inconsistency two market versions. In fact several explanations exist for this apparently inconsistent behaviour, linking motivations and interests to concerns of various market versions. In the case of the RSPO, for example, some take part, out of conviction – 'because the only recognised name out there is the RSPO' (Director of Sustainability Metrics and Performance Measures, Sodexo) – or out of interest, because it is the only option available. Others use RSPO membership to protect their image, whilst still claiming a 'palm oil-free' stance where needed for reasons of economic interest. Yet others seek to protect the palm oil boom from the emergence of alternative greener solutions. This participation in multiple market versions each demonstrating specific concerns, motivated by actors' multiple, different interests, also contributes towards overall market dynamics.

CONCLUSION

Sustainable concerns in the palm oil market can be seen to emerge through sets of entangled translation processes which attract and gather diverse entities and interests in an ever-evolving hybrid coalescence, that is, forests, orang-utans, inhabitants of and those living off the forest and peatland, smallholders whose livelihood depends on palm oil cultivations, other local inhabitants, industry growth, the protection of developing and developed countries, diverse dimensions and measures of sustainability and so on.

The market undergoes a constant shaping process and emerges progressively, excluding some entities, such as non-traceable oils or Nutella, and including others: labelled products, eco-consumers and mothers worried for their children's health. Interests and concerns, entangled in the market, on the one hand constitute the shaping process, within and between market versions, and on the other hand are shaped themselves by market forces at play, evolving and muting. These market versions can be seen to evolve and adapt, with market agents adjusting concerns to suit interests and even pursuing different sets of concerns simultaneously. The issue is not that of achieving a common, coherent whole, care, with shared concerns across the market. Rather it is one of the emergence of different market versions integrating multiple interests and concerns that include the permanently shifting component parts of the 'worlds of everybody'. Simplifications, agglomerations and transformations are the forces at play that bring to the constructed civilized market something of the multiple worlds and associated market versions composing it, whilst systematically 'betraying' to a degree each of them. This raises the question for future research avenues 'what role of care?' in the shaping of markets.

NOTES

1. As will be discussed later, drawing on this contraposition, alternative forms of sustainable palm oil market are emerging in addition to the RSPO, that is POIG.
2. The identification of HCV areas is based on six criteria: (1) a significant concentration of biodiversity; (2) large landscapes ecosystem; (3) rare, threatened or endangered ecosystems; (4) areas that provide basic services of nature; (5) areas fundamental to meeting the basic needs of local communities; (6) sites of cultural importance.

3. After start-up of a voluntary scheme in 1992 to improve forest management worldwide (FSC – Forest Stewardship Council), WWF have promoted similar systems such as the Marine Stewardship Council in 1999 and, in 2002 the Roundtable on Sustainable Palm Oil (RSPO). These are accredited under the International Association for Social and Environmental voluntary standard systems (ISEAL). New similar voluntary certifications are under study in other areas.
4. The eight principles are: (1) Commitment to Transparency; (2) Compliance with Applicable Laws and Regulations; (3) Commitment to Long-Term Economic and Financial Viability; (4) Use of appropriate Best Practices by Growers and Millers; (5) Environmental Responsibility and Conservation of Natural Resources and Biodiversity; (6) Responsible Consideration of Employees and of Individuals and Communities by Growers and Millers; (7) Responsible Development of New Plantings; (8) Commitment to Continuous Improvement in Key Areas of Activity.
5. In July 2012 a new online system for administrating the physical trade of Certified Sustainable Palm Oil (CSPO) was launched.
6. Namely, the four criteria applied to build the WWF palm oil buyers' scorecard in 2011 answered the following questions: (1) Is the company an RSPO member? (2) Did the company publicly commit to RSPO-certified sustainable palm oil? (3) Does the company disclose how much palm oil it uses? (4) How much of the palm oil used by the company is CSPO or is supporting sustainable production?
7. However, not all the wildlife organizations sustain the palm oil-free position. A case in point is the Sustainable Palm oil Platform (SPP) founded by the Zoological Society of London (ZSL) to facilitate communication between stakeholders, supporting the RSPO certified palm oil usage and consumption.
8. A similar law is also under discussion in Australia.

REFERENCES

AOCS (2012), available online at: http://lipidlibrary.aocs.org/market/palmoil.htm.

Araujo, L. and H. Kjellberg (2010), 'Shaping exchanges, performing markets: The study of marketing practices', in Pauline Maclaran, Michael Saren, Barbara Stern and Mark Tadajewski (eds), *The SAGE Handbook of Marketing Theory*, London: Sage, pp. 195–218.

Boons, F. and A. Mendoza (2010), 'Constructing sustainable palm oil: How actors define sustainability', *Journal of Cleaner Production*, 18(16/17), 1686–95.

Callon, M. (1986) 'Some elements of a sociology of translation: Domestication of the scallops and the fisherman of St Brieuc Bay', in J. Law (ed.), *Power, Action and Belief: A New Sociology of Knowledge?*, London: Routledge & Kegan Paul.

Callon, M. (1987), 'Society in the making: The study of technology as a tool for sociological analysis', in W. Bijker, T. Hughes and T. Pinch (eds), *The Social Construction of Technological Systems*, Cambridge, MA: MIT Press.

Callon, M. (1998), 'An essay on framing and overflowing: Economic externalities revisited by sociology', in M. Callon (ed.), *The Laws of the Markets*, Oxford: Blackwell Publishers.

Callon, M. (2009), 'Civilizing markets: Carbon trading between in vitro and in vivo experiments', *Accounting, Organizations & Society*, 34(3/4), 535–48.

Callon, M. and B. Latour (1997), '"Tu ne calculeras pas!" Ou comment symétriser le don et le capital', *Revue du MAUSS*, 9/1, 45–70.

Callon, M. and F. Muniesa (2005), 'Economic markets as calculative collective devices', *Organization Studies*, 26, 1129–250.

Cochoy, F. (2008), 'Faut-il abandonner la politique aux marchés? Réflexions autour de la consommation engagée', *Revue Française de Socio-Economie*, 1(1), 107–29.

de la Bellacasa, M.P. (2011), 'Matters of care in technoscience: Assembling neglected things', *Social Studies of Science*, 41, 85.

The Ecologist (2011), available online at: http://www.theecologist.org/News/news_analysis/967139/greenwash_and_spin_palm_oil_lobby_targets_its_critics.html.

FAO (2002), 'Small-scale palm oil processing in Africa', *FAO Agricultural Services Bulletin*, 148, 1010–365, Rome.

Fourcade, M. (2011), 'Cents and sensibility: Economic valuation and the nature of "Nature"', *American Journal of Sociology*, 116(6), 1721–77.

Fourcade, M. and K. Healy (2007), 'Moral views of market society', *Annual Review Of Sociology*, 33(1), 285–311.

Friedman, M. (1979), available online at: http://www.youtube.com/watch?v=RWsx1X8PV_A.

Geiger, S., H. Kjellberg and R. Spencer (2012), 'Shaping exchanges, building markets', *Consumption Markets & Culture*, 15(2), 1–15.

Hamprecht, J. and D. Corsten (2007), 'Supply chain strategy and sustainability: The Migros Palm Oil Case, Oikos sustainability case collection', in J. Hamschmidt (ed), *Case Studies in Sustainability Management and Strategy: The Oikos Collection*, Sheffield: Greenleaf Publishing.

Hirschman, A.O. (1982), 'Rival interpretations of market society: Civilizing, destructive, or feeble?', *Journal of Economic Literature*, 20(4), 1463–84.

Holt, D.B. (2012), 'Constructing sustainable consumption from ethical values to the cultural transformation of unsustainable markets', *The Annals of the American Academy of Political and Social Science*, 644(1), 236–55.

Kjellberg, H. (2010), 'Marketing on trial. The SAS EuroBonus case', in L. Araujo, J. Finch and H. Kjellberg (eds), *Reconnecting Marketing to Markets*, Oxford: Oxford University Press, pp. 181–203.

Kjellberg, H. and C. Helgesson (2006), 'Multiple versions of markets: Multiplicity and performativity in market practice', *Industrial Marketing Management*, 35(7), 839–55.

Kjellberg, H. and C.F. Helgesson (2007), 'On the nature of markets and their practices', *Marketing Theory*, 7(2), 137–62.

Kjellberg, H., A. Mallard, D-L. Arjaliès, P. Aspers, S. Beljean, A. Bidet, A. Corsín et al. (2013), 'Valuation studies? Our collective two cents', *Valuation Studies*, 1(1), 11–30.

Latour, B. (2004), 'Why has critique run out of steam? From matters of fact to matters of concern', *Critical Inquiry*, 30.

Latour, B. (2005), 'From Realpolitik to Dingpolitik: An introduction to making things public application', in B. Latour and P. Weibel (eds), *Making Things Public: Atmospheres of Democracy*, Cambridge, MA: MIT Press.

Law, J. (1997), 'Traduction/Trahison: Notes on ANT', Centre for Science Studies, University of Lancaster, available at: http//:www.comp.lancs.ac.uk/sociology/papers/Law-Traduction-Trahison.pdf.

MacKenzie, D. (2009), 'Making things the same: Gases, emission rights and the politics of carbon markets', *Accounting, Organizations & Society*, 34(3/4), 440–55.

Martin Persson, U. (2012), 'Conserve or convert? Pan-tropical modeling of REDD–bioenergy competition', *Biological Conservation*, 146(1), 81–8.

Morel, A. and B. Morel (2012), 'How could carbon credits for reducing deforestation compete with returns from palm oil: A proposal for a more flexible REDD valuation tool', *Journal of Sustainable Forestry*, 31(1/2), 11–28.

Nantha, H. and C. Tisdell (2009), 'The orangutan–oil palm conflict: Economic constraints and opportunities for conservation', *Biodiversity & Conservation*, 18(2), 487–502.

Nenonen, S., L. Cheung, H. Kjellberg, S. Lindeman, C. Mele, J. Pels, L. Sajtos and K. Storbacka (2013), 'Understanding market plasticity: The dialectic dynamics between stability and fluidity', The 2013 Naples Forum on Service, Ischia, Italy.

Nikoloyuk, J., T.R. Burns and R. de Man (2010), 'The promise and limitations of partnered governance: The case of sustainable palm oil', *Corporate Governance: The International Journal of Effective Board Performance*, 10(1), 59–72.

POIG Statement, available online at: www.greenpeace.org/international/Global/international/photos/forests/2013/Indonesia%20Forests/POIG%20Statement%2028%20June%202013.pdf.

Reijonen, S. and K. Tryggestad (2012), 'The dynamic signification of product qualities: On the possibility of "greening" markets', *Consumption Markets & Culture*, 15(2), 213–34.

Rinallo, D. and F. Golfetto (2006), 'Representing markets: The shaping of fashion trends by French and Italian fabric companies', *Industrial Marketing Management*, 35(7), 856–69.

RSPO (2003), *Closing Address*, Roundtable on Sustainable Palm Oil, 21–22 August, Mutiara Hotel, Kuala Lumpur, Malaysia, available at: http://rspo.org/files/pdf/RT1/Proceedings/Closing%20remarks.pdf.

Schouten, G. and P. Glasbergen (2011), 'Creating legitimacy in global private governance. The case of the roundtable on sustainable palm oil', *Ecological Economics*, 70(11), 1891–99.

Sheil, D., A. Casson, E. Meijaard, M. van Noordwijk, J. Gaskell, J. Sunderland Groves, K. Wertz and M. Kanninen (2009), 'The impacts and opportunities of oil palm in Southeast Asia: What do we know and what do we need to know?', *Occasional paper no. 51*, Bogor, Indonesia: CIFOR.

Stengers, Isabelle (1993), *L'invention des Sciences Modernes*, Paris: La Découverte.

Teoh, C.H. (2010), 'Key sustainability issues in the palm oil sector: A discussion paper for multi-stakeholders' consultations', Report commissioned by the World Bank Group, The World Bank and the International Finance Corporation, Washington, DC.

TWG (2011), 'Abuse of sustainability standards. An attack on free trade, competition and economic growth', available online at: http://worldgrowth.org/site/wp-content/uploads/2012/06/WG_Abuse_Of_Sustainability_Standards_9_11.pdf.

TWG newsletter, May (2013), available online at: http://worldgrowth.org/2013/05/the-green-development-oil-newsletter-issue-31-may-2013/.

von Geibler, J. (2012), 'Market-based governance for sustainability in value chains: Conditions for successful standard setting in the palm oil sector', *Journal of Cleaner Production*, 56(1), 39–53.

Wong, J. (2010), 'Sarawak a hotspot for palm planters', *StarBiz*, 8 March, B1.

5. Engaging diverging interests through pricing: the case of maize for bioenergy production in Germany

Jürgen Hauber and Chantal Ruppert-Winkel

INTRODUCTION

Markets are the result of ongoing efforts and activities by various actors to organize the exchange of goods. Within these efforts and activities the actors associate different and changing values and interests that should be realized within the organized market. These interests are not just about selling or buying a good with a specific value; the interests are also related to the issue of how the market orders goods, its design or its architecture (Callon, 1998a; 2007). As a consequence, markets can be seen as 'political projects' that are characterized by the struggle between different market actors to control the market (Fligstein, 1996; 2001). Related to different interests, multiple forms of market can be realized (see Kjellberg and Helgesson, 2006).

One product of the conflicts of interest and the struggle between firms is, referring to Weber (1978[1922]), the monetary price. It can be argued that in the process of forming a price actors are taking part in realizing the political project of a market, that is, the political interests of the acting firms emerge in the form of prices. To do this, different modes of engagement exist, one of which is situated in the performance of exchange (Kjellberg and Helgesson, 2010). Prices do not emerge mysteriously from 'the market' but they are 'constructed by the actors involved in the exchange' (White and Eccles, 1987, p. 985). From this point of view, the actors have to agree on a price to shape the exchange related to one or more specific interests. In the formation of price, different interests have to be balanced and aligned to each other so that an exchange comes into being. While the forces that structure prices are widely discussed (see for instance Beckert, 2011), the analysis of the practices taking place to form a price could help 'to better understand the processes through which prices, as well as the types of prices and their forms of realization in the market place, are made' (Çalışkan, 2010, p. 22).

The purpose of this chapter is to analyse how actors organize the practice of pricing in an exchange due to diverging interests, especially when the exchange is occurring in markets that can be seen as a political project. Our analysis focuses on the exchange of maize for the production of bioenergy in Germany and the realization of different interests underlying the actors' organizational efforts. The single market exchange is located in a value chain starting in resource markets and ending in end consumer markets (White, 2002). So, an exchange is part of a chain of interlinked markets. Due to this connection to different markets, diverging interests can over-flow into a single exchange (Callon, 1998b). In our case of the exchange of maize, what flows 'in' is on the one hand the market for maize as an animal feedstuff and on the other the energy market. The energy market in Germany is heavily influenced by interests enforced by political actors related to the goal to transform the energy system to a system mainly based on renewable sources (Hauber and Ruppert-Winkel, 2012). Our study shows that because of the connection to these markets within the exchange of maize a 'struggle of interests' can be observed related to the allocation of maize between the food and the energy market. We analysed how this 'struggle' is resolved during the organizing of the market exchange by fixing a price. On these grounds the research is focused on the market prac-tices that are conducted to realize the price, taking different interests into account. Thus, the chapter also contributes to our understanding of the practical efforts to produce market exchanges (Kjellberg and Helgesson, 2007a). Based on this research focus the chapter is structured as follows: first, existing perspectives on the practice of pricing are presented. Second, the empirical study design is introduced. Third, our case of the exchange of maize as part of two markets is presented. Fourth, the diverging inter-ests underlying the organizing efforts to bring an exchange of maize into being are analysed and two modes of how these interests are integrated in the exchange through the practice of pricing are presented. Finally, based on the empirical results, the practice of pricing is discussed, with a specific focus on pricing as a practice that serves to solve struggles of interests.

THE PRACTICE OF PRICING AND THE BALANCING OF INTERESTS

In economic theory prices are normally explained as the result of supply and demand. Changes in the curves representing supply and demand are expressed in changing prices. The market itself is the context in which the prices are determined (Çalışkan, 2007; Rosenbaum, 2000). In economic sociology attention has been drawn to the underlying structures that shape markets and prices (Beckert, 2011). Based on the concept of 'embedded-ness' (Granovetter, 1985) it is argued that the price is the result of the social structuring of markets through institutions, networks and cognitive frames (Beckert, 2011; Aspers and Beckert, 2011). However, apart from the general conclusion outlining the influence of social macrostructure there is 'very little research in economic sociology on pricing practices' itself (Aspers and Beckert, 2011, p. 29). Indeed, the structures which constitute prices or difference in the prices can be explained by the concept of 'embeddedness' but this does not describe the required efforts to realize a price 'on the ground' within a single market exchange. In the market exchange the practice of pricing itself comes to the fore, which contains all activities to set a price for the good or service that is traded.

Following Çalışkan and Callon (2010, p. 17) two 'striking facts' can be drawn from the studies on the practice of pricing: the first fact is 'that there is a multiplicity of prices which, at a given point in time, are available in markets and used'. The second one is that prices are 'calculated on the basis of other prices'. The existing prices are combined with each other in pricing formulas (or a pricing script, see Velthuis, 2005) to calculate the actual price of a good or service. The studies also show that material variables can play a decisive part in the formula; Velthuis (2005) for example demonstrates the significance of the size of paintings as an important parameter to setting the price in the art market. Another criterion highlighted by Çalışkan and Callon (2010) is the question of fairness that links the actors to the formation of a price. Referring to Muniesa (2003) and Guyer (2009) it is not the price but the modalities of calculation that determine the fairness of the practice of pricing. In an exchange situation the actors have to follow specific pricing norms to create a price that is perceived as appropriate (Velthuis, 2003). Furthermore, in market oriented pricing regimes the price must be formed under competitive conditions. It is seen as a characteristic of an ideal market and in this manner as a price to be held to be just. To recall Alexander and Alexander (1991, pp. 507, 508), a necessary precondition for the organizing of every exchange is that every 'commodity has an appropriate, or "fair" price'.

Altogether, the formulated price can be interpreted as an outcome of the already mentioned struggle between agencies trying to impose or defend their interests as a part of a mode of exchange (Kjellberg and Helgesson, 2007b). The struggle can be generally described as a gap between the interests of the different actors. In this struggle we understand interests in a broad sense (see Kjellberg and Helgesson, 2010) as 'things' that govern the activities. These 'things' can be ends that should be reached by realizing a price or the way (or means) to reach the price.

During this struggle pricing practices can serve as a normalizing practice to engage interests similar to a normative objective in the market exchange; that is how the fair price should be formed in the exchange. In this sense, the ruling price formula serves like a norm. Through putting the formula in place a guideline is established as to how the appropriate price should be (re)shaped according to the interests of some actors (see Kjellberg and Helgesson, 2007a).

For the analysis of the engagement of diverging interests through the practice of pricing we introduced the term of balancing based on the work of Kjellberg (2001). This notion helps us to describe how the different interests partake in the efforts of the actors to form a price. We choose the verb 'to balance' to highlight the non-linear character of these efforts; taking the presented discussion about pricing into account we assume that forming a price is not a linear process but one that unfolds in the making. The balancing of interests is conceptualized as part of the framing of a market exchange (see Callon, 1998b and Figure 5.1). Based on this framing, the actors associate different interests with the desired exchange situation; they try to introduce, for instance, a price formula (or pricing script, see Velthuis, 2005) that takes into account their interests related to the exchange situation. To do so, they have to persuade their exchange partners to take part in the market exchange following the proposed price formula in their pricing practice. A process of balancing starts: different interests related to the diverging practice of pricing have to be balanced, which means that some interests are engaged as relevant for the situation and others are disengaged as non-relevant or that interests are aligned with each other in the form of a compromise. In this sense, to balance means that in the process of realizing an exchange the actors have to frame each interest associated with the exchange. In this process, engaging relevant interests is a practice in itself and is part of the balancing effort. If the realization efforts are effective, a common practice of pricing, including a price formula, emerges; a mode of reaching a price is stabilized, the interests are balanced and all actors have committed themselves to acting as the formula prescribes. An exchange can be produced (Kjellberg and Helgesson, 2007a).

The framing of an interest as relevant or non-relevant can be seen as a part of the struggle, which Weber suggests. From this perspective the following consequences arise: actors balance different interests in their pricing practice in order to fix a price and consummate an exchange. Furthermore, we assume that the common practice of pricing integrates the relevant interests associated with the exchange. When the interests are

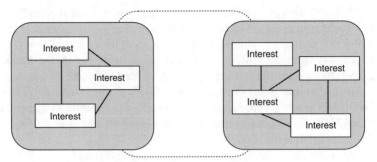

The actors associated different interests with
the desired exchange situation

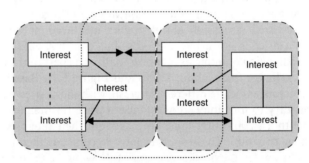

A process of balancing starts

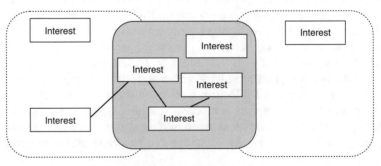

The interests are balanced as relevant and
non-relevant

Figure 5.1   Balancing as part of the framing of a market exchange

balanced it is expected that the struggle of interest is solved, a fair price is set, the exchange situation is stabilized and the local order of a market exchange is constituted (Beckert, 2009). It is assumed that by analysing the practice of pricing, a part of the struggle of interests underlying the marketization efforts can be identified.

EMPIRICAL STUDY DESIGN

The production of bioenergy has grown in Germany over recent years. This development has been part of a general process to transform the conventional energy system to a system mainly based on renewable energies (Hauber and Ruppert-Winkel, 2012). Previously, maize was mainly sold as agricultural feed; now maize is also increasingly used as a substrate for the production of bioenergy. As a consequence the exchange of maize can be part of two different markets: the food and the energy market. A 'struggle of interests' can be observed related to the allocation of maize between these two markets. Therefore, the market exchange of maize for the production of bioenergy is suitable for the analysis of the pricing efforts of the involved actors and their efforts to solve this problem.

The practices of pricing and the associated interests in this market are still under discussion and therefore can be identified in the making (Latour, 1987). Furthermore, the practice of pricing was analysed as a part of the overall process of organizing an exchange. Such openness provides space for a full exploration of the practice of pricing within a mode of exchange. The introduced notion of balancing helps us to improve the analysis of the interplay between different interests and the efforts underlying the process of pricing.

The best way to study practice is generally through participant observation, but interviews can also be an excellent means to reveal practices (see, for example, Reverdy, 2010). The combination of expert interviews and participant interviews can be particularly revealing. While experts spend a 'considerable amount of time in observing the practice', participants take part 'in the practice on an everyday basis' (Bueger, 2011, p. 16). Both types of interviews assist in reconstructing the interests that govern the activities of the actors involved. During the interviews the interviewees were given the opportunity to explain their own activities and the practice of pricing performed related to the interests they wanted to integrate; they clarified for instance that they had introduced a quality indicator in the price formula because they wanted to buy maize of good quality. With the help of the expert interviews, interests could be identified that originated from other market exchanges and formed part of the practice of the participants; for instance the interest to organize a stable exchange situation was connected to the interest of the stakeholders of the energy market to achieve security of supply for the energy market. Furthermore, the expert statements raised our awareness of specific interest constellations that the experts regarded as typical for the exchange of maize, for instance the interest of the biogas plant operators to introduce long-term contracts that included a calculable price for maize.

In a first step, nine market experts were interviewed. These experts were chosen because of their position within the German energy system relating to the issue of bioenergy and the exchange of maize. In their positions they not only observed the German energy system but as stakeholders they were also actively taking part in the forming of the relevant markets. They were representatives of relevant interest groups like the farmers' association or the biogas union, consultants for bioenergy projects or employees of energy providers. The question of how the exchange of maize is organized served as a starting point. They were asked to describe, from their point of view, their organizing efforts and the efforts they observed in practice. In addition, more specific questions were posed that were based on the introduced perspective on the practice of pricing, for instance questions about the organizing of the price, the relevant markets for the calculation of the price or how a fair price was calculated. With the help of these interviews an initial overview of the exchange of maize embedded in the energy system could be produced. Furthermore, a conference was observed. At this conference, experts of the bioenergy sector discussed different interests concerning the organizing of the exchange of biomass (also maize), especially around the interest of achieving security of supply for the production of bioenergy. The expert insights regarding the organizing of the exchange also allowed us to refine the questionnaire. The overview helped us to derive more specific questions for the second round of interviews. These new market-specific questions were integrated in the version of the questionnaire that we used for the interviews in the next round.

In the second round, concrete exchange situations were empirically investigated. They were identified by means of a study about the regional transformation process of the energy system in two German regions (see Hauber and Ruppert-Winkel, 2012). In these regions new technologies for the production of bioenergy were invented and therefore new exchange situations emerged. The novel character of the exchange of maize gave us the opportunity to analyse the practice of pricing as a new practice in the making, as the actors themselves perceived it. In these two regions we tried to investigate all exchange situations of maize, which were part of existing bioenergy production chains. In the end, 17 market actors agreed to take part in our study and were interviewed. These interviewees were actors selling their maize or buying it. Often they did both, because as biogas plant operators eight of them were also farmers, three of them were only biogas plant operators, four of them solely farmers and two of the interviewed actors were coordinators who helped to organize the exchange of maize.

Here, the question of how the actors organize the exchange of maize served as a starting point. Open questions gave the actors the opportunity to answer in a narrative way. They were asked to describe their organizing efforts. If it was necessary – because the actors had problems with the narrative form of the interview – market-specific questions were posed that were based on the expert interviews. The narrative form also gave the interviewees opportunity to express specific interests related to their organizing activities, for example, they could describe in detail the way in which the transport of maize to the biogas plant was organized, including their thoughts as to why they performed in the described way. In so doing, the open form of interviews helped us to detect the interests of the involved actors and avoided our account being dominated by our own interpretation. The interviews lasted between 30 minutes and one and a half hours and were recorded. Afterwards the interviews were transcribed verbatim.

Based on these two rounds of interviews the organizing of 12 separate situations of maize exchange could be described and analysed (see Figure 5.2). The transcribed data regarding the concrete exchange situations were complemented by the transcribed interviews of the nine market experts. The transcript data was managed and analysed with the help of the qualitative analysis software MaxQDA 2. The data was coded based on the initial theoretical perspective; however, during the analysis

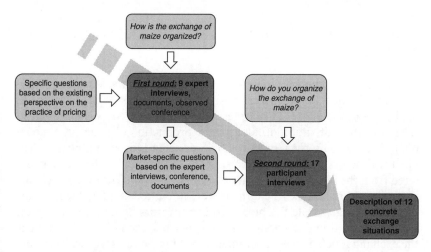

Figure 5.2   The two rounds of questions

new codes were inductively formed and old codes were revisited. Initial codes were, for example, codes related to the practice of pricing, such as market prices, price formula, quality indicator, the fair price; or related to the interests, like the interest to secure the supply of the biogas plant. Other codes were chosen to describe the exchange situation such as the code actor or artefact. Inductively formed codes were, for example, codes related to other practices that were mentioned by the interviewees and that were linked to the practice of pricing, for instance measuring quality, communication practices, harvesting practices or codes linked to new interests that were represented as part of the performed exchange situation, for instance the interest regarding contract duration.

In addition to the interviews, it would have been helpful to analyse documents that were produced by the actors themselves to realize the concrete exchange of maize (such as contracts, PowerPoint presentations). Unfortunately, for the farmers it was common not to prepare specific documents for the organizing of the exchange. Agreements were made on an oral basis and information was exchanged informally. Therefore, we used general documents regarding the exchange of maize (for instance legal texts, studies about the energy market in general, mentioned price statistics) or documents prepared by experts to gather additional data (for instance guidelines about how to fix a contract for the exchange of maize).

Based on the data, the exchange situations were mapped out; that is, the actors and the involved artefacts were pictured by their links and association to one another, and the interests enacted by the actors' activities to organize the exchange were identified, with a special focus on the practice of pricing.

THE EFFORTS TO ORGANIZE THE EXCHANGE OF MAIZE

The analysed exchange situations were mainly organized by practices linked to farmers, as the sellers of maize, and biogas plant operators as the buyers of the maize. The farmers were characterized by their practices related to the cultivation of land for the production of maize, the biogas plant operators by their practices of producing biogas and energy. The identified actors associated interests with the framed exchange that differed from the interests of the other actors with whom they were exchanging maize. For example, the farmers were interested in a flexible handling of the exchange, while the biogas plant operators aimed to stabilize the exchange situation in the long term. To persuade each other to partake in the exchange such a struggle of interests had to be resolved, which meant they had to organize which interests were relevant and which were not.

In order to illustrate this process in this section, first we introduce the exchange of maize as part of the energy system, because the struggle of interests within the exchange of maize is linked to the political project to transform the energy system in Germany. Second the characteristics of the maize exchange as part of two different markets are explained. After that, the different interests that are associated by the farmers and the biogas plant operator with the exchange of maize are introduced, and then the ruling price formula that was modified by the exchange partner in different ways is presented. Finally we analyse how the related interests were incorporated through the practice of pricing in order to organize the exchange of maize. Based on the different exchanges analysed, two different modes of pricing are identified. By comparing the two modes we show that the efforts to shape a price are associated with efforts to engage interests as relevant for the exchange situation or disengage them as irrelevant. The practice of pricing was the decisive activity to balance the different interests held by the actors. In the first mode this happened by performing an informal rule in the exchange situation, in the second mode by establishing a contractual fixed price in relation to investments made in the exchange.

The Exchange of Maize as a Concerned Part of the Energy Policy in Germany

As a resource for the production of energy, maize is an issue related to the energy policy in Germany. A general objective of this policy is to guarantee a secure energy supply for German society (stated in the 'Energiewirtschaftsgesetz' EnWG §1). In this sense energy markets should secure the supply of energy for the end consumers. In the case of the production of bioenergy, the secure supply of energy requires the stable supply of biomass, for instance of maize. Only through a stable supply to the biogas plant can a secure supply of energy be guaranteed. Furthermore, bioenergy is amongst the few renewable energy sources not dependent on weather conditions like wind or solar power. In a future energy mix with a high amount of renewables, bioenergy plays the role of a stabilizer, that is, to even out the fluctuation of wind and solar energy in the power supply system. Therefore, as a concern of energy policy, the goal of a stable production of bioenergy postulates a stable exchange of maize, and seen this way, an interest of stability is politically framed as relevant to the exchange. The energy policy reflects the desire of the majority of the German population who see security of supply as one of the most important characteristics of the electricity that they purchase (Kress, 2013).[1] The importance of a stable supply of biomass, for instance of maize, can also be explained by the influence of the Renewable Energy Act (REA) in Germany.[2] Through this law every producer of renewable energy receives, over twenty years, a fixed feed-in-tariff and the network operator is legally obliged to feed the produced electricity into the grid. In short, the REA stabilizes the market for renewable energy regarding the price and the quantity of sale. This means that biogas plant operators can sell whatever electricity they can produce at a fixed price. Consequently, to calculate profitability the operators are interested in a stable supply of biomass in terms of price and volume. The link between the exchange of maize and the exchange of electricity is enforced by bonuses that are paid in addition to the feed-in-tariffs if the plant operators use renewable resources like maize. Another source for the interest of stability regarding the supply of maize is rooted in the investment required to build a biogas plant. The biogas operators generally have to take out a loan to build the plant. To safeguard the loan, the bank normally demands objective evidence that the supply to the plant, with resources like maize, is secured.

> 20 years [contract duration] are the premise for financing a biogas plant. If the bank is doing the financing, then they want to have planning reliability and then they are asking how we can ensure that we get maize in the long term. (Biogas plant operator)

It can be stated that for the exchange of maize the interest of stability is relevant. The interest is rooted in the link to the downstream energy markets, which are influenced by the REA, the end consumers' demand and the objectives of German energy policy. In the exchanges of maize analysed, the interest of stability regarding the amount and the price of maize was relevant for the biogas operators. The importance of stability becomes even more obvious if the characteristic of maize as a 'flex crop' is highlighted.

The Exchange of Maize as Part of Two Markets

The observed struggle of interest also has one origin in the characteristic of maize as a 'flex crop'. Flex crops are crops like soya, palm oil, sugar cane or maize that can be used for the production of food as well as energy. As a consequence, the exchange of maize can be linked not just to the bio-energy market but also to the food market. As a flex crop maize is the raw material for the production of food or the production of energy.

Some varieties of maize are seen as more suited for one of the markets, but in the investigated exchange situation it was the same plant on the same cultivated land, and the only distinction that was made by the farmer was the time of harvest. As a resource for the production of energy, maize is normally harvested four weeks earlier than if the maize is utilized for the production of food. When the maize is harvested later, the maize cob has more time to mature. This is central for the utilization of maize as agricultural feed because the cob is the part with the highest food value, while for the production of energy the quality of the whole plant is crucial.

The exchange of maize as a resource for the production of energy is realized between the first and second production steps of a typical bioenergy production chain (Schaper and Theuvsen, 2006), that is, between the production of maize and the transformation of maize to biogas. The transformation process occurs within a biogas plant. In the plant the biogas is piped through a pipeline to a combined heat and power unit (CHP). In the CHP unit the biogas is transformed into power and heat. Normally the electricity is fed into the national grid while the heat is transported through a local heating grid. As part of the food production chain, maize is basically used to produce agricultural feed for meat production. In the analysed regions the maize was sold to farmer cooperatives which store the maize and distribute it to livestock owners or feed mills. Taken together, the exchange of maize can be pictured as part of two production chains, that is, as an exchange interlinked with two markets (Figure 5.3).

However, not all maize produced is brought to market; often maize is cultivated by farmers to feed their own livestock such as pigs and cattle. Accordingly, a farmer can take part in an exchange to sell the maize to a biogas plant operator or to a farmer cooperative, or he can grow maize for feeding his own animals. Biogas plant operators normally participate as buyers in the exchange of maize, but can also be farmers and cultivate maize for energy production. In these cases, operators need not buy all their biomass on the market. Operators that do not own agricultural land, however, have to purchase all their biomass, mainly maize, from farmers.

In 10 of the 12 concrete exchange situations analysed, the biogas plant operator is also a farmer. These operators were cultivating maize for the production of energy as well as buying maize from other farmers. In the

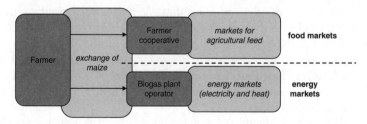

Figure 5.3   The exchange of maize as part of two markets

two remaining exchange situations, the biogas plant operators were enterprises investing in bioenergy production sites and buying all their maize or
other biomass on the market.

   In all analysed exchange situations one common struggle of interests
could be identified that had to be resolved in order for the exchange of
maize to come into being. It could be described as a struggle between the
interest of flexibility and the interest of stability. It originated from the
aforementioned concerns about stability in the German energy system and
the characteristic of maize as a 'flex crop'. This does not mean that this
was the only relevant struggle of interest in the organizing of the exchange
but it was the struggle most prominently noted by the involved actors;
for example, it was the central topic at the observed conference. We will
show how these interests are integrated in the exchange through the practice of pricing. But first, the conflict is presented as it was observed in the
concrete exchange situations.

A Struggle of Interests Regarding the Organizing of the Exchange of Maize for the Production of Energy

For the biogas plant operator the interest of stability was part of the
frame associated with the market exchange of maize. This interest was
existential; without a stable supply of biomass like maize the plant would
be useless.

> Point one is always the security of supply. A location [for a biogas plant] is
> useless if I don't have the biomass, especially close to the plant. (Expert, Energy
> Provider)

   Furthermore, the market price had to be stable as well, so that the price
was calculable in the long term. The biogas operator was also interested in
a stable quality linked to the dry matter of maize.

   As a consequence, he had an interest in decoupling the maize market for
bioenergy production from the food market, which meant that he wanted
to create a buyer's market for maize that was exclusively supplied for the
production of bioenergy and characterized by stable quality and price. As
an instrument to decouple the maize exchange from the downstream food
markets, the biogas operator was interested in closing long-term contracts
with the farmers regarding the exchange of maize. Through such a contract the biogas plant operator would be untouched by price changes on
the relevant crop markets.

   But the farmers wanted to be independent too, in this case independent
of contractual commitments, and therefore avoided long-term binding

contractual relationships. Consequently their interest was to exchange the maize without signing a contract.

> The contract isn't lucrative to me. What's the deal if I have a contract for 10 years now? 10 years always the same price [for maize]? But what is happening if the price for maize on the global crop market is going up to 30 or 40 EUR, and I have 10 tons? Then I am better off selling the maize to the global market rather than to the regional one. (Farmer)

The absence of a contract also gave farmers the opportunity to react to price trends in the market related to food or to energy respectively. With a long-term contract the farmer, in contrast, would commit himself to cultivating maize on part of his land; he could not cultivate, for instance, grain if the price of grain rose. In line with the tendency to avoid contracts, the farmers were also interested in a flexible handling of the price and the amount of maize traded. First, they wanted to be able to decide in the short term if they needed the maize for feeding their own cattle, especially if the harvested quantity did not prove satisfactory. Second, if they decided to sell their maize they wanted to receive a good and fair price, which meant a price that was higher than the price on the global market for crops. If the price on the global market was higher, the farmers wanted to be free to supply that market. They wanted to have the opportunity to decide each year which market to sell their maize to.

> I decide it, each time in August if I sell the maize for the production of bioenergy or as maize for agriculture feed. This year I sold the maize for the production of bioenergy, that was because of the weather. The weather was decisive, because the maize cob hadn't the quality to sell as maize for agriculture feed. But at this moment I wouldn't close a contract. That's clear. (Farmer)

Therefore, the objective of the farmers was to sustain two seller markets for their maize, a market for maize for the production of bioenergy and a market for maize as agriculture feed. Related to the interest of flexibility, the farmers were not interested in selling just maize, they also wanted to be flexible regarding the issue of crop rotation.

However, the interest of stability was also relevant to the farmers because they wanted a stable price for maize if one of the two sales opportunities were perceived as unattractive in the long term. Furthermore, they also had an interest in keeping the regional biogas operators as buyers in order to maintain the market for maize biomass. And the maintenance of this market could only be achieved if the biogas operators were profitable in the long term. As noted above, such long-term profitability on behalf of the operators depends on stable prices and a stable supply of maize.

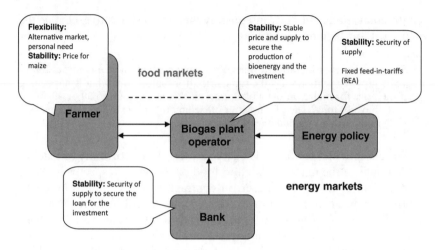

*Figure 5.4   The struggle of interest in the exchange of maize for the
                production of energy*

As a consequence, the interests of stability and flexibility are inextricably
linked for the farmers. They did not want to commit themselves to one of
the markets, that is, they preferred to be flexible in their choice of participation, but they also preferred a stable price to make their choice easier.
However, in order to enjoy flexibility the farmers need to offer some
measure of stability for the biogas plant operators, because the operators
are the ones who create the basis for their flexibility. Through the investment in the plant they create the demand for maize, and so, the alternative
to the feed market.

   Looking at a typical exchange situation between a seller and a buyer
and taking into account the depicted linkages of the exchange with the
energy system, a struggle between the interest of flexibility and stability
can be identified (see Figure 5.4). Within the organizing of the exchange
this struggle has to be resolved. The interest to secure the supply of the
biogas plant with maize was part of the frame the biogas operator associated with the exchange of maize. The interest was strengthened by German
energy policy and the interest of the bank that approved the loan to build
the biogas plant. The interest to be flexible regarding the utilization of
maize (personal need or alternative market) was part of the frame the
farmer associated with the exchange. To have a stable price was part of
both frames, the difference being that the farmer preferred a stable price in
both seller markets while the biogas operator's interest was focused on the
price for maize linked to the downstream energy markets. In the framing
of the exchange the actors have to organize which interests are relevant,

which are excluded and how the interests are aligned to each other to create a local order of exchange.

Within the analysed exchange situations two different modes of solving the described struggle of interests were identified: one in which the interest of flexibility was primarily integrated in the exchange, and one in which the interest of stability was framed as relevant. The first one was based on ten identified concrete exchange situations, the second one on two. However, the second mode was also the common mode mentioned by the experts. In both modes the practice of pricing was central to balancing the differing interests. Therefore, a price formula needed to exist that could be applied in exchange situations.

The Performed Price Formula

In the analysed exchange situations a ruling price formula to find the price for maize for the production of energy could be identified. In the formula the relation of the maize exchange to two different markets was represented and the two markets were associated with each other. Therefore, in the price formula an image of the global crop market[3] was integrated as a minimum price. The price in the global crop market was known through the prices indexed by the regional farmers' association or through personal enquiry in professional farmers' journals or on the Internet. On the Internet the actors could compare the regional price with prices on the global market or professional agribusiness web pages. While this market defined the minimum price, the maximum price was determined by the prices in the downstream markets on which the produced energy was sold as electricity or for heating, minus the calculated energy production costs. The price for electricity was a stable variable in this formula because of the fixed feed-in-tariffs guaranteed by the Renewable Energy Act (REA). Together the two prices defined a possible price space between a maximum and a minimum price. In the practice of pricing, the minimum price was integrated by the farmer while the maximum price was part of the calculation the biogas plant operator performed. The exact price within the price space was found by comparing the price boundaries with the price that was normally paid on the regional market for maize for bioenergy production. That price was normally known through communication with other farmers or operators of biogas plants. In the end, the price of maize had to be higher than the actual price in the global crop market and lower than the price in the downstream markets minus the energy production costs (Figure 5.5).

The concrete price paid to the supplier of maize was furthermore linked to the quality of the maize in terms of its dry matter. A specific dry matter of around 32–33 per cent received the best price, other qualities

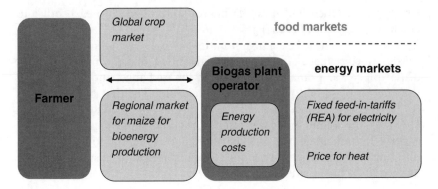

Figure 5.5   The organization of the price formula

received less. Through the link between quality and price, the interest of the biogas plant operator in a stable quality was integrated into the exchange situation. A good and fair price was therefore also linked to a specific quality that has to be demonstrated during the exchange in a transparent manner.

However, in the analysed exchange situations the price formula was smoothly modified by the actors' efforts to solve the outlined struggle between flexibility and stability to their advantage. It had to be balanced if the interest of flexibility or the interest of stability dominated the exchange.

Solving the Conflict through Specific Modes of Pricing

The balancing of flexibility and stability by an informal rule of pricing

One identified mode to solve the struggle of interests was typical for exchange situations in which the biogas plant operator also cultivated maize to produce energy himself. Typically he purchased the remaining amount from other farmers. The mode was characterized by the fact that the farmers integrated their interest of flexibility into the exchange situation. The farmers did not sign a contract, but they verbally guaranteed to deliver maize to the biogas plant operator. Because no contract existed, theoretically the farmers were still flexible to choose between two seller markets. When the harvest season started, the farmers could compare prices in the global crop market and the regional maize market and sell in the market offering the highest price.

The biogas plant operator could only ensure stability of supply by guaranteeing that he would always pay a better price than that offered in the global crop market.

No, we don't have a contract or something that commits us to the biogas plant operator. If I see that the price of maize for food is higher than what he is paying, then I can talk to him and see if he wants to link the price to the price that is paid for other crops on the market. (Farmer)

This guarantee served as a rule to stabilize the supply of the biogas plant for the continuous production of energy. The rule was common and was enacted in all analysed exchange situations. The farmers were in this favourable negotiating position because the market of maize for the production of bioenergy is usually a regional market because of the high transportation costs. The biogas plant operator depends on a regional supply of maize; transport from another region would be too costly. Unlike the farmer, the biogas plant operator has no alternative, while the farmer can sell the maize as agricultural feed to regional farmers associations, which were paying the price represented by the global crop market.[4] Thus, the rule reflects the dependence of the biogas plant operator on the regional supply of maize.

Regarding the price formula, the informal rule had the following consequence: the biogas plant operator guaranteed that the price of maize was always higher than the minimum price as a variable in the price formula. Then the price was perceived as 'good and fair'. The significance of the rule was enforced by past experience. The biogas plant operator had already demonstrated his willingness to pay a better price than that paid in the global crop market. So, he was well known for paying a 'fair and good price', which was equal to a good partnership.

When the grain costs 6€ or 7€ [in the global crop market] it is no problem. Then you can pay 25€ or 30€ for maize, then you get maize as much as you wanted, [. . .] this year we paid 29€, the last year 28€, the first year 28€. In the second year we paid 30€, at this time the price in the global crop market was rising, therefore we paid 30€. (Biogas plant operator)

This positive image of the other as a good and fair exchange partner was also associated with the exchange of fermentation residues. The suppliers of maize were only eligible to receive fermentation residues in proportion to the amount of maize supplied. These residues were used instead of chemical fertilizers, in effect linking the value of the paid price to the value of the fermentation residues. The value of the residues was derived from the market price for the chemical fertilizer that was substituted. Also, in some of the analysed exchanges the farmers were asked to take part in the harvest or in the transport of the maize with their technical equipment, such as lorries. This was in the interest of the farmers because they could utilize their lorries, and in the interest of the biogas operator because he did not have to employ a subcontractor.

In summary, the interests of flexibility and stability regarding the exchange situation were balanced through the integration of the rule that the price of maize for bioenergy production is always higher than the price for maize in the global crop market. The validity of the rule was associated with the personal image of the other as a good and fair exchange partner. The biogas plant operator had already demonstrated the validity of that image in the past with the result that a good partnership was also possible in the future. Theoretically, the farmer still had the opportunity to sell his maize in the market offering the best price, but the possibility that the best price was the regional price for maize for energy production was, thanks to the rule, very high. In the end the flexibility was still integrated in the exchange situation because the global market for the crop remained relevant to the situation and could not be disengaged permanently.

The integration of stability by contractual fixed prices in relation to investments
The second mode of exchange was typical for exchange situations involving biogas plant operators who had no land to grow their own maize. They had to purchase all of their maize in the market. In contrast to the first mode, in this mode the biogas operator could enforce the integration of the interest of stability within the exchange situation through long-term contracts. The stability was associated with the security of supply and a fixed price so that the costs for the bioenergy production were calculable. The price was fixed by freezing it for the duration of the contract, the supply by the commitment of the farmer to grow maize for the biogas plant operator on a defined part of his land. In the contract negotiation the price was also calculated by adopting the common price formula, that is, the minimum is defined by the global crop market and the maximum by the prices in the downstream market regulated by the REA, minus the production costs. But with the signing of the contract the price formula was suspended for the contract period (in general 10 to 20 years). Thus the associated market images for the calculation of the price were not relevant for the exchange situation any more. Through the contract, the exchange between the farmers and the biogas plant operator was isolated from the global crop market and also from the regional maize market.[5] The concrete exchange was personalized as a relation between both contractual partners. Metaphorically speaking the exchange is frozen according to contractual terms negotiated by the farmers and the operator with regard to both markets.

With the fixing of the price in the contract, the informal rule that the price for maize for bioenergy production must be higher than the price of maize in the global crop market was invalidated. Therefore, in this mode, the price changes in the global market become irrelevant. Linked to the fixed price, a preferred quality for maize was defined (also about 32–33 per cent dry matter) and a defined amount of fermentation residues were exchanged. The interest in a stable quality and the purchase of fermentation residue were integrated through the forged link to the price. Also the opportunity to work for the biogas plant operation during harvest and transportation was related to the price.

The biogas plant operators were able to enforce long-term contracts because they linked the interest of stability with other interests which associated the farmer with the realization of a concrete exchange situation. They persuaded the farmers to join the exchange by presenting points of connection, which gave the farmers the opportunity to integrate their own interests within the exchange situation. The first point of connection was the interest of the farmers to have stable prices in the long term. This interest was linked to the image of the global crop market as very volatile. The stable price was now guaranteed through the contract in the long term, and the volatile crop market was disengaged. However, in the contract the farmers were only committed to grow maize for the biogas plant operator on part of their land, therefore they could still cultivate other crops on their remaining land and sell them to the food market for prices indexed by the global crop market or use them for their own purposes. As a consequence the farmers could still be flexible although the interest of stability was integrated within the exchange. The second point of connection was more fundamental. It was in the interest of the farmer to have the opportunity to sell their maize on two different markets. As the biogas plant operator was the only potential buyer of maize for the production of bioenergy in the region, the operator could align this interest to his interest in long-term contracts. In comparison with the buyers of the first mode the operators in this mode could choose the location for their investment because they were not tied to a piece of land. Only the contractual fixed stable price and stable amount of land for the cultivation of maize made the investment in the biogas plant worthwhile. Therefore, the contract was a necessary condition for both exchange partners, on the one hand for the constitution of the biogas plant operators as a buyer in the region through investing[6] and on the other hand for the farmers to create a new seller market for their maize.

> . . .and yes, I participated in the negotiation about the credit for the investment, and a plant is only financed if the supply is secured, and therefore the farmers have signed the contracts to secure the supply for the biogas plant. (Biogas plant operator)

In summary, the interest of stability could be integrated into the exchange because the interest was framed within the exchange situation as relevant to the farmers as well as to the buyers. The interest of flexibility was disengaged, but the biogas plant operator took into account that the farmer could realize the interest regarding another exchange situation. The interest of stability was linked to the interest of a stable price, which secures the investment of the biogas operator. Through the secured investment a second market for maize emerged, which gave the farmers the opportunity to sell some of their maize to an alternative market.

The Practice of Pricing in the Centre of the Struggle

These findings show that one of the decisive points in solving the struggle of interests was the efforts to shape the price of maize in the exchange situations. These efforts can be summarized as the practice of pricing. As part of the practice of pricing a price formula was used to calculate the price. Through the performance of the formula the exchange was related to the prices of the global crop market, the downstream energy markets and a regional market of maize and to a personalized image of the exchange partners. These images served as devices helping to realize a price.

As part of the realization of the price, the actors had to balance their differing interests. The farmers wanted to be flexible regarding the selling of maize so that they could decide if they wanted to sell it to a biogas operator or in the market as maize for agricultural feed. Therefore, they were interested in the flexible handling of the exchange, including a flexible price formula that took into account the prices in both markets. The biogas plant operators, in contrast, wanted stable prices, a stable supply and long-term relationships. With regard to the balancing of flexibility and stability, two modes of pricing could be identified. In the first mode the conflicting interests were balanced through an informal rule that guaranteed that the price of maize for the production of bioenergy was always higher than the relevant price for maize as an agricultural feed. In the second mode the two interests were balanced through a contractually fixed price and volume of maize. The stable supply secured the investment of the biogas plant operator to build the plant and created an additional market for maize for the farmers. As the farmers did not commit themselves to producing maize for the biogas plant operator on all their land they were still flexible to react to new trends in the global crop market.

Linked to the price and its calculation were other practices that were entangled with interests related to the framed exchange situation. For example, the biogas plant operators gave the sellers of maize a benefit by receiving fermentation residues that could be used as fertilizer. Or the farmers were paid to transport maize to the biogas plant during the harvest themselves, thus utilizing their own equipment and thereby receiving a higher end price.

The end price paid was the outcome of the practice of pricing that forged associations between different interests and to other practices that influence the valuation of the exchange. The price was the outcome of balancing the interests that the involved actors framed as relevant. Therefore, a mode of pricing also displays different ways of how interests in markets are being realized, not only about the interests to buy or sell a particular good.

DISCUSSION

Based on the empirical findings, it can be argued that for the integration of different and diverging interests, price formation plays a central role because differing interests are configured around the price. In calculating the price, the actors enact images of markets, align their interests related to the price, and take into account practices that are associated with the perception of the price. The pricing process is a process of solving conflicts of interest; as Weber (1978[1922], p. 108) said, '[m]oney prices are the product of conflicts of interests and of compromises'. The conflicts and the related struggle do not emerge from assessing the value of the goods (see Beckert, 2009), but from different interests associated with the question of how a market exchange should be organized. The efforts in the marketization process are not only about 'forming clear subjective values for the goods in the market' (Koçak, 2003, p. 8) but also about framing the exchange in the market.

As a result of the performed pricing practices, prices were formed that were perceived as good and fair by the participating actors. The price was determined to be so because it was realized through the accepted price formula that was associated with the exchange of maize for the production of bioenergy. The fairness depends, as Guyer (2009) and Muniesa (2003) stated, on the modalities of calculation; this was in the analysed case that the price formula referred to the markets that were framed as relevant for the market exchange. In this sense, a price formula works as a 'judgement device' (Karpik, 2010), but with the following difference: it is not only the product that is judged by referring to some quality indicators but also the price.

In the realization of the price the actors follow this formula and adapt it to their specific interests, in one case to the interest of flexibility, in the other to the interest of stability. In the formula different prices and their markets are connected to the exchange, while the exchange is isolated from others so that the exchange is disengaged from uncontrolled overflows (Callon, 1998a). A separation is occurring; in our case the exchange of maize was separated through the guaranteed higher price or the contractual fixed price formula in an exchange of maize as a resource for the production of energy and as a raw material to produce agricultural feed. However, the excluded prices, markets and interests are still underlying the exchange process and are potential sources for renegotiation. They can overflow into the defined exchange situation – for example by introducing a new price formula or by changing the price formula because of new emerged interests in the connected markets (for example the energy market) – and can destabilize the balance found between the interests (Callon, 1998b; Kjellberg, 2001).

The second mode of price formation, which links pricing to the configuration of a buyer through the investment in a biogas plant, illustrates the importance of a second statement by Weber (1978[1922], p. 108), that prices are 'the result of power constellations'. In this mode, the investor could enforce his interests (long-term contract, stable price and stable quantity of maize) because of the possibility to constitute himself as a buyer or not. It was this alternative to invest in another location or exchange that gave the actor the power to engage his interests. The farmers did not have such an alternative because they are immobile because of their land. It was only when the biogas plant operators were already constituted that the power constellation was shifting. In that case the farmers could participate in an alternative exchange, the exchange of maize as agricultural feed. The biogas plant operators, in contrast, were dependent on the regional supply of maize. Only the knowledge of this constellation provides the farmers with the power to establish the first mode of pricing and enforce their interest of flexibility.

The source of power can be interpreted as 'relations of domination' (Çalışkan and Callon, 2010, p. 13): in the first mode it is the relation between the farmer and two seller markets; the farmers have an alternative market while the operators are dependent on one market. In the second mode it is the relation between the ability to invest and the potential location for the establishment of a regional maize market. The operators can offer the farmer a second market for maize.

It is becoming apparent that in our case such relations were not based on the unequal power of calculating agencies, as Çalışkan and Callon (2010) proposed, but whether or not an alternative existed, first regarding the market on which to sell and secondly regarding the location in which to invest (and where to create a seller's market). Due to these asymmetries, the respective actors possessed the 'performative power' to realize their 'pricing script' (Storbacka and Nenonen, 2011, p. 243; Velthuis, 2005,

p. 117). That script was then perceived as the dominant script in the market, with the result that the other actor experienced that the price that was arrived at was not necessarily something forced upon him. Power was not based on constraints but on the implicitness of an established script to set a price (see Han, 2005).

From this perspective and as the results show, the price not only provides a crucial point of orientation for actors (Aspers and Beckert, 2008; Fourcade, 2004), but it is also the outcome of a balancing process between their different interests emerging within the exchange situation. Prices are the product of 'relations of domination', of the efforts to solve interest conflicts and arrive at a compromise, for example a stable price as a 'good price'. The price is part of a 'political project' and a desired state of the world. From this perspective, the price can be an entrance point for organizing a 'concerned' (that is politicized) market exchange. In our case, through the practice of pricing, the energy market and its interests became apparent in the exchange of maize. A stable amount of supply in exchange of a stable price in the long term was framed as relevant to secure the supply for the energy consumer. The price thus represents the maize market's connection to the energy system.

Such a political discussion is not about changing the framework of a market through normalizing practices but is realized in each single exchange, that is, the exchange itself is part of a political struggle between sellers and buyers. Each exchange incorporates on the one hand the struggle to find a good and fair price and on the other hand the struggle over the question of what markets and what market-related interests are relevant to realize a price. In our case the struggle was whether the exchange of maize is an exchange dominated by the interests that are relevant for the energy system or an exchange dominated by the farmers' interests, who wanted to serve as producer for two markets. With the engagement of stability the energy market became the leading market, from which the exchange and their actors are governed (Aspers, 2011; Gereffi et al., 2005). The farmers became part of the energy industry and so did the exchange of maize.[7] As a result, maize is framed as a resource to produce a stable amount of energy and not just as a resource for the production of food; a differentiation that is still open to political discussion.

CONCLUSION

Our analysis suggests that pricing is a struggle to solve conflicts of interests, in our case between the interests of flexibility and stability. It was shown that in our case for the creation of a stable exchange, and so for a market, a successful resolution of that struggle is necessary. In this regard a mode of pricing is produced that contains the performed price formula and that realizes the price for the good traded. The relevant interests are integrated while the non-relevant interests are dis-integrated. But the dis-integrated ones are still present in the exchange situation and are a potential source for disturbance within the exchange, even to the point of preventing the exchange. The pricing is conceptualized as a continuous process of balancing different interests with the goal to pacify conflicting interests associated with the exchange. To understand the realization of a price and the efforts to balance different interests through it, the question of power comes to the fore. Our results provide evidence that the engagement of specific interests is a result of the power the actors have in an exchange situation. Therefore, a valuable question to pursue in the future could be how power is influencing the engagement of interest during the realization of a price and what the sources of such a pricing power are. For future research on market exchange, this means that the dividing line between politics and the economy is blurring, and a new focus is set on the political aspects of pricing.

ACKNOWLEDGEMENTS

This chapter was written as part of the research project 'Renewable Energy Regions: Socio-Ecology of Self-Sufficiency' funded by the Federal Ministry of Education and Research of Germany (BMBF).

NOTES

1. In a representative survey conducted by Kress (2013) in two administrative districts in Germany, nine out of ten respondents declared that the security of supply was important or very important regarding the electricity they purchased.
2. The REA was introduced in Germany with the goal to support a sustainable energy supply through the enhancement of the renewable energy supply.
3. The global crop market serves as a reference. This market represents the prices for different crops like maize or wheat. So the market demonstrates the value of maize and alternative crops that could be cultivated by the farmer.
4. The global crop market serves more as an index or device and not as a real market to which the maize is sold because it would also be too expensive for the farmers to transport the maize to other regions.
5. An alternative to the fixed prices mentioned by the interviewed experts was to integrate a formula into the price calculations within the contract; then the relevant images of markets could be indexed. But in practice this case wasn't found.
6. This circumstance is related to the fact that the costs for maize increase massively with the distance between the potential exchange partners.
7. 'An *industry*, as we define this notion today, is a set of markets, one of which is the core or leading market, and to which other markets are auxiliary.' (Aspers, 2011, p. 33).

REFERENCES

Alexander, J. and P. Alexander (1991), 'What's a fair price? Price-setting and trading partnerships in Javanese markets', *Man*, New Series, **26** (3), 493–512.

Aspers, P. (2011), *Markets*, Cambridge: Polity Press.

Aspers, P. and J. Beckert (2008), 'Märkte', in Andrea Maurer (ed.), *Handbuch der Wirtschaftssoziologie*, Wiesbaden: VS-Verlag, pp. 225–46.

Aspers, P. and J. Beckert (2011), 'Value in markets', in J. Beckert and P. Aspers (eds), *The Worth of Goods: Valuation and Pricing in the Economy*, Oxford: Oxford University Press, pp. 3–38.

Beckert, J. (2009), 'The social order of markets', *Theory and Society*, **38**, 245–69.

Beckert, J. (2011), 'Where do prices come from? Sociological approaches to price formation', *Socio-Economic Review*, 1–30.

Bueger, C. (2011), 'Praxiography in international relations: Methodological implications of the practical turn', draft paper prepared for presentation at the third Conference of the World International Studies Committee, Porto, Portugal.

Çalışkan, K. (2007), 'Price as a market device: Cotton trading in Izmir Mercantile Exchange', in M. Callon and F. Muniesa (eds), *Market Devices*, London: Blackwell Publishing, pp. 241–60.

Çalışkan, K. (2010), *Market Threads: How Cotton Farmers and Traders Create a Global Commodity*, Princeton and Oxford: Princeton University Press.

Çalışkan, K. and M. Callon (2010), 'Economization, part 2: a research programme for the study of markets', *Economy and Society*, **39** (1), 1–32.

Callon, M. (1998a), 'Introduction: The embeddedness of economic markets in economics', in M. Callon (ed.), *The Laws of the Markets*, Oxford: Blackwell and *The Sociological Review*, pp. 1–57.

Callon, M. (1998b), 'An essay on framing and overflowing: Economic externalities revisited by sociology', in M. Callon (ed.), *The Laws of the Markets*, Oxford: Blackwell Publishers and *The Sociological Review*, pp. 244–69.

Callon, M. (2007), 'What does it mean to say that economics is performative?', in D. MacKenzie, F. Muniesa and L. Siu (eds), *Do Economists Make Markets? On the Performativity of Economics*, Princeton, NJ: Princeton University Press, pp. 311–57.

Fligstein, N. (1996), 'Markets as politics: A political-cultural approach to market institutions', *American Sociological Review*, **61** (4), 656–73.

Fligstein, N. (2001), *The Architecture of Markets. An Economic Sociology of Twenty-first-century Capitalist Societies*, Princeton and Oxford: Princeton University Press.

Fourcade, M. (2004), 'Price and prejudice: On the practical culture of economic theory', unpublished manuscript, Berkeley, CA: University of California, Berkeley.

Gereffi, G., J. Humphrey and T. Sturgeon (2005), 'The governance of global value chains', *Review of International Political Economy*, **12** (1), 78–104.

Granovetter, M. (1985), 'Economic action and social structure: The problem of embeddedness', *The American Journal of Sociology*, **91** (3), 481–510.

Guyer, J. (2009), 'Composites, fictions and risk: Towards an ethnography of price', in K. Harrt and C. Hann (eds), *Market and Society: The Great Transformation Today*, Cambridge: Cambridge University Press, pp. 203–20.

Han, B-C. (2005), *Was ist Macht?* Stuttgart: Reclam.

Hauber, J. and C. Ruppert-Winkel (2012), 'Moving towards energy self-sufficiency based on renewables: Comparative case studies on the emergence of regional processes of socio-technical change in Germany', *Sustainability*, **4** (4), 491–530.

Karpik, L. (2010), *Valuing the Unique: The Economics of Singularities*, Princeton and Oxford: Princeton University Press.

Kjellberg, H. (2001), *Organising Distribution. Hakonbolaget and the Efforts to Rationalize Food Distribution, 1940–1960*, Dissertation, Stockholm: EFI.

Kjellberg, H. and C-F. Helgesson (2006), 'Multiple versions of markets: Multiplicity and performance in market practice', *Industrial Marketing Management*, **35**, 839–55.

Kjellberg, H. and C-F. Helgesson (2007a), 'The mode of exchange and shaping of markets: Distributor influence in the Swedish post-war food industry', *Industrial Marketing Management*, **36**, 861–78.

Kjellberg, H. and C-F. Helgesson (2007b), 'On the nature of markets and their practices', *Marketing Theory*, **7**, 137–62.

Kjellberg, H. and C-F. Helgesson (2010), 'Political marketing: Multiple values, performativities and models of engaging', *Journal of Cultural Economy*, **3** (2), 279–97.

Koçak, Ö. (2003), *Social Orders of Exchange: Effects and Origins of Social Order in Exchange Markets*, PhD thesis, Stanford: Stanford University.

Kress, M. (2013), 'Akzeptanz erneuerbarer Energien und Beteiligungsmöglichkeiten der Bürger in EE-Regionen. Ergebnisse einer wiederholten telefonischen Bevölkerungsbefragung', unpublished manuscript, in progress.

Latour, B. (1987), *Science in Action: How to Follow Scientists and Engineers through Society*, Cambridge, MA: Harvard University Press.

Muniesa, F. (2003), *Des Marchés comme Algorithmes: Sociologie de la Cotation Electronique à la Bourse de Paris*, PhD dissertation, Ecole des Mines de Paris.

Reverdy, T. (2010), 'The unexpected effects of gas market liberalization: Inherited devices and new practices', in L. Araujo, J. Finch and H. Kjellberg (eds), *Reconnecting Marketing to Markets*, Oxford: Oxford University Press, pp. 158–81.

Rosenbaum, E.F. (2000), 'What is a market? On the methodology of a contested concept', *Review of Social Economy*, **58** (4), 455–82.

Schaper, C. and L. Theuvsen (2006), 'Die Zukunft erneuerbarer Energien: Eine SWOT-Analyse', in ÖGA Tagungsband 2006 *Ländliche Betriebe und Agrarökonomie auf neuen Pfaden*, Vienna.

Storbacka, K. and S. Nenonen (2011), 'Markets as configurations', *European Journal of Marketing*, **45** (1/2), 241–58.

Velthuis, O. (2003), 'Symbolic meanings of prices: Constructing the value of contemporary art in Amsterdam and New York galleries', *Theory and Society*, **32**, 181–215.

Velthuis, O. (2005), *Talking Prices: Symbolic Meanings of Prices on the Market for Contemporary Art*, Princeton, NJ: Princeton University Press.

Weber, M. ([1922]1978), *Economy and Society*, Berkeley: University of California Press.

White, H. (2002), *Markets from Networks, Socioeconomic Models of Production*, Princeton, NJ: Princeton University Press.

White, H. and R. Eccles (1987), 'Producers' market', in J. Eatwell, M. Milgate and P. Newman (eds), *The New Palgrave: A Dictionary of Economic Theory and Doctrine*, London: Macmillan, pp. 984–6.

6. Credible qualifications: the case of functional foods

Frank Azimont and Luis Araujo

INTRODUCTION

This chapter addresses how the credibility of a new form of qualification is established. Our empirical setting is functional foods and its struggles to establish itself as a product category, halfway between foodstuffs and pharmaceuticals. Functional foods can be broadly defined as foods which claim a specified health benefit. Claims to health benefits invoke a different form of justification from those traditionally used in the food industry. For example, suggesting that chewing gum freshens breath is one thing but claiming it reduces tooth cavities is quite another. The standards required to establish health claims in functional foods bring this category closer to pharmaceuticals than food, where claims are justified on the basis of strict standards and closely regulated.

Our starting point is the notion of credibility, how it is established and consolidated across multiple arenas, as well as how it relates to markets. In science, the seminal work of Latour and Woolgar (1979) and Knorr-Cetina (1982) describe how scientists establish cycles of credibility amongst their peers and funding agencies, converting different types of resources (for example data, publications or money) as they build, accumulate and capitalize on credibility. More recently, Lehenkari (2003) and Penders and Nelis (2011) investigate how credibility is established in the world of corporate science, where private firms invest in basic science as a way to create new products as well as establish the credibility of claims made by their products.

We position credibility as an integral part of the process of defining the qualities of a good (Callon et al., 2002). The qualities of a good are here seen as the outcome of a process of qualification rather than a set of intrinsic and universally agreed properties. As Callon et al. (2002, p. 199) put it: 'Talking of quality means raising the question of the controversial processes of qualification, processes through which qualities are attributed, stabilized, objectified and arranged'. The focus on qualification processes opens up important issues regarding the work involved in attaching qualities to goods. There is no reason, for example, to restrict qualification work to a limited set of actors (for example those on the supply side) or to expect qualification processes to succeed as a matter of course. The establishment of the qualities of a good involves the acceptance of claims about its properties. Those claims may appeal to common knowledge, as is the case with the vast majority of fast-moving consumer goods, but may also involve more complex and contested forms of credibility, including the use of scientific knowledge. And, these claims may be subjected not just to common laws (for example regarding packaging, advertisement claims) but also to other forms of scrutiny (for example regulators).

Our purpose in this chapter is to examine these more complex forms of qualification. In particular, we are interested in how firms establish the credibility of claims to particular qualities. In our case, these qualities take the form of the health benefits claimed by functional foods and how these qualification efforts brought marketing and corporate science together. The relationship between marketing and corporate science has been addressed mainly in the context of pharmaceutical companies. Applbaum (2009; 2011) and Sismondo (2010) argued that, in recent decades, the role of marketing in pharmaceutical companies has expanded to the point where it now occupies an important role in determining R&D priorities. But, whereas this line of argument is often used to criticize the current state of affairs in the pharmaceutical industry, we look at how the interdependencies between marketing and corporate science develop in an emerging and contested product category, and how this leads to new ways for establishing credible quality claims.

The structure of this chapter is as follows: in the second section, we focus on the notion of qualification and how products are qualified. In the third section, we explore the relationship between corporate science and qualifications and discuss how scientific knowledge is mobilized for the pursuit of credibility strategies. The fourth section describes the research methodology employed in our empirical studies. Our empirical data, based on two phased studies, features in the fifth and sixth sections. The first phase, based on secondary data, describes the history of functional foods and its emergence as a product category. The second phase takes a company perspective, focusing on a European food multinational that made significant investments in functional foods. The penultimate section places the empirical results in a broader frame and the last section offers some concluding comments.

QUALIFYING PRODUCTS

Lancaster (1966) introduced into economics the notion of goods as a bundle of characteristics that consumers valued in different ways. Utility was derived from these characteristics and not from goods themselves. More importantly, the characteristics possessed by goods were seen as objective attributes shared by all consumers. As Lancaster (1966, p. 134) remarked: 'the personal element in consumer choice arises in the choice between collection of characteristics only, not in the allocation of characteristics to the goods'. Kotler (1967, p. 289) extended this definition by looking at products as 'bundles of physical, service and symbolic particulars to yield satisfaction or benefits to the buyer'. Since Copeland (1924), marketing practitioners and theorists have been concerned with how to relate product characteristics to marketing strategy. Aspinwall (1962) and Miracle (1965), amongst others, proposed several refinements to product classification schemes in order to strengthen the link between different classes of goods and appropriate marketing strategies.

These early approaches tell us something about a product's qualities but next to nothing of the processes through which these qualities are revealed. Callon et al. (2002) observe that the establishment of product characteristics often requires heavy investments (for example in formulating a product's content, in production equipment) and that agreement on those characteristics is often hard to achieve. In addition, product characteristics are not settled once and for all. As a product travels from design offices, to factory floors, logistics hubs and retailers' shelves, it undergoes multiple rounds of qualification.

The notion of qualification blurs the classic distinction between supply and demand, in which suppliers inject objective qualities into goods and buyers simply decide on their rank preferences for those qualities. Qualification processes undertaken by a variety of market professionals bridge this gap between supply and demand, by successively incorporating multiple and often different versions of demand in their work (Barrey et al., 2000).

Méadel and Rabeharisoa's (2001) story of how orange juice bottles reach supermarket shelves exemplifies a sequential, multiple and distributed process of qualification. Dubuisson-Quellier (2010) uses the example of a food company to show how different functional areas within a food producer mobilize forms of expertise, data and metrological devices to sustain divergent qualifications of the product and its intended customers. The alignment between product qualities and demand is always in flux and there is no need for a consensual agreement on quality for the product to reach retailers' shelves.

Dubuisson-Quellier (2013) shows how other types of actors, namely social movement organizations, can help introduce new modes of qualification into markets (for example through labelling strategies) aimed at changing consumption habits. But the literature surveyed so far does not address the establishment of claims about product qualities or how those claims are made credible. In many cases, claims about product qualities (for example through advertising) are strictly regulated (for example through advertising standards bodies). In the remainder of this chapter, we will address potentially more difficult qualification cases regarding products that claim to confer specific health benefits to consumers and look at how those qualifications are established.

SCIENCE AND QUALIFICATION

This section addresses the role of corporate science in establishing product qualifications and focuses on the investments required to sustain credible qualifications. The role of corporate science in establishing product qualities is both obvious and elusive. At one level, for many contemporary products, scientific knowledge is involved in the formulation of a good's intrinsic qualities (for example its chemical composition, its technical specifications). Scientific knowledge is equally involved in the qualification trials that verify and regulate a good's claimed qualities (for example a vehicle's CO_2 emission ratings). But the role of scientific knowledge is hardly confined to these activities. In many other cases, scientific knowledge is mobilized to appeal to what Callon et al. (2002, p. 199) called the extrinsic quality of goods – that is 'not only are the qualities shaped by the device used to test and measure the good (and therefore depend on the choice and characteristics of that device) but their formulation and explanation also generate evaluations and judgements which vary from one agent to the next'. It is the role of corporate science in this that we are mainly interested in. But first, we will briefly review what we know about the role of corporate science in commercial organizations.

In discussing the role of formal organizations in knowledge production, Vaughan (1999) lamented that, for science and technology studies, organizations remained a largely invisible backdrop to action. For Vaughan, organizations are important for understanding knowledge production because: they configure people, resources, technologies and work practices; set up motivational and incentive systems that facilitate the development of certain types of knowledge and discourage others; and establish relationships with third parties that both complement and reinforce particular logics of knowledge development.

It should be noted that Vaughan's (1999) discussion is couched in the terms of 'organization' rather than a specific type of organization. As Penders et al. (2009) remark, knowledge production is hardly confined to academic or non-profit institutions. A significant part of scientific research is carried out in corporate laboratories, although this is hardly reflected in science and technology studies despite the odd history of corporate R&D (see Hounshell and Smith, 1988).

The contrast between science as carried out in the public sphere and the science-for-profit undertaken by corporations cannot be reduced to antinomies between disinterested versus interested knowledge production. Large corporations often employ large numbers of scientists and engineers who are active researchers and contribute regularly to peer-reviewed journals. Universities and publicly funded research establishments interact with scientists employed in the private sector in many high-technology sectors such as the life sciences or nanotechnologies. Universities promote industry cooperation through partnerships, science parks and so on. But scientific work in corporations, as Penders et al. (2009) note, is hardly confined to the natural sciences and extends to applied social sciences such as consumer studies and marketing, whose development owes a large debt to corporate investments. To study corporate science is thus to understand how scientific practices within corporations co-evolve with publicly-funded science as well as other practices related to, for example, markets and regulators.

Sismondo (2010) provides an illuminating account of how scientific and marketing practices intersect in the pharmaceutical industry. Doctors have been warned that the only type of credible evidence for the therapeutic effect of drugs is that produced by randomized control trials, meta-analysis and systematic reviews (Bohlin, 2012). In this world, companies are involved in producing evidence to get their products past a strict regulatory regime, but also have to use this evidence as part of their efforts to persuade physicians to prescribe their products. As Sismondo (2010) concludes, clinical research in pharmaceutical companies has to be able to display its credentials to be able to convince markets that it is an integral part of scientific medicine.

Pharmaceuticals thus provide an interesting case on how corporate science takes part in establishing intrinsic product qualities as well as producing assessments and evaluations that form an important part of marketing drugs to physicians. Lehenkari (2003) focuses on a hybrid case, falling between fast-moving consumer goods and pharmaceuticals. The case concerns the introduction of Benecol, a margarine which claims to lower cholesterol. This claim had to be based on scientific research because it impacts on general health. When scientific proof is established, the claim can be inscribed on packaging labels.

Lehenkari (2003) describes the creation of credibility as a cyclical process, with different forms of evidence deployed to mediate between different discourse systems. What counted as evidence was not restricted to scientific arguments but involved other forms of representations such as mass media advertisements. Credibility in one arena (for example science) needed to be translated into another (for example marketing). As Lehenkari (2003, p. 520) explains: 'Research does not have an intrinsic value that automatically confers credibility, but rather is dependent on how well negotiations are carried out and on what basis research results are assessed'.

Penders and Nelis' (2011) study of Unilever shows how the corporation deals with the claims its products make in the areas of nutrition, food and health. The production of claims in this setting is achieved by a variety of means, from peer-reviewed publications to accreditations from regulatory agencies and product endorsements. Unilever invests significant resources in research leading to peer-reviewed publications. Publications are important because they help the company's credibility as a knowledge producer and as corporate citizen, as well as backing up the claims made by its products. But the engineering of credibility, as Penders and Nelis (2009) and Penders (2013) show, does not stop with academic peers or key opinion formers in science. Outside science, strategies to accrue credibility such as peer-reviewed publications have little currency.

In these cases, credibility extends to regulators, retailers and consumers through the use of multiple strategies. Although these strategies are treated as separate processes, the boundaries between them are often porous. Penders and Nelis (2011, p. 508) explain: 'Credibility engineering by Unilever is a practice in which science, regulation and marketing meet, in which scientists, regulators and consumers are addressed side by side and in which scientific facts and persuasive strategies are mobilized alongside one another, and in which universal claims are made personal'.

The race to produce product claims involves corporations investing in basic science to bolster their credentials as part of the very establishment they are trying to sell to (for example doctors, nutritionists). Corporate science, whilst fulfilling many of the functions we may associate with academia and non-profit institutions, interacts with a variety of other corporate functions, namely sales and marketing, to address different audiences requiring different forms of persuasion of which scientific evidence is but one type of evidence. In these worlds, there are no clear-cut divisions of labour. Corporations are involved in producing and consuming scientific evidence to further their interests. Consumers may resort to a wide variety of sources to establish what counts as a healthy diet, for example (Penders and Nelis, 2011). Regulators play a vital role in approving marketing claims, compelling the disclosure of information about product qualities through advertising and product labelling, and thus influencing consumption patterns (Schleifer, 2013). Much the same can be said of third parties' certifications, which often play an important role in product qualifications (Loconto and Busch, 2010; Busch, 2011; van der Kamp, 2011).

In short, qualification is closely linked to how the credibility of claims about qualities are made and sustained. In many product categories, qualification is undertaken by a host of market professionals distributed across multiple, mainly commercial actors. But other types of actors often intervene in this qualification process. For example, governments intervene through the regulation of advertising claims or the enforcement of labelling rules (for example, 'smoking kills'). Third parties such as standards and certification institutions may further contribute to qualification through labels or seals (for example organic produce). Social movements or consumer organizations campaign for the introduction of particular forms of qualification (for example fair trade).

In specific product categories, such as pharmaceuticals, scientific knowledge is heavily implicated in qualifying products, and corporate science plays a key role in establishing product qualities, obtaining regulatory approval and participating in the development of the scientific disciplines. The most challenging cases, as we have shown, are hybrid cases – that is products that fall in between these two extremes. These are products whose qualities need to be backed up by credible evidence and the credibility of those claims needs to be established with a variety of audiences. It is in these cases that the link between qualification and credibility is least well understood. In the next section, we will briefly describe the methodology of our study before introducing our empirical material.

METHODOLOGY

The race to produce credible claims is easy to observe in the food industry and in particular in the functional foods segments. Functional foods are broadly defined as foods that have proven health benefits. This type of product market is therefore particularly interesting to identify how such claims can be established. The collection and analysis of empirical data comprised two phases. The focus of the first phase was the history of functional foods. This phase of the study involved mainly desk research and involved the consultation of numerous books, articles and publicly available policy documents. The history of functional foods can be traced back to a number of different countries and to particular government priorities, long before major corporations became involved. In particular, we trace this history back to time periods of food shortages around World War II and how nutrition became a salient public health issue.

At the same time, the history of functional foods is tied up with concerns of defining and regulating the category. This phase of the desk research focused on the processes that led to the promulgation of standards at national and international levels, namely at the European Union level. To track the controversies and the progressive stabilization of the vocabulary that defines the key food categories and in particular functional foods, our study has focused on the projects run by DG Health and Consumers (SANCO) of the European Commission that is in charge of food safety. It is within this instance that we can observe how a consensus was progressively created in Europe. To understand the substance of these debates and what decisions were taken as a result, we traced the minutes of the task force created to define what counts as evidence in food safety. These minutes were consulted through the website of the DG SANCO.

The second phase of our study comprised fieldwork in one major food producer, a multinational company with a strong presence in many European markets, the geographic focus of our study. This part of the study built on a significant degree of collaboration with the company over a long period of time, involving the first author. During this period, we collected numerous materials including training manuals, PowerPoint presentations and other forms of documentary evidence from the consumer and medical marketing departments. These materials were identified in two types of meetings: meetings where managers discussed the positioning of their brands, and in particular defined their benefit ladders; and meetings where the same managers discussed what claims could be made on behalf of their products.

Twelve in-depth interviews of one and a half hours each were conducted with medical marketing, legal affairs, science experts and consumer marketing managers. We talked to heads of department because of their ability to impact decisions within steering committees at the highest level. We also talked to operational managers in charge of running medical trials, building scientific cases and defining the claims for health care professionals and consumers. This range of interviews with managers across three food-related business units provided us with rich data on how the company approached markets for different food categories and the infrastructures it built to address the requirements of those markets. The emphasis on this phase of data collection was to understand how the company attempted to comply with evolving requirements in the functional food area and how it built a scientific and marketing organization to cope with these challenges.

THE EMERGENCE OF FUNCTIONAL FOODS

The food industry has long been concerned with proposing foods with organoleptic benefits to consumers. In other words, producers have long since tried to differentiate their products through claims about taste.

In Europe, at the start of the twenty-first century, a new trend emerged when food producers started to promote aggressively the functional qualities of the ingredients present in their products. The emergence of this trend and the mechanism through which these claims have been pursued is interesting because it represents a major shift in terms of how these claims are justified. This shift involves the use of a particular technique, Randomized Control Trials (RCTs), which are more commonly associated with evidence-based medicine.

The emergence of the term 'functional foods'[1] is located in Japan (Kwak and Jukes, 2001a; 2001b; Ashwell, 2002). In the 1980s, the Japanese government financed research programmes on food with the aim of analysing their health benefits. In 1991, Japan produced legislation on food for Specified Health Uses (FOSHU). The objective of the legislation was to slow down the rising health costs and encourage the Japanese to consume more fibre and calcium (Japanscan, 1998). The contemporary emergence of functional foods is the result of a combination of several factors, such as the ageing population in developed countries, the increasing autonomy and willingness of people to take initiatives regarding their own health, as well as the opportunities generated for food producers to sell value-added products by claiming particular health benefits (Kwak and Jukes, 2001a; Ashwell, 2002).

But before specialists could speak of functional foods, the first official food regulations can be traced back to 1942 in Canada (Ashwell, 2002). They were part of a wartime nutrition programme aimed at improving Canadians' health despite restricted food availability. The prevention of nutritional deficiencies was the main objective of the guidelines that followed. It was only in 1982 that the Canadian nutritional guidelines integrated the concept of functional foods, defined as a type of nutrition designed to reduce the incidence of chronic diseases.

Between the 1950s and the 1980s, researchers systematically explored the link between foods and chronic disease. In the 1970s, authorities in North America and Europe started to set up nutritional guidelines with specific targets such as the reduction of cardiovascular diseases and cancer. In France, for instance, the national plans for health nutrition (PNNS I and II) are examples of this type of guideline, with a strong focus on over-nutrition rather than under- or malnutrition. These programmes emerged at the beginning of the 2000s (WHO, 2008).

In the last 20 years, researchers have established that foods contain much more than calories, proteins, carbohydrates, vitamins or minerals as we are frequently reminded by health magazines and websites (Ruby, 2006). Research centres on functional foods popped up all over the world. Numerous countries have initiated innovation programmes to develop foods with functional benefits. Europe, in particular, seems open to functional claims about foods, resulting in public administrations' efforts to define what functional foods are.

At first, functional foods developed without any official definition. The wish to stress the functional benefits of particular substances led to various denominations and concepts: nutritional health, designer food, pharmafood, medifood, vitafood and so on. This overlap led Kwak and Jukes (2001b) to suggest that regulatory control should follow a horizontal approach based on health claims rather than a vertical approach associated with the sector the food is associated with.

Progressively, a stabilized term became accepted: functional foods. To qualify as functional, food must contain a substance with proven positive effects on health, an idea developed within DG SANCO. A further qualification was added: functional foods are conventional foods that deliver physiological benefits beyond the basic nutritional functions, such as a benefit related to the reduction of chronic diseases. These benefits have to be demonstrated and documented scientifically (Aggett et al., 1999; Kwak and Jukes, 2001a; Ashwell, 2002). This precise qualification of functional foods made them more visible, more unified as a category, and thus contributed to accelerate the positioning and development of new food products with health benefit claims. In the dairy industry, for example, Danone promoted the favourable benefits of bifidus on intestinal transit. Unilever companies promoted the benefits of vegetal sterols contained in margarine to reduce cholesterol. Numerous players in the fish industry have stressed the benefits of omega-3 fatty acids in reducing the risk of heart disease.

Consequently, a second type of distinction emerged (Aggett et al., 1999). Broccoli, onion, olive oil and some types of fish are functional foods as they contain several components with health benefits, such as sulphoraphanes, flavonoids or omega-3. These have been labelled 'intrinsic functional foods' in contrast to other types of foods whose benefits are derived from industrial processes. These are called functional foods by addition or 'extrinsic functional foods'. Some foods have also been systematically enriched, such as flour or pasta, to prevent potential deficiencies in specific nutrients. Various types of justification are used to support enrichment processes such as the weakening of certain foods through industrial processes that need to be rebalanced. In other cases, such as in Canada, public health policies require common foods such as white flour, corn semolina or pasta, to be enriched with folic acid. This practice is aimed at improving the intake of foliates by pregnant women and reduces disorders of the neural tube for newborn babies (Ruby, 2006).

Within the European Union, a large project called FUFOSE (Functional Food Science in Europe) was initiated to promote scientific research on functional foods. This project, led by ILSI, was started in the early 2000s, with a broader scope than the ones in North America. Further to the idea of reducing the risk of diseases, the European project includes the notion of improving health and well-being.

For FUFOSE, a functional food can be:

- A natural type of food whereby one component has been naturally raised through techniques of culture. For example, a variety of strawberry, rich in anti-oxidant, could be created. Omega-3 eggs also fall into this category, when the content in omega-3 is improved through poultry feeds.
- A type of food that has been enriched through addition with one beneficial component. Fruit juices can be enriched in calcium or milk can be enriched by adding omega-3.
- A type of food whereby one ingredient has been withdrawn to reduce the negative effect on health. Biscuits without trans fats are an example of this kind.
- A type of food in which one component has been modified chemically to improve its positive effects on health. The hydrolysation of proteins in formula milk for babies, for example, reduces the risk of allergies.
- A type of food where the bioavailability of one or several ingredients has been increased to allow a better absorption of a beneficial component.
- Any combination of the above.

This project has allowed a convergence of interests between food producers, scientific bodies and consumers concerned with the relation between the consumption of food and its impact on health. The question of how to prove health benefit claims became a central issue (ILSI, 2002). Functional claims require the ability to demonstrate the effects of functional foods on health. Biomarkers have to be defined as indicators of real or potential modifications within functional systems (organs, cellular and sub-cellular tissues) that can be used alone or in combination to trace the evolution of health and the exposure of populations to certain ingredients. These markers should allow the observation of effects, including in those situations where the time lag between the consumption of one ingredient and its effects would be long. A classification of markers soon emerged: markers of an exposition, markers of the target function and its biological response, markers of intermediary reactions (linked to the reduction of the key driver of a particular risk). In the case where the claim would support the reduction of a disease risk, the proof should be based on validated markers of the disease itself (ILSI, 2002).

If the work required to establish the denomination 'functional' foods has been a somewhat convoluted process, the one used to identify markers was even more complex. Still, this did not stand in the way of food producers communicating through TV advertising the beneficial health effect of their products, raising a legitimate question on the part of consumer associations: what is the legal framework that regulates such claims? In many countries, consumer associations, but also public bodies such as health ministries and drug and food administrations, were in the early 2000s calling for a regulatory framework against which these claims could be checked and validated.

At first, producers suggested that the presence of one ingredient that can promise to deliver a health benefit would suffice. In the case of chewing gum, for example, the presence of xylitol or any other polyalcohol would be enough to explain why this product would have an impact on cavity prevention. The impact of polyalcohol on the prevention of tooth cavities has been established scientifically (Ruby, 2006). But what are the quantities of a substance required to observe particular effects? Indeed, the presence of one ingredient says nothing about the quantities needed to reach a desired effect. Efforts to define functional foods across a number of countries led public bodies to progressively require greater rigour in demonstrating health claims before using them in advertising, for example (Kwak and Jukes, 2001b).

In this context, the role of regulators has been crucial for both consumers and competitors within the sector to dispute unproven claims. The proposed implementation of legislation that would force producers to substantiate their health-related claims led to a debate on how to establish the scientific basis of such claims. Establishing a scientific frame would help define the validity of claims and consequently help consumers to make valid choices and reduce market confusion. In June 2002, the General Directorate for Consumer Health (DG SANCO) at the European Commission published a draft proposal about functional claims in nutrition and foods. This proposal served as a basis for negotiations between EU member states in the second half of 2003. The tools involved to establish scientific claims emerged and were further defined in a second project called PASSCLAIM (Process for the Assessment of Scientific Support for Claims on Foods), also coordinated by ILSI Europe. This second project built upon the principles defined within the publications arising out of the FUFOSE project. PASSCLAIM aims at creating a consensus document containing criteria to assess the scientific basis for claims on foods, and disseminating it amongst scientists, producers, consumer groups and regulators.

Only in December 2006 did regulators at the European Union reach a consensus and vote on a law that grounds the foundations of a European harmonization regarding the rules to follow in terms of health and nutritional claims. Through this legislation, the EU wishes to ensure that all claims are substantive and scientifically justified. They stress that 'applications for the authorisation of health claims should adequately demonstrate that the health claim is based on and substantiated by generally accepted scientific evidence, by taking into account the totality of the available scientific data and by weighing the evidence' (Commission Regulation (EC) No 353/2008 of 18 April 2008). They define that 'well-designed randomised controlled trials (RCTs) provide the most persuasive evidence of efficacy, allowing strong inferences' (Gallagher et al., 2011, p. 19). Three sets of laws are issued under the articles 13.1, 13.5 and 14. The EFSA (European Food and Safety Administration) received the mandate to check the claims' validity of already launched products, as well as receiving and validating all filed requests for the launch of new products in European markets.

In summary, consumers and governments have shown great interest in this type of food, particularly in light of ageing populations wishing to stay healthy for longer and of the rising costs of healthcare across most of the developed world (Kwak and Jukes, 2001a). This interest has been largely triggered within a context where chronic diseases increase dramatically, together with the social trend of taking care of one's health (self-care).

The food industry has often been blamed for serving consumers with too fatty, too sweet or too salty foods. This industry regards functional foods as a strategy to improve its image and also to generate further profits. In the early 2000s, the market for functional food was said to represent nearly €100 billion of sales and, following a steep growth curve, was expected to reach €150 billion by 2010 and represent nearly 5 per cent of the total food expenditures in the developed world (Aroq, 2004).

For public bodies, this legislation proved to be helpful too. It allowed health authorities to promote the benefits of particular types of foods to prevent the onset of costly to-care-for chronic diseases, such as cardiovascular ailments, cancer, diabetes and obesity. It appears from this short history that traces the emergence of functional foods that the universe of the food industry has started to resemble more and more the world of pharmaceuticals. Claims to health benefits have to be substantiated scientifically. They have to be approved by an official organization (the EFSA, in the case of Europe) before marketing claims can be made.

HEALTHY FOODS: A COMPANY PERSPECTIVE ON FUNCTIONAL FOODS

After describing the development of functional foods, a look at an individual company will help show how these trends have affected business

practices. The second part of our study focuses on how a large corporation addressed the issue of credibility in promoting its functional foods.
Healthy Foods (a pseudonym) is a corporation that operates in the nutrition sector with three business units. First, it produces and sells foods to
consumers; secondly, it offers baby nutrition to mothers through health
care professionals (HCPs) such as paediatricians, general practitioners
(GPs) and pharmacists. And lastly, it offers advanced medical nutrition,
aimed at supplementing medical treatments for diseases such as cancer.

Healthy Foods is a relevant site of study because it operates in three different business areas with contrasting situations with respect to functional
foods. In advanced medical nutrition, there is no controversy regarding health benefits, as the products are covered by the rules that apply
to the pharmaceutical industry. Foods sold to consumers are another
polar case where one would not expect scientific evidence to play a key
role. The case of baby nutrition is particularly interesting because at first
sight, powder and breast milk are substitute goods. However, upon closer
inspection, one soon discovers that an organism such as the World Health
Organization (WHO) regards breast milk as unique and recommends that
exclusive breastfeeding is practised for babies up to six months of age (see
http://www.who.int/topics/breastfeeding/en/).

As producers started to compare their formulations to breast milk, they
moved into a sphere where they had to produce evidence on how close they
can get to breast milk. This became all the more relevant when they started
to claim that their milk has a positive effect on health versus dairy milk.
For instance, the formulation of industrial baby milks is based on dairy
milk and may cause babies to experience poor digestion. Some producers
claim that partially hydrolysed formulas make milk easier to digest. They
even claim, in the case of babies with a dairy milk protein allergy, that
extensively hydrolysed formula may be needed so the milk is unlikely to
cause an allergic reaction.

The requirement to compare manufacturers' milk to breast and dairy
milk made baby milk something other than mere food. Baby milk has
become a type of food in which one component has been modified
chemically to improve its positive effects on health, thus meeting one of
the criteria identified by FUFOSE to declare a substance a functional
food.

To take full advantage of these claims and to be able to manage them in
the most appropriate way, both scientifically and legally, Healthy Foods
added to its historical consumer marketing function an entity called
'medical marketing'. This entity was divided around three major departments: marketing, whose role consists in contributing to market understanding, developing offers and promoting them amongst a community of

health care professionals (HCPs), targeted for its prescriptive power; the medical sales force, whose mission is to present the company's offerings to doctors in face-to-face interactions; and lastly, medical affairs, which is the department in charge of running scientific research to justify the functional claims made by the company's products. This is also the department that verifies that marketing messages comply with existing regulations. Our study focuses on medical marketing (as described above), the entity that takes into account scientific evidence to promote milk when it is sold to a community of HCPs.

What Type of Science do HCPs Consider?

Healthy Foods addresses a mixed audience of consumers and HCPs such as paediatricians, neonatology specialists, midwives, GPs and nutritionists. In the medical marketing part of the organization, market specialists describe their targets with in-depth studies. The large and heterogeneous population of HCPs displays different attitudes and behaviours towards prescribing or recommending products. Typologies are thus built to create clusters of more homogeneous HCPs and qualify their propensity to recommend a specific brand of baby milk, for example. In one given country (for example, the UK) there may be up to 58 000 HCPs that can be grouped around the following criteria: (a) HCPs totally opposed to prescription; (b) HCPs who are partly open to prescription based on pragmatic considerations (for example the product helps the patients even if it only has a placebo effect); (c) HCPs who based their prescriptions on what they consider very strict scientific criteria; and lastly (d) those HCPs who accept to prescribe the product of one specific supplier (for example Healthy Foods or a competitor).

These clusters indicate the type of information that an HCP will expect to receive from producers, either through specialist magazines or sales reps, before engaging in a conversation with the parents of a child. The clusters also signal the type of evidence requested by these professionals before they accept to recommend a particular product or brand of baby milk as well as characterize the type of sales devices medical visitors should be equipped with when meeting doctors, for example.

Some HCPs have great empathy towards mothers and feel comfortable recommending milk whose scientific claims are very limited, provided the baby and the mum feel relieved. Other HCPs will only propose products whose claims are substantiated by strict scientific protocols. But even in this case, studies carried out by Healthy Foods show differences across HCPs: immunologists would accept as proof of effectiveness protocols that include *in vitro* experimentation,[2] while paediatricians only accept human intervention studies. These internal studies also rank the prestige and authority of scientific journals according to the various types of HCPs.

These observations on the attitudes and behaviours of HCPs have an impact on the way research programmes are developed and implemented at Healthy Foods. Most research programmes are costly and often lead to uncertain results in terms of commercial exploitation. Scientific results can only be achieved in the long term whereas Healthy Foods traditionally expects short-term results. Faced with similar constraints, competitors of Healthy Foods made a strategic choice to use generic claims, based on broader research programmes with a weaker scientific basis, but delivering a better return on investment, in line with traditional expectations in the food sector. The engagement of a firm in scientific research is subject to a risk analysis that oscillates between managing expectations on financial return and the scientific expectations of the medical community. The choice of Healthy Foods was, over the last decade, to invest in credible scientific research in the medical and baby nutrition departments.

How can the Strength of Product Claims be Assessed?

In an industry where producers talk to HCPs, competition to demonstrate the scientific basis of product claims is fierce. Marketing and sales people spend a significant amount of effort to prove why their products are better than those of their competitors. Over the years, specialists within the medical affairs department have built a method that allows them to qualify the claims made by competitors to HCPs. This method, as the director of medical affairs explained, is largely based on the work of Guyatt and Rennie (2002) who argue that expert opinions without explicit critical evaluation, based on physiology or on studies carried out on animals, lead to weak statements. They also argue that arguments become progressively stronger through a series of case studies, studies with a control case, cohort studies, RCT studies and ultimately, meta-analysis. According to the director of medical affairs, it is helpful to acquaint the marketing and sales teams with this variety of scientific studies to show that science feeds on controversies and requires the progressive settlement of controversies through different forms of empirical studies. Thanks to this approach, marketers and sales people are trained to formulate strong statements and defend them in front of doctors who contest them with notions emanating from their professional training or promoted by competitors of Healthy Foods.

This easy-to-use method is based on an ordinal scale designed to score the strength of a scientific argument. The first level of the scale qualifies as 'weak' an argument stating that an ingredient known for producing a

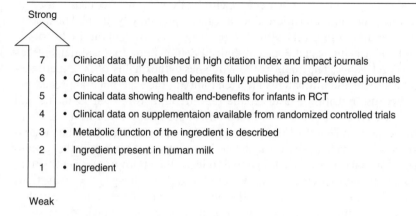

Not all science is powerful science: From weak to strong science

Strong

7 • Clinical data fully published in high citation index and impact journals
6 • Clinical data on health end benefits fully published in peer-reviewed journals
5 • Clinical data showing health end-benefits for infants in RCT
4 • Clinical data on supplementaion available from randomized controlled trials
3 • Metabolic function of the ingredient is described
2 • Ingredient present in human milk
1 • Ingredient

Weak

Source: Healthy Foods, adapted from Guyatt and Rennie (2002).

Figure 6.1   How to build strong statements

positive effect is present in the product, even if the benefit has not been proven in a real usage situation. Level 2 is used when a product contains an ingredient present, say, in breast milk, and when it is claimed that if the product has the ingredient profile of breast milk, it is then close to the ideal standard. At level 3, the metabolic function of the ingredient is documented. At level 4, clinical trials based on RCTs are carried out, leading to claims such as 'we could record a higher level of zinc in the plasma after a zinc supplementation'. At level 5, the link between a health benefit and a cause has to be investigated and established through a RCT. For example, a statement such as 'we could record significantly less atopic dermatitis in a population supplemented with prebiotics' should be demonstrated through the use of a RCT. At level 6, the results of studies carried out at level 5 have to be published in reference, peer-reviewed journals. The quality of a journal, based on its citation index and impact, allows a claim to reach the top score of 7. The scale, as enacted by Healthy Foods, helps the company argue against competitors' claims by proving that their evidence protocol is inadequate.

Marketers and sales people are not commonly trained to carry out the type of analysis described above. One might argue that this is not their job either. But still, they have been able to engage in a conversation at this level with different types of HCPs. It took Healthy Foods a significant amount of effort to make these market professionals familiar with research methods and the processes involved in assessing the validity of a statement.

Healthy Foods put in place training actions to help these populations understand that the statement 'scientifically proven', frequently used in advertising communication, does not mean anything by itself. The quality of a research study, as Healthy Foods stresses, lays first in the quality of the statement being tested. One can indeed demonstrate that a statement has weak relevance. The quality of research lies in the quality of the experimental protocol and ultimately in the reliability of the experimental procedure.

Because nutrition is a discipline that attempts to mirror medicine and because HCPs are involved in recommending infant milk formulas, scientific experts at Healthy Foods promoted what they considered to be the gold standard of evidence-based medicine. Training sessions were further organized for marketers and sales people to learn the appropriate scientific language. It was expected that they would be able to engage in conversations with doctors, not so much on the physiological processes involved when using baby milk, but on the experimental processes involved in research about infant formulas. The RCT protocol in general, and in particular the four major types of bias (selection, performance, attrition and detection) became core concepts selected to be central to these training sessions.[3]

As all players within the food industry, Healthy Foods has been exposed to the regulatory constraint of having to demonstrate its health benefit claims, using a protocol resembling the one widely used in the pharmaceutical industry. When filing its cases with the EFSA, the company was exposed to a variety of situations. In two of its divisions, teams were well prepared for this challenge. Numerous studies had been conducted and the appropriate scientific evidence amassed. A few cases with reasonable chances of success were filed and most of them approved.

In contrast, the consumer goods division put forward a number of cases for EFSA validation that had to be withdrawn. Healthy Foods was forced to destroy all communication materials that referred directly or indirectly to health benefits, and it was widely believed that the negative reputational effects that followed went well beyond the consumer goods division.

A year after these events, Healthy Foods estimated that the investments required to establish the health claims of functional foods were too high. The marketing of functional foods was partly divested and investment proposals aimed to exploit health benefit claims were to be carefully scrutinized from then on.

DISCUSSION

The case of functional foods throws up a number of interesting issues regarding how credibility is established for claims about product qualities.

The definition of functional foods presented a few classificatory challenges to scientific communities, regulators and legislators. If functional foods could be seen as providing health benefits over and above conventional nutritional values, and as contributing to the prevention and/or treatment of disease, the encroachment on medicine's traditional domain became inevitable (Kwak and Jukes, 2001a).

In the marketing of pharmaceuticals, as Sismondo (2010) notes, the target audience is clearly physicians. They act as gatekeepers between pharmaceutical companies and patients. Credibility is established through peer-reviewed publications using well-established procedures in medical science. In the food sector, as Penders and Nelis (2011) remark, peer-reviewed literature and the highest standards of scientific evidence are not widely deployed as marketing tools.

The establishment of standards, through the European Food Standards Agency, was a long and tortuous process that had a strong impact on the establishment of a market for functional foods which, crucially, included norms for making credible claims about product qualities. Standards provided an arena within which health benefit claims could be established and vigorously contested by other players, including competitors and regulators. The case of Benecol related by Lehenkari (2003) took place prior to the establishment of standards in this field, and contrasts with our story in the sense that strong medical evidence backing the product's health benefit claims neither led to regulatory approval by the US Food and Drug Administration, nor to the market success in the US. The emergence of standards for credible claims, based on established scientific knowledge, made it easier for functional food manufacturers to align their scientific and market practices with the pharmaceutical industry.

Healthy Foods embraced the challenge of establishing qualification claims with important investments in research, sales and marketing as well as links between these functions. These investments would allow the company to produce claims about their products that could be backed up by scientific evidence and complied with regulatory guidelines. As in the Unilever case related by Penders and Nelis (2011), R&D, sales and marketing, and regulation at Healthy Foods were joined together to engineer credibility for specific product claims.

Our study of Healthy Foods goes beyond these general observations and adds greater detail concerning how these joint efforts are carried out in practice. This is best exemplified by the formation of a medical marketing unit and the role of medical affairs in tandem with marketing and sales. The concerted effort to equip market professionals with skills in recognizing different forms of scientific evidence and tailoring their arguments in interaction with different types of HCPs represents one example of how medical marketing recognized differences in what counts as a credible claim. The attempts to segment HCPs and target them with different messages according to the type of evidence they are likely to be most sensitive to, is another example of the tight alignment between science and marketing at Healthy Foods promoted by the medical marketing unit. In the case of Healthy Foods, credibility comes in many different shapes and sizes depending on the audience targeted. As we showed, HCPs themselves turned out to be a highly diverse audience susceptible to different forms of persuasion based on quite different types of evidence.

The example of Healthy Foods also illustrates the problems of reconciling these different forms of establishing credible claims across different businesses. The company's portfolio encompassed baby, medical and consumer nutrition businesses. Whereas baby and medical nutrition followed the path of hybridization, bringing the company closer to the standards of the pharmaceutical industry, the traditional food side of the business operated in a looser regulatory environment, where claims to health benefits were more diffuse and subject to less exacting standards of evidence. When it came to submitting health benefits claims to the EFSA, two of the business units were well versed in the types of evidence required to obtain regulatory approval. The same could not be said about the food side of the business and some of its attempts to obtain regulatory approval for functional food products fell by the wayside, leaving the company to write off significant investments in promotional materials. These failures led the company to become wary of further investments in functional foods, scaling back its ambitions in this area.

CONCLUSIONS

The history of functional foods and the case of our focal company, Healthy Foods, illustrate two major issues related to our understanding of qualification. First, the process of qualification of functional foods as a generic category took a long time and involved a large number of actors, including corporations and public bodies at the national and transnational levels. The qualification process was far from linear or uncontroversial. It involved considerations about science, legal rules and regulations, health policy agendas and the desire of the food industry to diversify into new, more profitable market niches. Eventually, consensus emerged around the notion that to qualify as functional, food must deliver physiological benefits beyond its basic nutritional properties. But, to be able to claim functional qualities, manufacturers had to be able to demonstrate the credibility of their claims in scientific trials.

This case of functional foods generates broader questions related to the notion of qualification, namely its political and contested character. Who is involved in qualification processes, what role do they play, how is that role legitimized and by whom? In our case, the role of corporate science and its alliance with national and transnational agencies was vital in establishing the product category and providing a platform for developing a business of functional foods. But relationships between business, regulators and science are often riddled with tension and controversy as recent examples of qualification of functional foods attest.

Secondly, the case of Healthy Foods demonstrates just how complex and expensive the move to functional foods proved to be for a manufacturer. A new department of medical marketing coordinated all activities related to demonstrating the credibility of the claims made by the company's products. Not only did health claims made concerning the company's products have to be validated by the EFSA, but the scope and strength of those claims also had to be calibrated against the concerns, interests and skills of a variety of audiences. Traditional processes of market segmentation were used for calibrating marketing strategies as well as deciding what type of evidence could be deployed to make credible claims about a product's qualities. Marketing and sales people had to be trained to understand different types of scientific evidence and learn how to successfully deploy them to engage different audiences. All these processes required large investments and the wisdom of those investments was to be severely tested as the failures of the consumer division of Healthy Foods demonstrated. And they produced not a unique qualification, but a series of loosely related qualifications with different standards of evidence deployed to back up the claims that underpinned those qualifications.

In short, the case of functional foods sheds new light on the distributed and contested nature of qualification processes. As our empirical material suggests, qualifications need to be credible. But credibility means different things to different audiences; what counts as compelling evidence in one forum might be dismissed as substandard in another. Lastly, building up capabilities to play the credibility game requires major investments on the part of those who are tasked to certify claims but, just as importantly, on the part of those who wish to advance claims about their product's qualities. As Healthy Foods discovered much to its cost, credibility is a high stakes game.

NOTES

1. The key milestones of the history of functional foods have been detailed by the International Life Sciences Institute (ILSI). ILSI is a non-profit, worldwide foundation established in 1978 to advance the understanding of scientific issues relating to nutrition, food safety, toxicology, risk assessment and the environment, and is affiliated with the World Health Organization (WHO). By bringing together scientists from academia, government, industry and the public sector, the ILSI seeks a balanced approach to solving problems of common concern for the well-being of the general public and tracks the emergence of new phenomena that can possibly have an effect on human beings' health, including food trends.
2. *In vitro*: (of biological processes or reactions) made to occur outside the living organism in an artificial environment, such as a culture medium (source: http://www.dictionary.com).
3. In statistics, a bias is a systematic error or deviation in results or inferences from a true value. In studies of the effects of health care, the main types of bias arise from systematic differences in the groups that are compared (*selection bias*), the care that is provided, exposure to other factors apart from the *intervention* of interest (*performance bias*), withdrawals or exclusions of people entered into a study (*attrition bias*) or how outcomes are assessed (*detection bias*). Reviews of studies may also be particularly affected by *reporting bias*, where a biased subset of all the relevant data is available (source: The Cochrane collaboration, http://www.cochrane.org/).

REFERENCES

Aggett, P.J. et al. (1999). 'Scientific concepts of functional foods in Europe consensus document'. *British Journal of Nutrition* 81: S1–S27.

Applbaum, K. (2009). 'Is marketing the enemy of pharmaceutical innovation?' *Hastings Centre Report* 39(4): 13–17.

Applbaum, K. (2011). 'Broadening the marketing concept: Service to humanity, or the privatization of public good?' In D. Zwick and J. Cayla (eds) *Inside Marketing. Practices, Ideologies, Devices*. New York: Oxford University Press, pp. 269–98.

Aroq (2004). *Global Market Review of Functional Foods – Forecast to 2010*. Aroq Limited.

Ashwell, M. (2002). *Concepts of Functional Foods*. Brussels: ILSI Press.

Aspinwall, L.V. (1962). 'The characteristics of goods theory'. In W. Lazer and E.J. Kelly (eds) *Managerial Marketing. Perspectives and Viewpoints*. Homewood, IL: Richard D. Irwin, pp. 633–43.

Barrey, S., F. Cochoy and S. Dubuisson-Quellier (2000). 'Designer, packager et merchandiser: Trois professionnels pour une même scène marchande'. *Sociologie du Travail* 42(3): 457–82.

Bohlin, I. (2012). 'Formalizing syntheses of medical knowledge: The rise of meta-analysis and systematic reviews'. *Perspectives on Science* 20(3): 273–309.

Busch, L. (2011). *Standards: Recipes for Reality*. Cambridge, MA: MIT Press.

Callon, M., C. Méadel and V. Rabeharisoa (2002). 'The economy of qualities'. *Economy and Society* 31(2): 194–217.

Copeland, M.T. (1924). *Principles of Merchandising*. Chicago, IL: Arno Press.

Dubuisson-Quellier, S. (2010). 'Product tastes, consumer tastes: The plurality of qualification in product development and marketing activities'. In L. Araujo,

J.H. Finch and H. Kjellberg (eds) *Reconnecting Marketing to Markets*. Oxford: Oxford University Press, pp. 74–93.

Dubuisson-Quellier, S. (2013). 'A market mediation strategy: How social movements seek to change firms' practices by promoting new principles of product valuation'. *Organization Studies* 34(5–6): 683–703.

Gallagher, A.M. et al. (2011). 'A standardised approach towards PROving the efficacy of foods and food constituents for health CLAIMs (PROCLAIM): Providing guidance'. *British Journal of Nutrition* November 106(Suppl. 2): 16–28.

Guyatt, G. and D. Rennie (eds) (2002). 'Users' guides to the medical literature: A manual for evidence-based clinical practice. *Journal of Medical Library Association*. Chicago, IL: American Medical Association.

Hounshell, D.A. and J.K. Smith (1988). *Science and Corporate Strategy: DuPont R&D, 1902–1980*. New York: Cambridge University Press.

ILSI (2002). 'Functional foods, trends and future'. *British Journal of Nutrition* 88(Suppl. 2): 233–5.

Japanscan (1998), *Functional Foods and Drinks in Japan*, Leatherhead: Leatherhead Food Research.

Japanscan (2005). *Food Industry Bulletin*. 23.

Knorr-Cetina, K.D. (1982). 'Scientific communities or transepistemic arenas of research? A critique of quasi-economic models of science'. *Social Studies of Science* 12(1): 101–30.

Kotler, P. (1967). *Marketing Management. Analysis, Planning and Control*. Englewood Cliffs, NJ: Prentice-Hall.

Kwak, N-S. and D.J. Jukes (2001a). 'Functional foods. Part 1: The development of a regulatory concept'. *Food Control* 12(2): 99–107.

Kwak, N-S. and D.J. Jukes (2001b). 'Functional foods. Part 2: The impact on current regulatory terminology'. *Food Control* 12(2): 109–17.

Lancaster, K.J. (1966). 'A new approach to consumer theory'. *Journal of Political Economy* 74(2): 132–57.

Latour, B. and S. Woolgar (1979). *Laboratory Life: the Social Construction of Scientific Facts*. Thousand Oaks, CA: Sage.

Lehenkari, J. (2003). 'On the borderline of food and drug: Constructing credibility and markets for a functional food product'. *Science as Culture* 12(4): 499–525.

Loconto, A. and L. Busch (2010). 'Standards, techno-economic networks, and playing fields: Performing the global market economy'. *Review of International Political Economy* 17(3): 507–36.

Méadel, C. and V. Rabeharisoa (2001). 'Taste as form of adjustment between food and consumers'. In R. Coombs, K. Green, A. Richards and V. Walsh (eds) *Technology and the Market: Demand, Users and Innovation*. Cheltenham, UK and Northampton, MA, USA: Edward Elgar, pp. 234–53.

Miracle, G.E. (1965). 'Product characteristics and marketing strategy'. *Journal of Marketing* 29(1): 18–24.

Penders, B. (2013). 'Mythbusters: Credibilising strategies in popular nutrition books by academics', *Public Understanding of Science*, May.

Penders, B. and A.P. Nelis (2011). 'Credibility engineering in the food industry: Linking science, regulation, and marketing in a corporate context'. *Science in Context* 24(4): 487.

Penders, B., J.M.A. Verbakel and A.P. Nelis (2009). 'The social study of corporate science: A research manifesto'. *Bulletin of Science, Technology & Society* 29(6): 439–46.

Ruby, F. (2006). 'Qu'est-ce qu'un aliment fonctionnel?'. Available at: www. PasseportSanté.net.

Schleifer, D. (2013). 'Categories count: Transfat labelling as a technique of corporate governance'. *Social Studies of Science* 43(1): 54–77.

Sismondo, S. (2010). 'Linking research and marketing: A pharmaceutical innovation'. In V. Quirke and J. Slinn (eds) *Perspectives on Twentieth-Century Pharmaceuticals*. Oxford: Peter Lang, pp. 241–56.

Van der Kamp, M. (2011). *Enacting Standards in Organic Agriculture*. Unpublished PhD dissertation. Lancaster University, Lancaster.

Vaughan, D. (1999). 'The role of the organization in the production of techno-scientific knowledge'. *Social Studies of Science* 29(6): 913–43.

World Health Organization (2008). *WHO European Action Plan for Food and Nutrition Policy 2007–2012*. Report, Copenhagen, Denmark, WHO Regional Office for Europe.

7. Designing better markets for people at the bottom of the pyramid: bottom-up market design

Ronika Chakrabarti and Katy Mason

INTRODUCTION

The purpose of this chapter is to investigate how actors come together in a collective effort to design a market *bottom-up* in the context of developing markets that are subsistence based and/or at the Bottom of the Pyramid (BoP). Drawing on Dewey's Process of Inquiry, an ethnography is performed in the turbulent delta of the Sundarban (translated as 'beautiful forest') Islands. Findings show how methods of inquiry can inform bottom-up market design to unfold ways to see what a market *is* and what it can *become*. A bottom-up approach to design is vital to allowing market creation to occur organically and inductively rather than being determined a priori or being superimposed onto a market.

There have been many calls for academics and practitioners alike to develop markets at the BoP. Companies have been urged to make products and services accessible to consumers earning less than $2 a day. For example, much praise has been given to Procter & Gamble's efforts – making individual sachets of shampoo and soap available in small quantities, at low costs, in remote markets. However, this follows a top-down approach to market design whereby companies work out what they can offer to the poor or to vulnerable consumers.

This chapter first explores the concerns raised about BoP markets and contrasts these with discussions in the subsistence markets (SMs) literature. If we are to further the *business for poverty-reduction* agenda, we need to better understand the middle ground, and how we design markets that bring genuine benefits for the poor. Second, we therefore ask 'how are market interventions designed in a context of BoP?' By addressing this question we investigate how social values come to inform interventions, and how these can be used to unfold and shape practices that transform people in poverty into active consumer-producers in market systems.

The chapter thereby contributes to an understanding of bottom-up market design by showing how an inquiry process is performed and how a market constructed for the good of the people that are of concern. The ethnographic study reported here followed the efforts of villagers, NGOs, scientists and academics as they engaged in a process of inquiry so that they might design a market that brought benefits for communities. This market-making effort followed a tsunami in the Sundarban Islands that transformed the space into a desolate landscape, removing traditional means of income for inhabitants. Market actors worked together to make judgements about the *facts* that they had to deal with and their *concerns* about how they would live in this new post-tsunami world. We see how both facts and concerns shaped their actions in designing and enabling their engagement with a market.

CONCERNING CONCEPTUALIZATIONS OF MARKETS

BoP Markets and Subsistence Markets or Markets as 'Bundles of Practice'

In the marketing literature two distinct but sometimes overlapping perspectives have been adopted in understanding markets that involve low-income consumers: BoP markets and subsistence markets. Kolk et al. (2013) ask, 'What has become of the BoP concept?' In general, BoP research is grounded in the observation that there are over three billion people in the world that need to clothe, feed and shelter themselves and their families, but who have less than US$2 or US$1 a day to live off (www.worldbank. org; www.un.org). BoP populations are generally associated with developing countries in India, South Asia, South America and Sub-Saharan Africa.

The traditional Bottom (or Base) of the Pyramid literature has explored how companies might re-conceptualize those at the BoP as being a market worth their attention. The argument is that as there are so many people in this position that their available expenditure, when gathered together, is well worth a marketing effort (see London and Hart, 2010; Prahalad, 2006; Prahalad and Hart, 2002). By making products and services cheap, small and accessible companies could connect with such markets and improve the lives of people at the BoP while, at the same time, growing their business (see, for example, Singh et al., 2009). Conceptualizing BoP markets purely as a new site to make money has sometimes come at the expense of the poor rather than to serve and empower the poor (Karnani, 2007a).

In contrast, the conceptualization of subsistence markets (SMs) focuses on how consumers trade in local economies, with a focus on understanding existing community practices (Viswanathan and Rosa, 2010; Viswanathan et al., 2012). The SMs literature focuses on exchanges in their own right and is not motivated by these contexts being new markets. This is a very relevant distinction from BoP markets. Furthermore, SMs are *bottom-up*, as the starting point of these markets are at the much neglected micro level but the end points are not necessarily at that level. Trade is for basic goods in order that consumers are not dependent on connections with the industrialized world. This shifts the focus from the firm as producer to the consumer as producer-consumer (Karnani, 2007b). For example, in their study Abdelnour and Branzei (2010) describe how a subsistence market for Dafuri communities developed affordable fuel-efficient stoves. In this intervention women were empowered with skills for the use and local production of stoves, and trained other Dafuri women to become producers and active participants in the production, distribution and consumption of stoves.

Distinguishing subsistence markets from BoP is important, as the former frame a very different kind of market formation. Much of this work has its roots in the Development Studies literature (see Sen, 1999) and so the site of intervention is often geographically bounded and local. As such, there have been concerns that while such initiatives might be useful, they are limited in their ability to pull people out of poverty. Table 7.1 summarizes the differences between these two literatures.

Table 7.1   The differences between conceptualizations of BoP market interventions and subsistence market interventions

BoP market interventions	Subsistence market interventions
Driven by multinational firms as a viable business option linking strategy with poverty alleviation	Driven at the grassroots level by the 'poor' as a bottom-up approach to intervention. The micro level of the market place is analysed, e.g. daily exchanges, relationships, roles of producer-consumers at the subsistence-level, coordination of resources, community empowerment etc.
Interventions are located between the formal and informal economy	Interventions are located in the local economy and focused on community practices
Interaction is one-to-many (Western firm selling to local firms/resellers and/or consumers)	Interaction is dyadic (one-to-one, groups to groups, communities to communities/ NGOs /governments)

Contributions to market conceptualization have also been made by the growing body of market studies literature in economic sociology (Callon, 1998; MacKenzie et al., 2007) and marketing (Kjellberg and Helgesson, 2007; Araujo et al., 2010). Here markets are conceptualized as bundles of practices and can be applied to subsistence contexts (see Lindeman, 2012). With the intention to show how market design can be performed bottom-up we draw on these ideas to suggest that it is helpful to conceptualize BoP markets and SMs as bundles of practices.

WHEN BoP MARKETS NEED DESIGNING

In 2009 a tsunami hit the Sundarban Islands in West Bengal, India. In a few moments the islanders lost their homes, their livelihoods and means of feeding and protecting themselves. Roads and houses were washed away, goats and chickens perished and the salt from the sea penetrated the land, rendering it infertile *'for at least three years'* (United Nations Educational, Scientific and Cultural Organization (UNESCO)). The Government of India wanted to help and NGOs tried to provide immediate relief from hunger and the imminent threat from wildlife (the Sundarbans, which have been awarded the status of a world heritage site, are the home of the Royal Bengal tiger and crocodiles). Unless the islanders produce food and a trade surplus they will not survive. This chapter will describe how the *'first author'* visited the Sundarban Islands as a researcher to perform inductive data collection and worked with islanders, NGOs and other actors to understand and design interventions that would 'make a market' for the islanders of Gosaba.

Adopting an ethnographic, practice-based approach (Araujo et al., 2008), multiple agencies involved in a process of inquiry were studied as a way of understanding how they performed the designing of a market. Attention was given to what actors did to create a market that had the specific purpose of engaging them in the exchange of sustainable offerings. Practices, the established ways of doing or saying (Reckwitz, 2002), became the unit of analysis. Interest in what actors actually did and said, as well as in the material tools used in the landscape was considered. In addition, written discourse (NGO reports, accounting systems, special focus reports, farmers' book-keeping for yield productivity, lease agreements, graphical maps outlining land plots for the development of a training centre and so forth), interviews, photo documentation and data collected from key agencies were analysed. The *'first author'* was situated in Gosaba for a month and became part of the inquiry process.

The designing of a market is not seen here as the centralized envisioning of a market that is then enacted through the coordinated effort of a single manager. In other words, there is no normative understanding of market design as a 'design–implement–evaluate' process. Rather, what the study reported in the chapter revealed was a process of inquiry that the NGOs engaged in, that the villages shaped and in which academics, scientists and governments became enrolled in. Recognizing that different approaches to market design exist, this chapter draws on the ideas of Dewey's (1910) notion of 'pragmatism' to explain how actors made judgements about what they should do – the next pragmatic or innovative step in making lives better by enabling communities to engage with some form of market. Romme's (2003) 'organization as design' is also drawn upon and these approaches complement one another. Whereas Romme speaks of design instead as a normative unfolding process of action towards an imagined ideal, Dewey's framework is useful when faced with extreme conditions, critical events or some kind of indeterminate situation that renders us temporarily unable to act, and of how inquiry can re-order and reframe social values and concerns.

Romme's (2003) notion of design assumes that we know the problem (yet it does state the problem of *knowing the problem*) and focuses on creating and experimenting with solutions. In contrast, Dewey's process of inquiry does not know the problem and explores deeply how the order of social values can frame problems. Understanding market design as a process of inquiry recognizes that we need to work hard to understand the *indeterminate situation*, the problems that this situation presents and the concerns of the actors involved.

The narrative of Gosaba's recovery is not yet finished. However, it has become a narrative of how, from 'nothing', 'something' can unfold: the islanders found the means (with the help of scientists) to introduce new fertilizers into the lands that made the barren soil productive and learn new skills of pisciculture and goat management to produce goods for the market. None of this could have happened without efforts to engage in bottom-up market design. The following section presents a brief description of the work the actors did to understand how they could design activities that brought them to market and what this imagined market needed to be like in order to work in this challenging setting. We then analyse the case presented through the framework of Dewey's five phases of inquiry to show why things turned out as they did, and importantly to reveal how the market design process came to the fore. We conclude by considering implications for market design in BoP markets.

DESIGNING MARKETS BOTTOM-UP THROUGH A PROCESS OF INQUIRY

Initially governmental agencies, from India and overseas, intervened to invoke post-disaster recovery and humanitarian services on the islands. These services involved evacuation of islanders to safe regions of the Sundarbans for temporary shelter, food and medical attention. Once the storms had subsided, the islanders waited for the national weather service to provide information and advice before it was deemed safe for boat services to resume. Transport links across and between the islands had been devastated.

An inquiry into the conditions of land and infrastructure (coastal and road transportation) was initiated by UNESCO. They went to Gosaba island to assess the conditions of the agricultural land which had previously been used for subsistence farming. Soil experiments determined soil health and future yield capabilities. UNESCO's findings revealed abnormally high salinity levels within the soil. Scientists forecast that the land would be fallow and unyielding for the next two to five years. This became an important 'fact' in the market design. It raised serious concerns for the villagers, due to their lack of knowledge and insight into the techniques and tools necessary for maintaining animal health (livestock and fishery) in saline conditions, and how to rebuild ponds.

Another important 'fact' was that NGOs had a history of supporting islanders in the Sundarbans. Long before the tsunami, an extensive women's self-help group (SHG) programme in Gosaba was facilitated by a local NGO,[1] which the local women were keen to restart. These groups took pride in their capabilities to earn and save monies collectively in SHG bank accounts, which gave them purpose and status on the island. In the aftermath of the tsunami, women raised concerns over a lack of work and earnings that were previously generated from goat herding and livestock. These concerns extended into deeper anxieties of '*self worth*' and '*what else they could be doing*' to tap into saved monies and to perhaps start new forms of working practices. One idea suggested was 'learning tailoring' to trade saris and blouse pieces.

Ideas and concerns were raised at village meetings with NGO field workers, academics and sometimes visiting scientists. A melting pot of '*facts and concerns*' was created and assembled by the NGO and academics. In order to make things happen, the NGO found itself in a position where it had to oppose the scientific facts of land infertility and question, reorder and reconstruct new facts that would allow villagers to act and help themselves. Moreover, the '*first author*' met a university graduate – from a leading Kolkata institution within the local community. After the tsunami he had returned to the island to help his father with running the family's agricul-

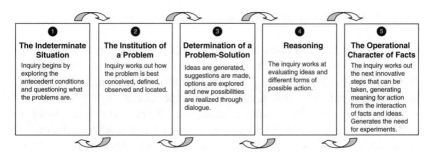

Figure 7.1 *Dewey's (1938) five-step inquiry process as an analytical framework to explore market design*

ture business. Despite his degree, he had found himself having to become a farmer once again. He spoke about his concerns over the well-being of his father and the helplessness of the islanders who felt they were being forgotten. It mattered to him that academia paid attention to Gosaba's situation and he wanted to bring concerns 'out of the Sundarbans and into the wider world' so that they could be explored and so that new ways of doing things on the island might be imagined, connected and realized.

From all these concerns and dialogues an inquiry process began. The job for the researchers and the NGO staff was to gradually unpack problems and frame positive steps forward. The inquiry process using Dewey's (1938) five steps as an analytical framework (see Figure 7.1) is presented next to explicate how concerns and matters of fact were used to work out, design and unfold market practices for the villagers of Gosaba.

ANALYSING THE ETHNOGRAPHY USING DEWEY'S FIVE STEPS

The five steps of inquiry presented in Figure 7.1 highlight the practices that enabled the people at the BoP to engage in marketing practices (of production, distribution and sales of goods), which in turn made the markets in which they participated what they became. The inquiry process is therefore a process of market design for the villagers and the other market actors at the BoP. Before the tsunami, there was a market in the Sundarbans, near to Gosaba Island. Villagers had to travel by boat to the island of Gotkali where a produce market enabled islanders to trade their surplus produce. However, after the tsunami access to the market was impeded. Market design, for and by the people of Gosaba, was therefore about creating a market they could be part of and reassembled into.

Stage 1: the Indeterminate Situation

Dewey's (1938) notion of an indeterminate situation is premised on doubt and that the 'irritation of doubt' causes us to struggle to attain belief. Without doubt there is no inquiry. Inquiry enables us to construct beliefs and understand how situations can be experienced as a whole in the context of Gosaba. In search of belief, the villagers, the NGO workers and the researchers needed to draw on the background and history of the islands and what it was like to live there. Inquiries reveal numerous experience-based facts: if a market is going to work, then facts about the environment need to be taken into account.

The environment can present challenges though even for a small, local market. In order to trade, the villagers must feel part of the market, be able to travel there and be able to produce goods for trade. Not only do the Sundarbans face difficult weather fronts and tsunamis, there is also an 'assaulting' ecosystem at play. The islands have experienced complex land cultivation, the need for scientific forestry management and are host to a national park, which offers protection to many exotic animals including the indigenous Royal Bengal tiger. The Sundarbans have been the site of many scientific studies and conservation initiatives and have historically had a significant tourism industry. The future horizon involves continuing environmental research with attention being paid to increasingly unstable weather conditions of the area. Stretching along the coast of India and Bangladesh, the Sundarbans are a collective of mangrove forests, water and landmasses. The mangrove forests act as shock absorbers along the coastlines, protecting local communities from the impact of storms. The coastal ecology of the Sundarbans makes it the second most cyclone prone area in East Asia (Danda, 2012).

What becomes clear from the inquiry is that it is not just the villagers and their need for a market which frames the indeterminate situation, but that the island encompasses a type of situation that is indeterminate in nature and representative of a doubt-inducing ecological 'space'. On the one hand, the island protects the densely populated Bay of Bengal and its livelihoods from the worst extremities of nature, acting as an effective coastal defence and natural bio-shield. Yet, the islands remain under constant threat, not only from the destruction of its lands as a result of natural disasters but by man's activities, including land reclamation, logging and shrimp farming. Its mangrove forests are being destroyed faster than any other ecosystem on earth, removing an essential barrier between the sea and the land (Juniper, 2013; Suhkdev, 2013; Sanjayan, 2013). The situation we find 'is not a single object or event or set of objects and events' but rather we find that market actors will need to work within this 'environing experienced world – a situation' (Dewey, 1938, LW 12:72) to take into account what is or is not sustainable to design a market 'place'.

The facts that are also important to consider include: the villagers live in poverty at the BoP, with limited access to healthcare and finance. They had previously made a living as subsistence farmers, fishermen and livestock handlers with no access to social security, pensions or help for the sick. In small communities, people helped each other. The tsunami wrecked normal life, washing away local roads, homes and much of the existing island infrastructure. The soil was contaminated and the villagers had nothing to trade, no means of production and felt unable to help each other.

This particular assemblage of facts shapes action and becomes part of the market design process. Facts play an important role in the market design process. Facts are partial to given experiences, polemic in nature and provide multiple measures that are disputable in their validity. Facts represent the production of scientific certainty by being 'prematurely naturalized objectified' (Latour, 2004: p. 227). In this view, matters of fact are found to be associated with worldviews that are inherently specialized, narrow-minded, scripted, historically bounded and set within precise repertoires of attitude and attention (Latour, 2008). Storbacka and Nenonen (2011) describe how markets become scripted by assemblages of facts and suggest that such assemblages can create mental models that prevent innovation and the exploration of new possibilities. In certain instances matters of fact can be dangerously unrealistic and unjustified. Overcoming a worldview premised on facts continuant with matters of concern that are more 'becoming' and mutable becomes important in the second stage of inquiry in market design.

Stage 2: the Institution of a 'Problem'

The second stage requires the situation to be seen in some way as problematic and worthy of attention. The fact that the inhabitants of Gosaba cannot survive without external aid is seen as a problem. Progress from merely knowing about a situation to the framing of a problem that matters now takes place: facts are assembled. When understanding a problem bottom-up, facts may need to be repositioned as concerns, as the knowledge of what 'is' becomes disputable, and what should be the focus of the inquiry is highlighted. Facts describe the history and nature of the Sundarbans determining its ecological conditions, but concerns about how people will survive and trade on the Sundarbans can be acted upon.

Earlier in the chapter we presented several facts, but also many concerns. The most prescient concerns were that villagers could not produce

goods for trade because of the infertile land. Villagers were also concerned that they could not trade because they could not reach existing
markets. To help with the 'infertile land' problem, the NGO began to
pursue this line of inquiry into the concerns of 'trade and market design'.
Importantly, these two concerns are linked and so Dewey's point of
understanding the 'whole context' is brought home: if the villagers cannot
produce goods from the land, they cannot trade and be part of a market.
Thus, matters that are of concern are set within the indeterminate situation of the Sundarbans, with the impact of weather and the extreme conditions within which the villagers now live becoming important facts in
the market design problem.

As the tsunami destroyed Gosaba's connections to wider markets, both
on the Sundarbans (in Gotkali) and beyond (in Kolkata), two problems
are now framed: how to produce (anything) on Gosaba, and where to sell
it. These problems generate further inquiries: what resources do the islanders have to produce anything with? How could they travel to trade, where
could they go, at what cost?

In other words, the inquiry generates a scenography of concerns. It
reveals that ecologically, animal welfare and the livelihoods of the islanders are now well below the poverty line (BPL). The NGO evaluative tools
for assessing where help is needed must show that nutrition and food production is urgent. Observing the 'facts of a case' constitutes the terms of
the problem. The observations surrounding the aftermath of the disaster
highlighted a multitude of changes to people's everyday lives as they were
temporally relocated in protected enclosures provided by agencies until
housing was rebuilt. The migration of farmers (who were typically island-
based subsistence growers) left their families to go to the neighbouring city
(Kolkata) or larger cities in other states.

'Interventions' to determine matters of fact and concern on Gosaba
Island were led by multiple agencies: market practitioners, NGOs, governing bodies (local/state level and internationally funded). The intention
was to work out how problems could be conceived and located. Scientific
interventions took the form of soil experiments, which determined the
fallowness of the land. These limitations of the land posed problems of
nutrition, income generation and marketability for the people of Gosaba.
At one time crops such as chili and dhal (lentils) were staple providers
of nutrition and income. Dipalidi, a mother and breadwinner residing in
Gosaba Island, reinforces this:

> Before the illa (tsunami) I had to do two hours of dhal and chili cultivation
> a day which would feed us and then lead to extra sales. Now, none of us are
> generating money but we don't want to leave the island. This land is Maya
> (illusion). No fish, no vegetables are growing or being grown here, so how can

we live? The illusion is like a fruit tree. You see a fruit tree should provide fruits and we are here in hope of those fruits. We could go to Kolkata tomorrow and be a maid, earn money and get good food on our plates every day, but we want to live out our karma (work) and do what we can here in the Sundarbans.

Although matters of fact develop cases for the institution of problems, these problems need to be instituted in ways that allow for matters of concern to emerge. Instituting a problem means that the group works collectively on the framing of the problem as well as collectively accepting the problem as the problem to be solved. The analogy of the fruit tree is interesting as it suggests that concerns (e.g. high salinity levels, lack of nutrition) should be disputable and ongoing until closure is found and fruits are produced again in a functioning market environment.

Latour (2004) claims that matters of concern have to be 'liked'. In the process of inquiry for market design a clear link emerged between Dewey's notion of the institution of a problem and of those problems turning into the Latourian notion of concerns. Here concerns shape discussion and take forward relevant matters in a 'likeable' way among the people and the agencies involved in the design of BoP markets and/or subsistence market-places. Problems should lead to suggestions, discussions and debate over what should be included or dismissed; what data is selected or rejected and how they can be revisited and refined in an iterative way.

Stage 3: Determination of the Problem-solution

The next stage of inquiry is to gather together suggestions and ideas regarding how the problems identified in the previous stage might be solved. Successful inquiry needs a functional fit between facts, terms of a problem and ideas. Using concerns, actors shape ideas to fit the space between the 'facts' of the situation and the problem that concerns the market actors. If matters of concern become something by being 'gathered together', then it is useful to bring together the facts and the problems raised by the inquiry so far, to see if their assemblage suggests productive possibilities to the actors. In this way there seems potential to design solutions that are a good fit for the villagers and for the situation they find themselves in.

In Gosaba, meetings with villagers, farmers and self-help group leaders from other islands and NGO representatives explored possibilities. Designing markets progressed through the 'gathering of suggestions' as actors used a bottom-up-approach to work out what to do next (cf. Viswanathan and Rosa, 2010). The ideas that came up in meetings were often suggestions for solving a specific problem, for example the introduction of a new boat service in the morning to transport villagers and their

Figure 7.2   Ideas for land generation put into action: pisciculture and animal husbandry in Gosaba Island

goods to the island of Gotkali, where there was already a functioning market. This idea captures intention and reveals productive possibilities by showing what could happen and how. The facts, on the other hand, provide a framework within which the possibilities for action are fixed – and describe the present.

The gathering together of the different market agents allowed for the generation of ideas around the instituted problems of both *land regeneration* and *market access*. Just as factual conditions are understood by observation in the process of inquiry, so ideas were generated through observation. For land regeneration, suggestions were centred upon reshaping agricultural land to support new agricultural methods. The problem of soil salinity led to suggestions to use pesticides and fertilizers. However, chemicals are very expensive and BoP farmers did not want to take the risk of 'putting all their eggs in one basket'.

Further suggestions highlighted local knowledge about fishery (or pisciculture) and animal husbandry (involving goats and chickens). Both could be performed 'at home', meaning men could stay with their families instead of working in Kolkata. As the fit between the problem and the solution was shaped by concerns, villagers began to focus more attention on land generation ideas (Figure 7.2).

Fish-catching neighbourhoods, or *jailey paras*, operate as systems where people either hire boats by taking loans from a bank or pool together as

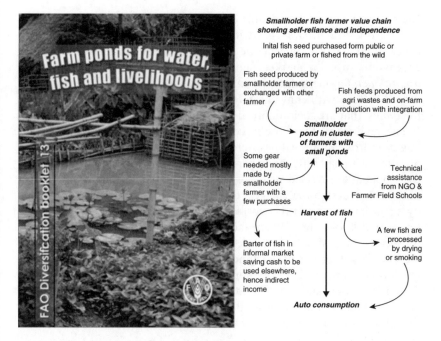

Figure showing photo with text "Farm ponds for water, fish and livelihoods" and "FAO Diversification Booklet 13" with the following diagram:

Smallholder fish farmer value chain showing self-reliance and independence

Inital fish seed purchased form public or private farm or fished from the wild

Fish seed produced by smallholder farmer or exchanged with other farmer

Fish feeds produced from agri wastes and on-farm production with integration

Smallholder pond in cluster of farmers with small ponds

Some gear needed mostly made by smallholder farmer with a few purchases

Technical assistance from NGO & Farmer Field Schools

Harvest of fish

Barter of fish in informal market saving cash to be used elsewhere, hence indirect income

A few fish are processed by drying or smoking

Auto consumption

Figure 7.3   FAO ideas of farm ponds for water, fish and livelihoods

a group and buy a boat for about 30 000 rupees. Although Gosaba Island was not considered to be a *jailey para*, with only 1500 fish catchers out of 4500 people inhabiting the area, the majority of families embarked on a process of either renting or owning a pond with typically one to two *bigha* of land. Relatively wealthier people on the islands, who worked as day labourers in households of city workers, could afford about ten *bigha* of land.[2]

NGO representatives had ideas too – of pisciculture training they had seen in other sites, in other countries. For example, part of the United Nations group working to reduce poverty in food and agricultural organization did significant work to understand how mini ecosystems could be developed around a pond, creating hydro-nutrition for plants that could not be cultivated using more traditional methods (see Figure 7.3).

What we see here is the potential for a BoP market design to be based around the introduction of new and improved processes for fish cultivation as a source of 'market potential' for the land and a 'route to market for the islanders through which they can be self-sufficient' (Sudhip, NGO trustee).

The group meetings, where solutions were explored, seemed to act as mini democratic forums where what was 'best' for the group (or at least what they felt most comfortable doing) could be explored. When Dewey asks the question '*what is the matter?*' he suggests that the '*matter*' is often a lack of imagination to generate important '*leading*' ideas. We argue that endeavours to make markets should not be constructed by what science (or the *facts*) alone authorize. Instead, the realities of existing problems should be read with conviction. Realities are sanctioned in and sustained by '*things*' that are socio-political in nature.

The realities of the Gosaba community and their ideas of how they might improve those realities were explored against and with the realities of others who had different experiences and knowledge and who, through their dialogue, revealed new possible ways of acting that work for the particular situation the villagers found themselves in. If ideas are stunted by a fact-based view of the world, market representations may be limited to existing knowledge. Where facts are inconsistent, and cause concern for actors, they should be contested, kicking off further trajectories of inquiry. Only then can we imagine or design new markets. In this way, the framework adopted here to explore a staged process of unfolding a market design is messier and more iterative than its presentation suggests, with actors constantly reframing problems, contesting facts and transforming them bottom-up into concerns that might have solutions.

Stage 4: Reasoning

Once solutions are suggested and ideas shared, the determination of facts and the formulation of the problem are worked out through a process of 'reasoning'. Here facts and ideas go through a co-evolution of sorts where facts may suggest new ideas, or ideas could suggest further need for the restatement or rejection of facts. In the case here, the reasoning of ideas by agencies, including the farmers, working women of Gosaba Island, NGO field workers, scientists and private enterprises, which rejected specific facts, instead cultivated new options for agricultural land regeneration. In doing so, a process of equating ideas by seeking out alternative types of chemical pesticides/fertilizers that might be affordable became part of the inquiry. If actors could find fertilizers that were 'affordable' but yet could promote crop yield in high-saline soils, then the fact of 'infertile land' would be overturned.

Similarly, a crop yield would remove an important barrier to market action. Extensive market research led to the discovery of a product called Tricostar (a natural fungus treatment for seeds which promotes crop health) by a local NGO. The actors (NGO representatives, farmers and pisciculturists of the island) attended workshops in Kolkata to learn how to use Tricostar in their farming practices. The workshop presented

Tricostar as a market offering and explained how the product should be used to grow crop yields.

In addition to crop cultivation, ideas for the development of training and demonstration hubs were raised. As villages began to practise pisciculture and use Tricostar, they hit problems that raised questions about pisciculture training and animal healthcare. A farmer called Benimadhav raised concerns over the health of his fish during a 'hut meeting'. Islanders had built the hut with support from the NGO, to encourage dialogue about the market effort. 'I have seen my fish suffering from rashes' (Benimadhav). If the fish were sick they would not make money at the market. A lack of skills in animal husbandry healthcare was also leading to market separation for the islanders. Mousanmi, an NGO field worker, said:

> Goats die due to worms on the island and this is a great loss as they are sold in the market place for 3000 rupees. It is a very profitable business but goat management requires the dispensing of medicines and the people do not know the processes involved.

This constant reasoning helps actors make judgements about what they should do in order to get to market. Animal and fishery welfare training was not an obvious step at first – but it became an important one. While facts make explicit what *is* there, reasoning helps the actors work out what is *not* there but needs to be put in place.

Reasoning also helped the researchers assess what new facts needed to be constructed. This is particularly pertinent where something only exists in the collective imagination. In the case of the Sundarbans, the construction of new facts through the potential of chemical seed treatment and the hut training centre as a hub for knowledge and skill development are both examples of newly constructed facts. And through the inquiry process became *facts in the making*.

Stage 5: the Operational Character of Facts: Meanings (or Experimentation)

In the final stage of inquiry, Dewey places emphasis on how the resolution of problematic situations requires putting solutions into practice. Here, experiments do not allude only to those typically found in laboratory settings but involve conditions that have conceptual guidance and functions, applied as solutions. In other words, market designers need to experiment.

In our inquiry, two types of experimental interventions were observed on Gosaba Island. Experiment 1 involved Tricostar, which was introduced to the islanders after an agreement between market agencies took place to allow a small trial of the product to be tested among selected sites on the island. As their crop yield increased, what became apparent to market agencies was that people at the BoP on Gosaba Island were spatially isolated and lacking the affordable means to leave the island and visit larger markets (that is, in Kolkata) to procure or sell products.

The Tricostar experiment yielded positive solutions for overcoming previously held facts about the land. Using a bottom-up approach it was decided by the local NGO that in December 2012 Tricostar would be bought for Gosaba Island at a reduced price, with a subsidy of 35 rupees. Once the product was brought onto the island, women's self-help groups (SHGs) on Gosaba would take the role of selling the product for approximately 60 rupees to farmers on the islands in order to gain a 25 rupee profit per bag. This would be their 'business model'. The Tricostar market became the first market to come to Gosaba Island. By testing their business model, the SHG hoped to drive demand, bringing islanders from surrounding Sundarban Islands to Gosaba, attracting external parties to source the product and then reselling it onto wider markets.

However, there was a critical drawback that was highlighted during the experiment. Islanders became concerned about the highly restricted and limited boat access to and from Gosaba:

> The time the boat comes into the island means that we can't make it to Gotkali market on time. As the boat arrives at 6.30 a.m. in the morning this is late for us as by then the majority of produce has been sold. It used to be 5 a.m. and this was much better (BoP Farmer).

Boat schedules were therefore contributing to the isolation felt by the islanders. Without effective transport services, a two-way flow between Gosaba and the market would be limited. To date, market agencies are in the process of undertaking more inquiry into how applications can be made to local authorities to allow for more flexible boat connections to and from Gosaba Island to other markets.

In Experiment 2, pisciculture training, a pisciculturist and NGO project facilitator attended a pond cultivation course in Kolkata during 2011. The purpose of this intervention was to train and provide this local figurehead with knowledge of up-to-date fishery- and animal-based healthcare and maintenance practices. Training enabled him to share his newly attained knowledge with local BoP producers. To facilitate local training on Gosaba, a pond was rented and underwent treatments in December 2011 and acted as a test space for demonstrations in practice. The island pisciculturist and NGO project facilitator Krishna stated:

> Training in fishery has taught me . . . to cultivate fish – one *bigha* area of land is needed to make a six to eight foot deep pond. The pond should be in a shape

of a bowl, similar to a bowl from which we eat our vegetables. The rashes which many of you have mentioned have affected your fish will continue and their heads will become fatter only if there is two foot of 'pap' (gaps) underneath your ponds. To make a pond, you must initially pump water out of it. Then let it dry for four to five days and fill the gaps with superphosphate. Remember to add four feet of water now into the pond, which you can get from another pond by a pumping device. From this point you will see cultivation and also a change of water colour from green to blue. Amis and Niramis fish are an example of fish that can be put into your ponds but to start with 15–20 000 rupees will be needed for cultivation.

Both experiments generated new objects or events. This represents new knowledge the community has brought into their design of the market. These 'things' or 'objects' add new meanings and connections to the experiences of islanders. For example, objects act as repositories of knowledge from where islanders can attain training and perform pisciculture (by renting ponds) and use social spaces and materials for knowledge sharing (the village hut). The translation of knowledge to islanders from the training courses illustrates how ideas, practices and knowledge can be further mobilized across sites. The mobility of ideas from training programmes will provide 'the resources to create solid ground for development that is both sustainable and which nourishes individuals and the social contexts in which they live' (Shudip, NGO trustee). Gosaba is developing a new training centre on the island and is transforming it into a knowledge hub for the Sundarbans. This showcases the potential to remove spatial barriers and allow for demand to be driven back onto the island. This will, in turn, reduce the spatial discrepancy and isolation of islanders on Gosaba by providing a two-way system of market exchange (Figure 7.4).

DISCUSSION: WHAT OF DESIGNING MARKETS FOR BoP CONSUMER-PRODUCERS ON GOSABA ISLAND?

By enabling the Gosaba islanders to become producers, they also become consumers. The first market they engaged with was a market that enabled them to be producers: purchasing Tricostar fertilizer. With the help of the NGO, the islanders began to trade Tricostar but needed boat connections with other islands and with mainland India, to ensure the market for Tricostar would be big enough. Experiments in trying to sell Tricostar on the island made the problem and solution clear.

Using the new boat connections meant islanders could travel to existing markets, at Gotkali and Kolkata. However, travelling to markets was problematic as it took time and villagers had to carry multiple items with

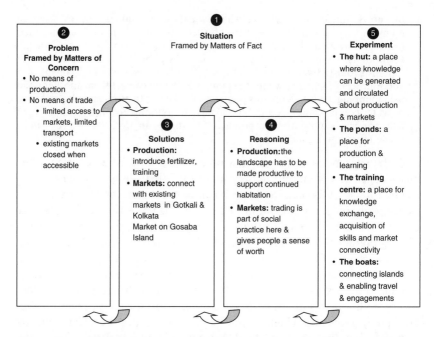

Figure 7.4   Designing markets through the process of inquiry: the role of facts and concerns in framing solutions and action

them. Those that arrived late to the market found many customers had already left and they could not sell their goods, which would then spoil. Market opening times were then understood to be critical for market connectivity and exchange. The Gosaba villagers needed to get to the market early (e.g. 5am), and engage with the market at its busiest time, to get a good price for their produce.

By becoming experts and having quality crops and healthy animals to sell, the reputation of a market can grow, and increase the entanglement of Gosaba islanders to other markets. As such, the pisciculture, animal healthcare and crop yield training are becoming recognized as worthwhile activities and part of the villagers' wider market practices.

Moreover, the imagined future for Gosaba islanders is now changing. The women of Gosaba, in their new roles as Tricostar produce-traders, see new possibilities through their engagement with buyers coming to the island. Further, they see women selling beautiful saris at the marketplaces and come back to the training huts and ask, 'How can we learn to sew? We can sell our tailoring in the market and incorporate the latest trends into our designs.' So market design continues to unfold as the process of inquiry goes on.

The unfolding of facts and concerns provides a growing understanding of what is valuable to market designers: the people at the BoP and/or SMs, the NGOs and the research teams. Much of what has been discussed here does not assume the inquiry works solely on solutions, rather focus is on the effort and value given by the different market actors into understanding and framing the problems that they face, and ordering these problems to privilege some as concerns that can be acted upon. While there is a deliberate effort to shift social norms, at the beginning there is no preconceived 'ideal' market model they work towards but rather they draw on a more abstract notion of market engagement. Any model that may be claimed to exist (in whatever form) comes out of the inquiry or market design process.

Romme (2003) also contributes to our understanding of what has happened in Gosaba through the efforts to design markets and enable engagement with them. Romme claims that organizations and systems are 'artificial objects' and as such our pragmatic focus is on changing or creating them rather than on diagnosing problems with them as existing objects. This is an important focus as it opens up opportunities for groups to imagine new ways of being and to work out what they might do or what resources, capabilities or expertise they might need to assemble and access in order to bring about an imagined other. As Banathy (1996, p. 20) explains, 'If solutions could be offered within the existing system there would be no need to design.' Thus our imagined market – a market that makes life better for the people at the BoP – is such an artificial object and an ongoing effort of the actors that perform and transform it. The material objects, the boats, the ponds, the fertilizer and the hut, reconfigured the actors as producer-consumers (cf. Viswanathan et al., 2010) and as it did so, the market in Gosaba began to transform into a network of connected market systems (Figure 7.5).

The findings suggest the need for new conceptualizations of BoP markets as market systems that sit somewhere between the more traditional models of BoP and subsistence markets. We show that, through the process of inquiry described here, practices that join up multiple market systems can be imagined and made real. This offers useful insights into how interventions may be developed to support trade, inform bottom-up policy-making and grow market initiatives in local sites of inquiry and then connect them to multiple sites and different kinds of markets (Figure 7.6).

The findings extend Lindeman's (2012) conceptualization of subsistence markets as community-based bundles of practices, by showing how bottom-up market design can allow for connections between market systems by opening up market actors' roles within subsistence markets and creating bridges into wider market systems (Figure 7.6c). The problematization process is necessary to work out how practices are bundled in the market.

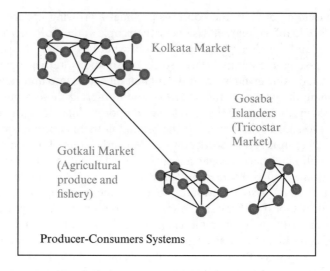

Figure 7.5   An unfolding market system, connected with and embedded in wider systems

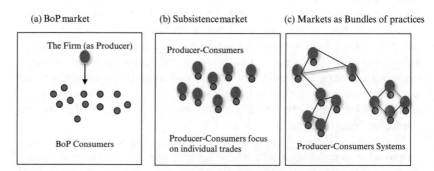

Figure 7.6   Three conceptualizations of markets at the BoP

It is through bundling that connections can be created between market systems at play. Problematizing allows for a shift between problems and market design to be made. By working out what are the right problems, the unpacking of what matters (for example, having boat access to get to the market on time and engage in political negotiations to achieve this) is revealed to allow for wider market connections to be made. Therefore, this study reveals how market problematizing and design is crucial for building and working out market connections that lead to practices that extend markets from within the community to wider market systems.

The important connections these market actors began to create, with other markets and on the mainland in Kolkata, show how market actors can move fluently across multiple systems. This is in keeping with Onyas (2011), who shows how these systems often share actors that are more or less active in one system than another at different times. This conceptualization enables us to build a bridge between the BoP and subsistence literature and helps us to think about how we might design markets – or at least perhaps interventions that shape market practices, in ways that work for the people trying to engage in them.

CONCLUSIONS

This chapter sees how methods of inquiry (Dewey, 1910) can inform bottom-up market design. In this way, inquiry feeds into the process of market design to unfold ways a market can be imagined, accessed, engaged with and transformed. The type of market considered in this inquiry is arresting as it is a shadow of what it is and was. It is important to work within these spaces at the BoP and within subsistence markets, in order to steer a more bottom-up approach to market making and design. By adopting a bottom-up approach, one can see what a market *is* and what it can *become*. Market design that is performed by various market actors is crucial to allowing market creation to occur organically and in a more inductive way as opposed to being determined a priori or being superimposed onto a market. Understanding market design as a process of inquiry is important for three reasons.

First, understanding market design as a process of inquiry and experimentation helps to make sense of a BoP market as a space for what it could be. This chapter demonstrates how BoP markets and subsistence markets have been theoretically set up as two contrasting things. The set-up of market practices here suggests that market design can create both types of market in terms of who is doing what and the practices that are being constructed. The market of interest is trying to become something, which is a combination of subsistence and BoP as a bundle of practices. As the notion of practices allows for a recursive performance, bottom-up design enables this performance to continue to happen and democratize what new social norms will be in the market. Problematizing and designing are therefore important for the bundling of practices and to create the right kind of market for the poor.

Although theoretically we need to stabilize differences between conceptualizations – as markets are living things. The usefulness of a bottom-up approach is found in the revealed transparencies of 'becoming a market'.

The need to slip between market combinations if necessary to design better markets is seen. Whether a market becomes framed into a BoP or subsistence market intervention, the design of a market needs inquiry to inform how it can appropriately address the concerns of the people (and societies) living with them (cf. Viswanathan et al., 2010). The movement from informal markets to larger market systems can be informed by the development of practices using a bottom-up approach and this can have implications for how individuals, communities, business systems (multinational and/or national), governments, NGOs, academics, policy-makers and so on can act to lift poverty and develop more sustainable markets.

Second, the role of inquiry has important implications for how we imagine and perform bottom-up design on hotly contested markets in the future. For example, markets in zones of war and conflict, where practices are being reshaped and normalized to cope with socio-political insecurities, or markets needing to be designed for low-carbon modes of transportation and renewable energy consumption, or markets that engage vulnerable consumers (cf. Piacentini et al., 2014), or those in the arts and social care that in times of austerity come under threat from the withdrawal of important market actors should be explored further. By using a process of inquiry in these markets we may stand to unfold market designs that work well for both the communities and institutions that perform them and offer insights into what matters and why in market design, and how the process of inquiry might lead to new and better ways of doing things. This chapter takes a tentative first step in the journey of understanding market design from the bottom-up and recognizes that this is an area ripe for further research.

Finally, bottom-up market design as an unfolding process of inquiry shows how the process can imagine and introduce new objects to configure market actors' practices in ways that make imagined markets become real (Araujo et al., 2010; Cochoy, 2008). The chapter has shown how a sustaining local NGO presence in an existing BoP market was vital for a process of inquiry and design through objects (such as the hut) to create a centre where learning can be shared, actors can be configured to adopt new ways of acting and performing markets. The localized body of knowledge encompassed by the NGO was used in a unique way to contest facts made by international NGOs (iNGOs) to draw out concerns, reconfigure practices and produce better versions of the market. In complex ecosystems, like the Sundarbans, more inquiry is needed to understand how market actors who are performing multiple interventions develop practices and representations to design better market futures. The pragmatism of market design, with its orientation towards the future, offers important insights for the making and shaping of BoP markets that bring real benefits for people at the BoP. Bottom-up market design as a process of inquiry has the potential to improve the way in which market futures are configured.

The research findings have real implications for how we might design markets bottom-up and understand assemblages as being part of and connected to other market systems and organizations in BoP settings. With calls for further research to explore, for example, bottom-up policy making (Viswanathan et al., 2012) and the need for revised laws that apply to informal market practices (Chakrabarti and Mason, 2012; Elyachar, 2005), it can be possible for the market design process to reconfigure existing systems in ways that enrol, include and engage those at the BoP who otherwise would not have the resources to act in such a system to become a part of its negotiated outcome.

NOTES

1. The genesis of SHGs in Gosaba was organized by the Kolkata-based NGO, Lokenath Divine Life Mission (LDLM) that was founded in 1985 by Baba Shuddhaanandaa Brahmachari (a former Professor of Commerce).
2. *Bigha* refers to a portion of land and this measure is commonly used to indicate relative wealth. As an estimation, 720 square feet is equal to one *quata* and 20 *quata* makes up one *bigha* of land.

REFERENCES

Abdelnour, S. and O. Branzei 2010. 'Fuel-efficient stoves for Darfur: The social construction of subsistence marketplaces in post-conflict settings'. *Journal of Business Research*, 63(6): 617–29.

Araujo, L., H. Kjellberg and J. Finch 2010. *Reconnecting Marketing to Markets*. Oxford: Oxford University Press.

Araujo, L., H. Kjellberg and R. Spencer 2008. 'Market practices and forms: Introduction to the special issue'. *Marketing Theory*, 8(1): 5–14.

Banathy, B.H. 1996. *Designing Social Systems in a Changing World*. New York and London: Plenum.

Callon, M. 1998. 'Introduction: The embeddedness of economic markets in economics'. In M. Callon (ed.) *The Laws of the Markets*. Oxford: Basil Blackwell.

Chakrabarti, R. and K. Mason 2012. 'Enabling practices: Making markets "worth the effort" at the Bottom-of-the-Pyramid', 2nd Interdisciplinary Market Studies Workshop, Dublin, Ireland, 6–7 June.

Cochoy, F. 2008. 'Calculation, qualculation, calqulation: Shopping cart arithmetic, equipped cognition and the clustered consumer'. *Marketing Theory*, 8: 15–44.

Danda, A. 2012. WWF. Available at: http://www.wwfindia.org/about_wwf/critical_regions/sundarbans/.

Dewey, J. 1910. *The Influence of Darwin on Philosophy, and Other Essays in Contemporary Thought*. New York: Holt; London: Bell.
Dewey, J. 1938. *Logic: The Theory of Inquiry*. New York: Holt; London: Allen & Unwin, 1939.
Elyachar, J. 2005. *Markets of Dispossession: NGOs, Economic Development, and the State in Cairo*. Durham: Duke University Press.
Juniper, T. 2013. 'BBC's Power of Nature'. Available at: http://www.bbc.com/future/story/20130212-sundarbans-natures-bioshield.
Karnani, A. 2007a. 'Doing well by doing good – case study: "Fair & Lovely" whitening cream'. *Strategic Management Journal*, 28: 1351–7.
Karnani, A. 2007b. 'The mirage of marketing to the Bottom of the Pyramid'. *California Management Review*, 49(4): 90–111.
Kjellberg, H. and C-F. Helgesson 2007. 'On the nature of markets and their practices'. *Marketing Theory*, 7: 137–62.
Kolk, A., M. Rivera-Santos and C. Rufin 2013. 'Reviewing a decade of research on the Base/Bottom of the Pyramid (BoP) concept'. *Business and Society*, 53(3): 338–77.
Latour, B. 2004. 'Why has criticism run out of steam? From matters of fact to matters of concern'. *Critical Inquiry* 30: 225–48.
Latour, B. 2008. 'What is the style of matters of concern?' Spinoza Lectures, University of Amsterdam, April and May.
Lindeman, S. 2012. 'Market formation in subsistence contexts: A study of informal waste trade practices in Tanzania and Brazil'. *Consumption Markets & Culture* 15(2): 235–57.
London, T. and Stuart L. Hart 2010. *Next Generation Business Strategies for the Base of the Pyramid: New Approaches for Building Mutual Value*. New Jersey: Pearson Education Inc., FT Press.
MacKenzie, D.A., F. Muniesa and L. Siu 2007. *Do Economists Make Markets? On the Performativity of Economics*. Princeton, NJ: Princeton University Press.
Onyas, W.I. 2011. 'Making and sustaining a "fair" coffee market: A market practice approach', paper presented at the 27th European Group for Organizational Studies conference.
Onyas, W.I. 2013. *Making and Sustaining a 'Fair' Coffee Market: A Market Practice Approach*, Lancaster University PhD thesis.
Piacentini, M.G., S.A. Hibbert and M.K. Hogg 2014. 'Consumer resource integration amongst vulnerable consumers: Care leavers in transition to independent living'. *Journal of Marketing Management*, 30(1–2): 1–19.
Prahalad, C.K. 2006. *The Fortune at the Bottom of the Pyramid: Eradicating Poverty through Profits*. Upper Saddle River, NJ: Wharton School Publishing.
Prahalad, C.K. and S. Hart 2002. 'The fortune at the Bottom of the Pyramid'. *Strategy and Business*, available at: http://www.cs.berkeley.edu/~brewer/ict4b/Fortune-BoP.pdf.
Reckwitz, A. 2002. 'Toward a theory of social practices: A development in culturalist theorizing'. *European Journal of Social Theory*, 5(2): 243–63.
Romme, A.G.L. 2003. 'Making a difference: Organization as design'. *Organization Science*, 14: 558–73.
Sanjayan, M. 2013. BBC's Power of Nature. Available at: http://www.bbc.com/future/story/20130212-sundarbans-natures-bioshield.
Sen, A. 1999. *Development as Freedom*. New Delhi: Oxford University Press.

Shove, E. and M. Pantzar 2005. 'Consumers, producers and practices'. *Journal of Consumer Culture*, 5(1): 43–64.

Singh, R., A. Rodolfo and S-C. Joseph 2009. 'Buying less, more often: An evaluation of sachet marketing strategy in an emerging market'. *Marketing Review*, 9: 3–17.

Storbacka, K. and S. Nenonen 2011. 'Scripting markets: From value propositions to market propositions'. *Industrial Marketing Management*, 40: 255–66.

Suhkdev, P. 2013. BBC's Power of Nature: Available at: http://www.bbc.com/future/story/20130212-sundarbans-natures-bioshield.

Viswanathan, M. and J.A. Rosa 2010. 'Understanding subsistence marketplaces: Toward sustainable consumption and commerce for a better world'. *Journal of Business Research*, 63: 535–7.

Viswanathan, M., J.A. Rosa and J.A. Ruth 2010. 'Exchanges in marketing systems: The case of subsistence consumer–merchants in Chennai, India'. *Journal of Marketing*, 74, 1–17.

Viswanathan, M., S. Sridharan, R. Ritchie, S. Venugopal and K. Jung 2012. 'Marketing interactions in subsistence marketplaces: A bottom-up approach to designing public policy'. *Journal of Public Policy & Marketing*, 31(2): 159–77.

Whitehead, Alfred North 1920. *The Concept of Nature*. Cambridge: Cambridge University Press.

www.worldbank.org

www.un.org

8. Articulating matters of concern in markets: (en)tangling goods, market agencies and overflows

Winfred Ikiring Onyas and Annmarie Ryan

INTRODUCTION

This chapter explores matters of concern and how they are articulated in markets. It centres on a coffee market connecting smallholder farmers in Uganda to an exporter called Good African Company (GAC). Of note in this setting are the attempts of the exporter to realize a version of the coffee market (which we will term 'the GAC market'), which is significantly different from the currently available mainstream market alternative for farmers (the sellers of coffee). Specifically, the GAC market involves the buying and selling of a more refined product: wet-processed coffee beans or parchment. To the farmers, however, coffee represents much more than just its material qualities; its value cannot be disentangled from its main use as a source of funding for educating their children. Hence, the role of education in the valuation of coffee becomes a matter of concern.

Responding to the call for research into subsistence marketplaces within the Market Studies domain (Lindeman, 2012), we draw attention to the market-making activities involving individuals who are earning barely sustainable incomes (Viswanathan and Rosa, 2010), who in our case are smallholder farmers. Following Viswanathan and Rosa (2010), we take a bottom-up approach to investigate the micro-level practices of buyers and sellers involved in the GAC market. We direct attention to the nature of matters of concern in this market; to the 'troubling, partially unknown' entanglements (Marres, 2007, p. 762), which threaten to disrupt market orderings (Latour, 2009). These *concerning* entanglements, to which market-shaping efforts are directed, form the analytical focus of this chapter.

Inspired by studies in anthropology, we examine the social entanglements of the focal good and the culturally specific meanings attached to it (Appadurai, 1986; Kopytoff, 1986; Zelizer, 1989). We explore the farmers'

conception of coffee as a multifaceted object with deeply entangled economic and socio-cultural dimensions including the coffee's significance in
the provision of school fees to the farmers' children, and as both a status
and inheritance object. However, only one aspect of this multifaceted
object is included or accounted for in the market version envisioned by
GAC: the economic dimension attached to the material qualities of coffee.
This points to a disjuncture between GAC's and the farmers' criteria of
valuation: GAC's valuation which only considers the economic value
emerging from the material qualities of coffee versus the farmers' valuation which takes into account the multifaceted dimensions of coffee. These
latter qualities, then, become overflows in the GAC market.

Of those socio-cultural entanglements, we focus our discussion on the
relationship between coffee earnings and the farmers' education of their
children. The reason being that their children's education is the primary
motive behind the farmers' involvement in coffee trade. Here, our interest is on how education can be considered as an overflow, whose exclusion from the GAC market potentially becomes a matter of concern.
Moreover, we investigate the disruptive, 'troublesome' role that actors
on the periphery (here the local coffee traders) play in amplifying the
education overflow to becoming a matter of concern in the GAC market.

The chapter is organized as follows: we begin with a discussion of
matters of concern in markets, including their inception. We then move
to our empirical account and outline the context to situate our discussion
of matters of concern and how they are taken into account in this market.
Next, we analyse the matters of concern in the GAC market. We draw
attention to what, who, when and how matters of concern are addressed in
this market. We do this by first examining the multiple framings of coffee
and the role of education in its valuation, and secondly, by investigating
the actors, interruptions and actions implicated in this regard. Further, we
trace and discuss these once distinct concerns for farmers as they become
entangled with their families and other actors in the GAC market. We
conclude the chapter highlighting the contributions of the work in terms
of market studies of subsistence markets.

MATTERS OF CONCERN AND THEIR ARTICULATION

Matters of concern are considered as 'problems which have not been
framed' so that no theories or available answers exist for them (Callon,
2009, p. 28). As such, they are characterized by strong uncertainty (Callon,
2009; Latour, 2009). As a concerned actor 'you don't know what situation

you're in nor what's going to happen if you take such-and-such a decision' (Callon, 2009, p. 26). And yet action and possible ways of rationalizing the problem are desired (Callon, 2009).

In attempting to define the problem at hand, a number of agencies and connections become involved. Through this process, their connections to the matter of concern and the activities they perform are made visible. This, Latour (2009, p. 24) points out, makes matters of concern 'take on the aspect of tangled beings', typified by numerous connections constituting the world they create and of which they become a part. Due to their lack of well-defined properties and boundaries, matters of concern give rise to 'unintended consequences [which] threaten to disrupt all orderings' (Latour, 2009, p. 25). With these characteristics, matters of concern might emerge as irresolvable issues (Callon, 2009), but where interaction and dialogue remain, they might also be a source of resolution. It therefore becomes imperative for the concerned actors to carefully formulate and frame matters of concern. Callon and Rabeharisoa (2008) suggest that this task involves the collective efforts of such heterogeneous actors as scientists or researchers, the concerned actors (whom they label as 'researchers in the wild'), politicians or regulators and other practitioners.

Articulating Matters of Concern

Building on Latour's work we address the articulation of matters of concern as a collective achievement of the actor-network. According to Latour (2005, p. 6) the matters that matter 'need to be presented, authorized, legitimatized and brought to bear inside the relevant assembly'. In this respect, the existing literature on matters of concern has highlighted their articulation in the public domain (Latour, 2005; Latour and Weibel, 2005; Marres, 2007; Callon and Rabeharisoa, 2008; Leino and Laine, 2012). Addressing matters of concern would, in situations such as the urban planning processes investigated by Leino and Laine (2012), involve a systematic approach of framing the main actors (that is, the planners) involved in planning, the issues articulated and the possibilities for the public discussion to evolve. Here the deliberations take place after each member of the participatory group brought matters of concern (relating to the key issue) to the table. As one would expect, the matters of concern are likely to change shape from the original version put forward by the articulator as part of this process. Leino and Laine (2012) attribute this outcome to the collective exchange of ideas, which translate the once distinct matters of concern into a collective, or possibly, a more divergent version of the 'original'. As such, matters of concern can involve trade-offs, especially when there is no agreement forthcoming (ibid.). As opposing groups of actors come together and deliberate over a common issue, they are encouraged to articulate and deliberate upon their respective concerns (what do they want?) with the aim of addressing and possibly finding a solution to the problem.

Our review of the extant literature on matters of concern reveals a focus on technoscience concerns including those relating to disease, the environment and politics (Callon and Rabeharisoa, 2008; Moser, 2008; Callon, 2009). There is a clear dearth of research regarding matters of concern in other fields. Consequently, this chapter ventures into a new area of research on matters of concern by focusing on their articulation in relation to subsistence markets. We do this by drawing on the defining characteristics of matters of concern to investigate troubling issues not specifically articulated in formal or public forums by concerned actors. The articulations we examine relate to the conflicting actions of market agencies and their attempts to resolve matters of concern by involving non-market actors. Specifically, we focus on market agents, goods and the relations between them as potential sources of overflowing (Callon and Rabeharisoa, 2008) whose entanglement to their respective worlds outside the market frame (Callon, 2005; Jensen, 2008) engender matters of concern.

THE GAC MARKET AND THE INCOME PROBLEM

Coffee is the highest export earner in Uganda, one of the leading exporters of coffee in the world (International Coffee Organisation, 2013a). GAC stands out from among 32 coffee exporters in Uganda (Uganda Coffee Development Authority, 2013) in being the only firm exporting coffee in its final form (roasted and packaged) to retailers in the UK and USA markets.[1] The firm sources coffee from farmers in the Kasese district, hence our focus on the market enacted at the farmer–exporter chain link in Kasese. Since the early 1900s, farmers in the Kasese district have grown and tend to produce unwashed, dry-processed coffee. This type of coffee is produced by first sun-drying the coffee cherries and then hulling them in order to remove the husks, thus revealing the unwashed green beans. The Kasese farmers sell unwashed coffee through numerous local traders and agents to exporters who are mainly based at the Ugandan capital, Kampala.

In 2003, GAC entered the Kasese coffee market and mobilized 14000 farmers (30 per cent of the Kasese farmers), organizing them into Producer Organizations (POs) consisting of about 50 farmers each[2] and eliminating local traders from the supply chain. The company introduced wet processing technology (hand pulpers), which enabled farmers to produce washed coffee, known as parchment. Wet processing essentially involves the use of pulpers[3] (machines that remove the skin off freshly harvested cherries) and substantial quantities of water. After removing the skin (pulp), the beans are fermented, washed and sun-dried. The resulting parchment is then sold to GAC which hulls the parchment, revealing wet-processed green beans. Globally, coffee is produced by either dry- or wet-processing methods and is primarily qualified on the basis of the material characteristics of the coffee. GAC, for example, only buys parchment that meets specific desirable qualities linked to the wet processes performed, as Tabu, a GAC official, explained:

> We look at the physical aspects: did you wash it [the parchment] well? If you washed it with little water, the parchment skin becomes a bit brownish. . .we will know that the farmer under-washed or used dirty water. They need to wash it about three times, until it is very white. The parchment needs to dry well, and the quality will be very good. If some of these things are neglected by the farmers, they impinge on the quality we had trained them about, and when they bring the coffee to sell, we tell them . . . "that is rejected, go back. You didn't learn well".

GAC's entrance into the Kasese district created two distinctive versions of the coffee market: the new GAC market (involving GAC farmers selling parchment to GAC) and the existing mainstream market (involving farmers selling unwashed coffee to traders). GAC and the traders compete to enrol farmers into their respective markets. However, the two markets overlap, with the GAC farmers producing (and selling) parchment and unwashed coffee in varying degrees. At the one extreme, the GAC farmers sell all their coffee to GAC plus a negligible quantity (of spoiled cherries or floats removed during sorting prior to the wet process) sold to the traders. GAC insists that these floats be removed so that only the good quality cherries are wet processed. At the other extreme, GAC farmers produce/ sell only unwashed coffee. Typically, these are farmers who obtain mortgaged loans from traders. Between these two extremes, farmers sell variable quantities of parchment and/or unwashed coffee depending on which offer (GAC's or the traders') they find more attractive.[4]

The coffee buyers, GAC on the one hand and the traders on the other, price coffee differently. GAC offers a price margin over unwashed coffee and a price cushion to stabilize the volatile prices[5] during the buying season. Market actors in the Kasese district recognize that GAC is the price-setter. The firm buys coffee only during the harvest seasons and reveals its price only at the start of the buying season. The traders on the other hand are price-reactive; they adjust their typically fluctuating prices, usually upwards, when the GAC buying season starts (but not high enough as to match GAC's price). The traders buy coffee all year round,

Table 8.1   Coffee farming seasons and buying seasons for GAC and the traders

Month	J	F	M	A	M	J	J	A	S	O	N	D
Season	Off-season		Minor harvest season			Off-season		Main harvest season				
GAC	Not buying coffee		Buying season			Not buying coffee		Buying season				
Traders	Buying season		Buying season			Buying season		Buying season				

even when it is still budding, and offer mortgaged loans to the farmers, particularly during the off-season when there is no income forthcoming from GAC. The farmers therefore encounter two income options: higher and stable incomes from GAC during the harvest (when there is ready demand for coffee and the need for income is not critical) versus lower and fluctuating incomes from traders (available when the farmers need it the most – during the off-season). Table 8.1 shows the coffee farming and buying seasons for GAC and the traders.

In the off-season, therefore, the higher GAC price ceases to matter, giving way to a much deeper concern among farmers for their children's education. As a result, the farmers usually make calculated choices, producing and selling parchment and/or unwashed coffee depending on when they need to pay for their children's education. June is usually the critical period for the farmers in terms of school fees. Ssali, a farmer in Nabisunsa village, explains:

> The amount of coffee sold to GAC depends on one's situation. If children are at school and farmers need money and there is no money in the village bank to buy coffee, they sell directly to [traders in] Kasese. E.g. one can sell 15 kilos to traders. . . Because of several demands, people mortgage a portion of their farms for loans from traders. E.g. UGX 100,000 for approximately 200 trees. . . Farmers apportion their farms [harvest] between GAC and traders. (Field note 1)

The village bank, mentioned by Ssali, is directly related to GAC's efforts to cater to the income concerns of the GAC farmers. Two years into its operations, GAC helped the farmers to start up village banks, also known as Savings and Credit Cooperatives (SACCOs), whose membership is open to farmers and POs. The banks, managed by the farmers themselves, were to provide the farmers with a source of funds as an alternative to obtaining funds from the traders. However, most village banks are yet to take off due to a lack of farmer savings. We will return to the role of these SACCOs in the GAC market in subsequent sections.

The price/income concern is further intensified in the GAC market due to the lengthy and strenuous process of producing parchment. For example, GAC requires farmers to engage in crop agronomy practices, carefully harvesting only the ripe cherries. In order to produce parchment, the farmers must engage in wet processing activities, strictly adhering to GAC's quality standards. Wet processing involves a series of activities which the farmers must perform, including sorting and floating cherries, pulping, fermenting, washing, drip-drying and sun-drying parchment. The entire wet process takes about two weeks.

A further complication linked to the GAC market is the location of the wet processing facilities. For the focal (Nakasero) PO studied, the processing store was centrally located at the Kitante homestead, which meant that most of the 50 farmers had to walk long distances through the mountainous terrain in order to process their coffee.[6] Conversely, dry processing is a much simpler and more straightforward process only requiring that farmers harvest and immediately sell their cherries to the traders. With two competing markets available for their coffee, farmers frequently make comparisons between the prices offered for parchment and unwashed coffee. At the same time, they consider unwashed coffee to be an inferior product compared to parchment due both to the limited attention paid to quality by the traders, and to the less cumbersome efforts involved in its production. This is a ranking that is also globally recognized and taken into account in pricing both products (International Coffee Organisation, 2013b).

As we shall see, the farmer's price/income concern goes beyond the boundaries of the two versions of the coffee market, and the goods exchanged therein, into a realm where socio-cultural entanglements (namely, education, status and inheritance) matter. We start to elaborate on this in the next section where we explore the multifaceted configuration of coffee, unveiling important entanglements and concerns to the GAC farmers in Kasese.

MATTERS OF CONCERN IN THE GAC MARKET

Figure 8.1 illustrates four issues guiding our analysis of matters of concern in the GAC market. We examine *who* addresses *what* matters of concern in the GAC market, as well as *when* and *how* they do so. The first subsection explores the 'what', identifying the sources of concerns. In the subsequent sections, we examine 'when' these issues arise, 'who' becomes involved and 'how' key actors respond. These issues are concurrently analysed under the heading 'Matters of concern: actors, interruptions and actions'.

what
likely sources of concerns

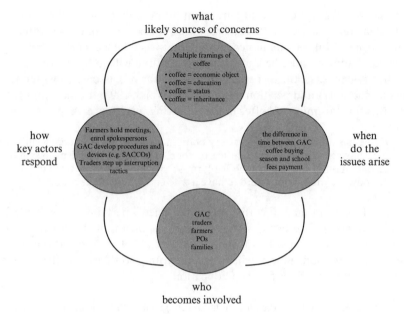

how
key actors
respond

when
do the
issues arise

who
becomes involved

Figure 8.1   What, who, when and how: four issues guiding our analysis of matters of concern in the GAC market

Sources of Concern in the GAC Market

The multiple framings of coffee
To the GAC farmers, coffee is an object with multiple connotations. Specifically, four distinct yet interlinked framings of coffee are discernible. First, the crop is considered an economic object whose value is established in different ways by GAC and the traders. GAC attaches economic value (or price) to the material qualities that parchment acquires during wet processing, such as its colour, scent and moisture content. The traders, on the other hand, attach economic value to coffee based on the current market price. Either way, the economic value obtained from coffee translates into the main source of income for the farmers.

The farmers, however, also frame coffee as a particular source of income, used for educating their children, which they perceive as their most pressing need. This second framing of coffee relates to education and is deeply entangled with the economic value of coffee as the farmers' allocation of incomes earned demonstrates. For example, the farmers (who practise mixed farming) spend the income earned from selling parchment on educating children while 'other monies' from bananas and animals are considered supplementary and are spent on household items like paraffin and soap (cf. Zelizer, 1989). 'If there was no coffee we would have nothing', one farmer, Mukisa, mentioned, adding that when he sees coffee flowering he feels happy because he knows that his children will go to school.

In a wider sense, the ownership of a coffee farm is associated with one's economic status and position in society (cf. Weiss, 1996). Lumu comments on this third framing of coffee in the following interview excerpt:

> If one has no coffee, then he is very poor. . . some people don't have land, so they have nowhere to grow coffee or food. These people end up becoming casual labourers working in coffee farms. . . if you have no coffee you are 'a nobody'. . . you cannot afford to have a wife and kids without coffee.

The fourth framing of coffee – as inheritance – pertains to the farmer's male offspring. The farmers' sons[7] inherit a portion of the coffee farms when they come of age. This framing is also related to the educational one: sometimes the sons inherit when they are young so that the coffee grown on their farm can cater for their education:

> Chwezi explained that the plots of land were given to them by their father when they were still children. He got his plot in 1980, which was when he planted these trees. He was told by his father that the coffee would educate him. . . 'Do you have another coffee farm?' I asked. Yes, he replied. It is his eldest son's coffee farm. The son is in secondary school [completing his O-levels]. During the holidays, this son maintains the farm. Otherwise, the parents normally work on the farm. Earnings from the farm are used for buying books and school uniforms. (Field note 2)

Signifying their social connection to coffee as the key source of livelihood for the community, the farmers typically locate their coffee farms adjacent to their houses. The food farms in contrast are located further away from the house, sometimes at a different farm plot miles away from the home.

The four framings of coffee just outlined (i.e. economic, education, status and inheritance) are connected, jointly depicting the contextually enacted meaning of coffee to the Kasese farmers. Of the four framings, the education framing emerges as central to the farmers' coffee world, featuring more prominently in their conversations with the lead researcher. For example, during the fieldwork the researcher noted that the farmers openly spoke about the low price of coffee that GAC offers, which in their view does not adequately cater for their children's education. In the next section, we therefore focus on the education framing, highlighting how it manifests as a matter of concern for the farmers in relation to the GAC market.

The role of education in the valuation of coffee

The multiple framings of coffee discussed above give rise to a matter of concern for the farmers in relation to the GAC market: a disagreement concerning what entanglements/qualities should be taken into account when valuing coffee. While GAC treats coffee exclusively as an economic object, the farmers consider the crop as an object with multiple entanglements. From the farmers' point of view, then, the GAC market frame only considers some aspects of coffee, excluding others that the farmers consider just as important (primarily, education).

The farmers articulate this concern mainly through their actions, for instance, in their decisions to sell coffee to the traders instead of GAC. We summarize in Table 8.2 the key interactions observed between GAC and farmers during the fieldwork. These interactions centre on the attempts by farmers and GAC to articulate and address the income and education matters of concern.

GAC is primarily concerned that the coffee meets specific desirable material qualities taken into account in its valuation. Specifically they want white, whole and unscented parchment of 12–13 per cent moisture content, as Tabu explains:

> There are some parameters we check [for] before paying them [farmers]: washing, moisture content, and appearance of the beans. Before weighing, we check [the parchment] so we that are sure of the product we are buying . . . We buy premium coffee; well-washed coffee, clean coffee without any stains.

GAC's consideration of material qualities in the valuation of coffee is characteristic of the qualification practices in the coffee industry. Because coffee prices are determined globally at the New York futures market, these desired qualities, also known as search attributes (Ponte and Gibbon, 2005), are globally standardized. Indeed, according to a senior GAC official, GAC considers various other factors when pricing coffee, including the New York price, foreign exchange rate, the price of unwashed coffee and the other (Ugandan) exporters' prices.[8] However, as we have shown earlier, GAC is trying at a local level to reconfigure the mainstream market by offering stable and higher prices.

The farmers, on the other hand, perceive (and/or experience) a lack of input in setting coffee prices, a feeling voiced when the researcher first met with the Nakasero PO farmers. Majugo, a GAC official present at the meeting, translated the farmers' sentiments:

> They [the farmers] explained that they needed someone to capture the problems they face so that they can negotiate prices, or that perhaps I could help them negotiate prices. . . the farmers believe that they are not getting the real prices. They

Table 8.2   Interactions between GAC and farmers observed during fieldwork

Event/activity	Purpose of the activity/ event	Issues discussed
A meeting between the GAC team (including a senior official from the head office and an international consultant) and the Nakasero PO farmers. The meeting took place just before the buying season started.	– To familiarize the consultant with the activities performed at the farms and at the processing store. – An opportunity for the consultant to interact with farmers.	– Farmers' concerns over the low price of parchment versus unwashed coffee. – School fees pressures on farmers. – The price of coffee in the subsequent buying season.
Three PO savings meetings attended by the Nakasero farmers.	– For farmers to save money in the PO and to repay PO loans.	– How to increase the PO savings. – Loan repayment.
Annual General Meeting attended by the Nakasero PO farmers.	– Substantive items in the agenda included Coffee processing, PO and SACCO savings.	– The motives behind farmers producing unwashed coffee, and how to address this problem. – How to increase the PO and SACCO savings. – PO and SACCO loan repayment.
The parents, teachers and students meeting. The lead researcher attended as the chief guest.	– To discuss matters concerning the PO children's education and performance at school.	– The parents' and students' concerns about education and students' performance at school.
Coffee transactions between farmers and GAC. For the Nakasero PO, it was Mukisa who delivered the coffee for sale. Most farmers sold the coffee individually, with the exception of one farmer-trader.	– Coffee transactions at GAC's field office.	– The material qualities of coffee considered by GAC. – Randomly emerging issues, e.g. SACCO savings and the price of parchment.

[the farmers] gave an example: some people sell 1 kilo of coffee at UGX 2000 while others sell at UGX 4000. They [the farmers] are aware that GAC is concerned about prices, but the question is: who fixes the price? To them [the farmers], the ideal is to have farmers fix the price they are to get for coffee. (Field note 3)

While this plea could be interpreted as simply an attempt to improve their bargaining position, it gradually became clear that the farmers' concern mainly derived from their educational framing of coffee. Specifically, the valuation of coffee in the GAC market yielded a 'troubling' situation for the farmers, threatening their children's education.

Matters of Concern: Actors, Interruptions and Actions

The farmers are making efforts to address the situation by framing education as a collective concern of the PO and their children as we illustrate in the next section. To accompany this rich description of the articulation of matters of concern in the GAC market we offer Figure 8.2. Here we use as a starting point GAC's market vision to create a sustainable alternative to the mainstream coffee market in Uganda as we have already shown. To achieve this aim GAC had to enrol farmers into their market. Since this required substantial changes in coffee farming and processing practices

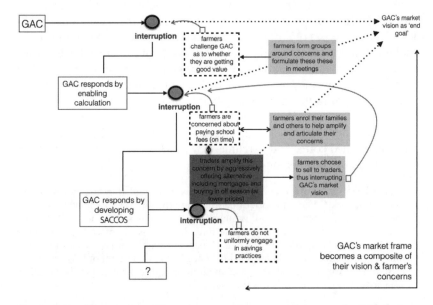

Figure 8.2   Illustration of how matters of concern shape markets and reconfigure actors

from what the farmers were used to, GAC's efforts were met with varying degrees of enthusiasm and sometimes resistance. In Figure 8.2 GAC is represented in the grey-lined boxes (left), whose actions (vision) were interrupted along the way when the farmers' matters of concern also became GAC's concerns. These points of interruption are represented as small circles. At each juncture we have a response to the matter of concern, which is depicted as a detour in GAC's market vision. The dash-lined boxes (mid) depict when the concern becomes GAC's concern; the light grey boxes (right) include 'backstage' actions by farmers; the dark grey box (mid) depicts the traders' (re-)actions. The arrows depict relations and connections between these.

In the ensuing analysis, we draw attention to four interlinked points of interruption: farmers confronting GAC over the value of parchment; the farmers' concerns about paying school fees (on time); the traders' actions to amplify the matter of concern; and the farmers' non-uniform saving practices.

Farmers confronting GAC over the value of parchment
The difficulty in establishing the relative value of parchment and unwashed coffee exacerbates the problem for farmers who continuously seek reassurance from GAC that they actually earn, for the same quantity sold, a higher value by selling parchment than they would by selling unwashed coffee. GAC attributes this misperception to the distinctive material qualities of the two types of coffee: as we shall see later, unwashed coffee in its final form (in the farmer–exporter trajectory) is sold as green beans, while parchment contains an additional covering (parchment) over the green bean.[9] The discrepancy in the value of parchment and unwashed coffee is of great concern to the farmers who continual challenge GAC to reassure them that they are getting good value by selling parchment. Majugo reveals that the farmers ask time and again 'if [we] sold the same quantities of unwashed coffee and parchment, with which coffee would [we] gain more?' Tabu offers a response to this:

> I have been telling [farmers] over and over again, and they are beginning to understand, that even if the price of coffee were the same (UGX 5000), the value they get from ours [parchment] is higher . . . 'when you sell to me at UGX 5000 a kilo, you are in actual sense selling only 800 grams of coffee beans because . . .. You are selling to me beans plus 20 per cent husks – husks which I have to remove [at the factory]'. They are slowly beginning to understand. When we go to seminars, we even crush the parchment in their [the farmers'] midst and they see for themselves that it is less [in quantity].

GAC has to deal continually with this recurrent confusion about whether farmers are actually getting more value for their coffee by selling parchment and not unwashed coffee. In his explanation, Tabu separates the two material components of parchment (husks and green beans) and values them separately, suggesting to the farmers that not only does parchment undergo further processing, but also that 'washed green beans' (an outcome of further processing/transformation practices performed at the GAC factory) attracts a higher value than parchment. Thus, in an attempt to justify the superior value of parchment over unwashed green beans, Tabu links one form of coffee, that is, parchment, to its subsequent form. In addition, GAC displays samples of parchment and green beans in the field office, which they use to demonstrate to farmers the material variations between the two types of coffee.

The traders on the other hand use underhand methods to entice farmers to sell to them, usually as the buying season is approaching. According to Tabu, the traders 'discourage farmers from pulping coffee'. The traders also misinform farmers – most of whom do not frequently visit the GAC field office – about the GAC prices. Kato explains:

> The traders told them that they were offering a higher price than GAC planned to offer when they [GAC] start buying coffee. Traders are now picking the mortgaged coffee. (Field note 4)

Evidently, GAC and the traders use different calculative approaches to persuade farmers to sell to them. As we previously alluded to, GAC only considers the material qualities of coffee when valuing coffee, a similar evaluation made when establishing the relative value of parchment versus unwashed coffee. The differing persuasive techniques only serve to increase the complexity of calculations that farmers need to make when evaluating their decisions to sell coffee in the GAC market and/or the mainstream market.

The farmers' concerns about paying school fees (on time)

Although free education is offered in Uganda through the Universal Primary Education (UPE) and Universal Secondary Education (USE) initiatives, the quality of education in these schools has widely come under scrutiny. Asankha and Takashi (2011), for example, recount the lack of basic school facilities such as desks, blackboards or toilets in rural secondary schools. Some farmers like Rwego therefore prefer to take their children to private schools where the education standards are higher (ibid.). Farmers with children in private schools must raise school fees, and like those with children in public schools, have to buy scholastic materials and meals as well. Since most of the farmers have large families (5–7 children on average), they have to spread their limited earnings from coffee to educate several children. This means that they are often forced to selectively allocate school fees to their children. Rwego's son, for example, mentioned that he had to miss school for one year after his O-levels because his father could not raise enough school fees for all the children.

It was not surprising, then, that most of the concerns raised by the farmers during the annual parents, teachers and students meeting had to do with the fact that they struggled to bear the costs of schooling their children. The farmers consider their children's education as needing careful attention if returns are to be achieved and negative outcomes avoided, such as students underperforming at school or dropping out of school entirely. The teachers in particular advised the students on a range of issues including peer pressure, alcohol and cigarettes, abstinence from sex and early pregnancy. They encouraged students to study sciences and arts and crafts, and to join discussion groups at school. As a way of motivating students to perform better at school, the teachers agreed to reward the best-performing students, and Kato asked the students to initiate this process by taking their end of term reports to the secretary (a student). The teachers' and parents' efforts aim to forestall any potential risks to their children's education, such as that experienced by one member who dropped out of school when she fell pregnant.

Kato's comment that UGX 1 million's worth of coffee is shared amongst ten children in the family, captures the extent of this need. During the parents, teachers and students meeting, the students recounted a number of problems they faced at school. Most of these stemmed from their parents' insufficient incomes. The main issues raised were: children going hungry at school, missing out on important learning activities at school and lacking the necessary scholastic materials. These problems pose a risk to the children's education, with likely concerns arising including children missing school or dropping out of school because their parents cannot pay school fees on time. The meeting helps farmers to shape their children's education and future so that they might successfully complete the education paid for using income from coffee.

Although GAC offers a higher price for coffee when they are buying, the education needs of farmers are present throughout the year, and actually become more pronounced during the off-season, when GAC is *not* buying coffee. Traders in the mainstream market are actively exploiting this mismatch, thus contributing to amplify the matter of concern raised by the farmers.

The traders' actions to amplify the matter of concern
The off-season, when GAC is not buying coffee, presents a critical period when the education needs of farmers are felt the most. Here, the traders

play a major role in amplifying the education matter of concern and making visible the failure of GAC to address this issue. They do so by offering farmers a number of advantages. First, they advance mortgages to farmers during the off-season when there is no income forthcoming from GAC. Therefore, when the school fees demands arise during the off-season, many farmers resort to selling unwashed coffee:

> Kato said that farmers had not been pulping [wet processing] coffee . . . He said that the farmers were discouraged as they had no money and GAC was not buying coffee during the off-season . . . they therefore had to mortgage their farms even with raw coffee . . . The problem is in the second term [which starts at the end of May] when farmers need money for kids' fees and [GAC] is not buying coffee. (Field note 4)

Moreover, the traders present several opportunities for farmers to earn an income at different points in the unwashed coffee trajectory. Unlike GAC which only buys parchment after all the wet processing activities have been performed, the traders purchase unwashed coffee in different forms: as budding cherries, fresh cherries, dried cherries and/or as hulled coffee beans. In addition, producing unwashed coffee is a much simpler and less cumbersome process compared to wet processing. Consequently, the flexibility offered by traders helps the farmers deal with the education needs, enabling them to raise school fees also during the off-season as field note 4 shows. The benefits gained from traders serve to illuminate the extent to which GAC's market model fails to accommodate the education needs of farmers. The lower but readily available income from traders comes at a cost to the farmers who have to forfeit the higher income from GAC in the subsequent buying season. Thus, a situation is created in which the farmers have to continuously calculate and choose to sell coffee to GAC and/or the traders as field note 1 above shows.

The role of the Producer Organizations
As a means of addressing their various concerns, the Nakasero farmers organize a number of meetings, creating a forum to discuss critical matters: to 'educate children; save for the problems; business; fight domestic violence; HIV/AIDS'. Two meetings stand out in the effort to address the income and education concerns of farmers: the savings meetings and the parents, teachers and students meeting introduced in the previous section. The savings meetings are by far the most frequently held, normally taking place every week, followed by the quarterly PO meetings and the annual parents, teachers and students meeting.

The PO and its regular meetings play an important role in translating the matter of concern from an individual concern to a collective concern of the Nakasero farmers, the majority of whom are kinsmen. The PO does this, for example, by facilitating farmers to pool resources (savings) and collectively raising and educating their children. GAC acknowledges the Nakasero PO's efforts, recognizing it as one of the best performing farmer groups, and attributing their performance to the kinship ties promoting harmony between farmers:

> Tabu commented that groups encourage joint action . . . 'You can't force them to work together'. . .He commented that the Nakasero PO has 'great potential'. He said this when I recounted to him what had happened at the Nakasero PO AGM and the parents, teachers and students meeting yesterday. He was quite impressed and mused that 'if only the other groups were as organized as Nakasero PO' . . . . He remarked that being family binds the Nakasero PO members together. 'With unity, they can achieve much', he commented. (Field note 5)

The Nakasero PO uses the savings to buy coffee from, and give loans to, farmers. At the start of the harvest season, the PO had accumulated UGX 8 million in savings and planned to spend UGX 2 million on buying coffee from farmers and give out the rest in loans. According to Mukisa, over 90 per cent of the members had loans with the PO and yet the savings levels were low. During the Nakasero PO Annual General Meeting (AGM), one farmer leader commented that the farmers were 'lazy to save money and yet children are advancing in education'. We see the PO savings meeting and SACCO performing similar roles although at different scales, with the PO collecting savings from individual farmers and the SACCO collecting from both the farmers and the PO. Although both saving mechanisms are managed by the farmers, the degree of autonomy varies. The PO savings are independently managed by farmers, but the SACCOs are closely monitored and supported by GAC. For example, as we have already shown, SACCOs (15 of them) were set up by GAC on behalf of the farmers. GAC also provides financial support to SACCOs as they slowly take off, as Tabu highlights:

> We [GAC] went ahead and assisted SACCOs by putting up signposts [having them printed]. We are still assisting them. We have assisted about seven of them to make proper offices. Because then, again, if we had left them they would not have known where to start . . . so what we did, we came here, got some little money, bought a few tables, a bookshelf, box files, staplers, pins . . . . I even went ahead and painted their offices; paid rent for six months; put up a signpost and then told the gentlemen to sit. Now they have started to recruit more because each sub-county can proudly say, 'we have our office, let's go and meet in our office'. That's how you empower peasants – through development; not speeches – these never work.

The role of SACCOs

SACCOs perform a critical role, particularly during the off-season, being used by GAC and farmers to address the income problem and counter the traders' offer of alternative income. Farmers (both individuals and POs) save in, and obtain loans from, the SACCOs, which present an alternative source of income to the traders' mortgages. Kato emphasized this during the AGM:

> If the SACCO had no money, then all the coffee would have gone to the trader .... If they ensured that the earnings from coffee goes to members [i.e. as savings in the SACCO], they would get loans from the SACCO and not from traders. (Field note 6)

Majugo concurs, encouraging farmers to save in SACCOs, a practice that is 'better than borrowing money [from the traders]'.

GAC hopes that the SACCOs will become autonomous so that farmers can obtain loans from their own savings/funds and stop mortgaging coffee to traders during the off-season. In principle, GAC encourages the farmers to voluntarily save UGX 200 of the price they offer at the SACCOs and even displays the recommended savings amount on a whiteboard at the field office entrance. This whiteboard stays in place for the duration of the buying season. The farmer leaders play a crucial role in implementing the saving mechanism, working hand in hand with GAC to encourage farmers to make the UGX 200 savings deduction. During the AGM, for example, Kato urged the PO members not yet registered with the SACCO to enrol as members.

However, not all the farmers make the recommended saving. Kato attributes the low savings to the seasonality of coffee which, he says, hinders farmers from making savings:

> During the off-season farmers have little money . . . It is time wasting as people save during the coffee season only to pay up loans obtained during the off-season. (Field note 7).

Some farmers, according to Mukisa, were inactive during the off-season and did not save, only starting to do so again during harvest when they had coffee to sell.

The SACCO, however, performs another important role that helps to consolidate the PO savings and address the income problem. It finances the PO's purchases of coffee from farmers, which coffee is then sold in bulk to GAC. The SACCO coordinator thus deducts the recommended saving from each farmer's earnings and credits this amount in the respective SACCO accounts. The SACCO thus facilitates the savings of registered members and, as field note 4 shows, directly substitutes the traders' mortgages by simultaneously providing income to farmers during the off-season. Mukisa explains:

> We manage to buy coffee even when the GAC is not operating [buying coffee]. For instance this coffee [he shows me the coffee inside his living room] . . . . At the moment GAC have not opened for the season. They start in August and they will buy coffee everyday . . . . This coffee [in the house] is bought from farmers in the group.

However, the SACCO struggles financially and is often in deficit owing to large number of debtors. At the AGM, Kato urged the debtors to repay their loans as the new school term was soon beginning:

> Kato says [to the farmers who had promised to settle their debts in early September]; 'the beginning of September is too far. The money is supposed to be used on 23 August when children go back to school. Other members also want to get loans in order to take their children to school' (Field note 8).

DISCUSSION: ARTICULATING MATTERS OF CONCERN IN THE GAC MARKET

The entangled nature of matters of concern in the GAC market makes visible the actors, relations and actions shaping this market (Callon, 2009; Latour, 2009). In line with Leino and Laine's (2012) assertion that each actor brings to the table specific matters of concern, our study illustrates how the coffee farmers bring with them their concerns when becoming sellers of coffee to GAC. But our study also shows how a matter of concern is translated from one form to another through market interaction. The matter of concern becomes entangled with the actors, takes on different forms and triggers diverse responses/actions. Initially, the focal matter of concern affected individual farmers, but was soon translated into a collective concern of their children and the PO, culminating in efforts to pool resources and frame the PO children's education. Thus the farmers are not only (a group of) sellers, but also become 're-formed' as a concerned group of citizens, or more specifically, parents of school-going children. For GAC, the *translated concern* is that the company is not able to provide timely income to farmers and risks losing them to the traders. The traders amplify this matter of concern by providing income to farmers during the off-season when GAC cannot.

The market actors respond to the (translated) matters of concern in diverse ways, generating uncertainty and disruption in the market(s) (Latour, 2009): will the price of coffee allow the farmers to educate their children? Will the efforts to act collectively and promote savings achieve the desired sustainable income? Will SACCOs succeed in retaining farmers in the GAC market? These questions may remain unanswered for the time being, but what is clear is that they continue to generate diverse actions on behalf of the concerned actors. The ongoing and troublesome existence of the investigated matter of concern points to a quandary in the GAC market and, while this may not develop into an outright crisis as Latour (2009) suggests, it remains a predicament in need of a resolution.

Leino and Laine (2012) depict the formal arrangements (i.e. public planning discussions) enacted to allow actors to articulate and address matters of concern. In contrast, our study portrays articulation as privileging the mundane, day-to-day interactive practices of actors illuminating their responses to troubling situations; troubling to GAC in the sense that they cannot definitively ascertain that farmers will produce parchment. This triggers GAC's ongoing explications to farmers that parchment indeed offers greater value than unwashed coffee. The farmers respond to the situation both by enrolling their families and others to help amplify and articulate their concerns, and by becoming calculative, choosing if and when to sell coffee to GAC and/or the traders.

Similar to Leino and Laine's (2012) observations, the concern over the valuation of coffee takes on an overlapping nature. For example, the farmers engage in conflicting production, qualification and exchange activities, depending on which one of the two markets (GAC or mainstream) offers them the income needed to educate their children. We thus see education permeating the boundaries of both markets, and indeed constituting a conduit between them as farmers evaluate which market to enter. Sometimes a farmer may operate entirely in the mainstream market for one season and in the next season almost exclusively sell to GAC. In yet another season, the same farmer might sell different proportions to both GAC and the traders. By tracing the diverse actions of concerned market actors, we are thus able to see how they contribute to shape those very markets.

The efforts of the actors to address the emerging matters of concern also shed light on the self-seeking and coordinative calculations of market actors. On the one hand, we observed how the matter of concern took on different shapes representing the interests of each actor (farmers, GAC and traders). On the other hand, we also observed that these interests, whilst self-seeking (Callon, 1999; Slater, 2002), were aimed at ensuring ongoing activity between market actors. All actors involved sought to coordinate actions and create durable associations (Araujo and Kjellberg, 2009). GAC and the traders, for example, each sought to ensure continued trade with the farmers. The farmers, too, coordinated their relations within the PO and with their children to collectively address their education and income concerns.

As part of their efforts to resolve the matter of concern, the concerned actors enacted at least three different market devices. Two of these devices, the POs and the SACCOs, were specifically geared towards market coordination. These devices allow the farmers to frame and translate the matter of concern into a collective concern of their families and the PO; they help to consolidate the associations between GAC and farmers; and they weaken the ties between farmers and the mainstream market. But the traders also have a powerful market device; mortgages, which they use to account for the failures of SACCOs. These market devices address the same concern and can thus be seen as complementary from the farmers' perspective. For GAC and the traders, however, they act in opposition to each other.

In all, we see how matters of concern permeate market boundaries and entangle various market actors, shaping their practices. Once a distinct issue linked to the socio-cultural entanglements of coffee, farmers and their families, the matter of concern now triggers responses from the associated actors in two competing markets.

CONCLUSION

In this chapter we offer an empirical account of how matters of concern shape markets by triggering diverse actions. We also show how one subsistence market is configured to take such matters of concern into account. We specifically trace the disagreements concerning which entanglements/ qualities should be taken into account when valuing a market object (in this case, coffee). Matters of concern can be seen here to be an important and insightful analytical device, revealing ongoing market-shaping activities that may otherwise be easily missed or discarded. We trace how multiple actors are introduced to or become involved in the market as concerns are articulated and 'dealt with'. The distributed and often obscure(d) nature of the efforts to articulate matters of concern in markets is also revealed here; that is, not all efforts to articulate concerns happen directly or contiguously. Farmers meet in groups to go over their income concerns. Traders visit farmers at the times that this problem is at its worst. Traders encourage them to migrate from the GAC market frame. GAC loses suppliers. GAC responds by introducing local savings banks (SACCOs). This is the to-ing and fro-ing involved in the articulation of matters of concern in markets, which is ongoing and occurs over time and space. It goes to show that the everyday practices of market actors (and what might first appear as non-market actors) matter, making visible the troubling entanglements disrupting and disordering markets.

At the heart of these issues are the deep entanglements of the economic and the social, which manifest in the complexities of coffee valuation. To the farmers, the clear-cut distinction between a social and economic world attempted by GAC is not very productive. Rather, they continually blur this distinction by taking actions that criss-cross market boundaries in search for a possible resolution of 'their' matter of concern. For example, the farmers find it necessary for their children's future to be 'recognized' as a matter of concern in the GAC market frame. Without this, their future and their children's future remain precarious.

Importantly, while the disputes regarding the qualification and valuation of coffee remain ongoing, trade between the farmers and GAC continues. Therefore we could say that, despite the dispute, there is trade where momentary detachments are being made. However, as we have argued, it is because of the disputes that the market is configured such as it is today.

The GAC market frame can then be characterized as a concerned market as it has been 'configured to take into account the various concerns that are associated with the unfolding of economic transactions' (Geiger et al., this volume). The actions and activities of GAC, farmers, traders and the researcher themselves have all been shaped by the 'education issue' put on the table by farmers acting within POs. Therefore while GAC may be viewed as a kind of 'social movement' or social enterprise (educating and organizing farmers, helping them to form banks, securing funding for pulpers and so on), many of these activities came about in response to farmers articulating their concerns directly and indirectly. That is, GAC's social enterprising character takes shape in responding to and dealing with farmers' concerns. From this we can see that the articulation of matters of concern is a collective outcome of multiple market actors' enrolment into, and involvement in the farmers' actor-network when the issues that matter are 'opened up for outside involvement' (Marres, 2007, p. 772).

Our study contributes to the emerging market studies on subsistence markets, responding to Lindeman's (2012) call for more debate and discussions on framing exchanges in these situations. We bring to light the efforts of subsistence market actors to frame markets by raising their concerns repeatedly vis-à-vis their various market partners. But, specific to matters of concern, we argue that these may not always be tabled for discussion or even be known in their entirety to transacting actors. Instead, market actors may enrol external actors to act on their behalf or help them articulate matters of concern to interested parties and 'extend their reach across space' (Raynolds, 2002, p. 408).

NOTES

1. The other firms export coffee in its raw form (green beans) mainly to the EU market.
2. The empirical material used for this chapter was collected during five weeks of ethnographic fieldwork in Uganda in 2010. After spending one week at the GAC head office/ field office, the first author spent two weeks studying the practices at the Nakasero PO. Specifically, the base for this part of the study was the Kitante homestead, home of Mukisa, a farmer leader at the Nakasero PO, who frequently interacted with GAC and other farmer leaders. At the Kitante homestead, there is a central processing store where some 50 farmers come to process coffee and hold PO meetings. Mukisa's own farm is also a demonstration plot where GAC visitors are often taken. In addition, three days were spent investigating the practices of farmers at a second homestead (Nabisunsa). Finally, additional observations of the (exchange) interactions between GAC and the farmers were made at the GAC field office.
3. Pulpers range from small-scale hand pulpers to large-scale washing stations.
4. In this study, we focus on the GAC farmers selling both to the GAC and to traders in the mainstream market.
5. World coffee prices are highly volatile and are determined globally at the New York futures market (Ponte, 2002; Kerr-Ritchie, 2006).
6. Located at the slopes of Mt Ruwenzori, the rugged mountainous terrain makes it difficult for these farmers to use the easier means (bicycles) for transport.
7. In their culture the girls do not inherit land, as Rwego clarified, because they get married into a different family.
8. This research, however, did not further investigate GAC's pricing mechanisms.
9. Later in the parchment coffee trajectory, at GAC's roasting plant, the parchment coverings are removed, revealing the washed green beans, which are then roasted, packaged and exported.

REFERENCES

Appadurai, Arjun (1986), 'Introduction: commodities and the politics of value', in A. Appadurai (ed.), *The Social Life of Things: Commodities in Cultural Perspective*, Cambridge: Cambridge University Press, pp. 3–63.
Araujo, Luis and Hans Kjellberg (2009), 'Shaping exchanges, performing markets: The study of marketing practices', in P. Maclaran, M. Saren, B. Stern and M. Tadajewski (eds), *The SAGE Handbook of Marketing Theory*, London: SAGE, pp. 195–218.
Asankha, Pallegedara and Yamano Takashi (2011), 'Impacts of universal secondary education policy on secondary school enrollments in Uganda', *Journal of Accounting, Finance and Economics*, **1** (1), 16–30.
Callon, Michel (1999), 'Actor Network Theory – the market test', in J. Law and J. Hassard (eds), *Actor Network Theory and After*, Oxford: Blackwell Publishers, pp. 181–95.

Callon, Michel (2005), 'Why virtualism paves the way to political impotence: A reply to Daniel Miller's critique of "The laws of the markets"', *Economic Sociology: European Electronic Newsletter*, 6/2 (February), 3–20.

Callon, Michel (2009), 'Elaborating the notion of performativity', *Le Libellio d'Aegis*, **5** (1), 18–29.

Callon, Michel and Vololona Rabeharisoa (2008), 'The growing engagement of emergent concerned groups in political and economic life lessons from the French association of neuromuscular disease patients', *Science, Technology & Human Values*, **33** (2), 230–61.

International Coffee Organisation (2013a), 'Exports of all forms of coffee by exporting countries to all destinations', available at: http://www.ico.org/prices/m1.htm, accessed 23 August 2013.

International Coffee Organisation (2013b), 'About coffee: Field processing, International Coffee Organisation', available at: http://www.ico.org/field_processing.asp?section=About_Coffee, accessed 23 August 2013.

Jensen, Torben E. (2008), 'Experimenting with commodities and gifts: The case of an office hotel', *Organization*, **15** (2), 187–209.

Kerr-Ritchie, Jeffrey R. (2006), 'Coffee's dark and bloody ground', *Nature, Society and Thought*, **19** (2), 207–16.

Kopytoff, Igor (1986), 'The cultural biography of things: Commoditisation as process', in A. Appadurai (ed.), *The Social Life of Things: Commodities in Social Perspective*, Cambridge: Cambridge University Press, pp. 64–91.

Latour, Bruno (2005), 'From realpolitik to dingpolitik or how to make things public', in B. Latour and P. Weibel (eds), *Making Things Public: Atmospheres of Democracy*, Cambridge, MA: MIT Press, pp. 14–44.

Latour, Bruno (2009), *Politics of Nature*, Boston, MA: Harvard University Press.

Latour, Bruno and Peter Weibel (eds) (2005), *Making Things Public: Atmospheres of Democracy*, Cambridge, MA: MIT Press.

Leino, Helena and Markus Laine (2012), 'Do matters of concern matter? Bringing issues back to participation', *Planning Theory*, **11** (1), 89–103.

Lindeman, Sara (2012), 'Market formation in subsistence contexts: A study of informal waste trade practices in Tanzania and Brazil', *Consumption Markets & Culture*, **15** (2), 235–57.

Marres, Noortje (2007), 'The issues deserve more credit pragmatist contributions to the study of public involvement in controversy', *Social Studies of Science*, **37** (5), 759–80.

Moser, Ingunn (2008), 'Making Alzheimer's disease matter: Enacting, interfering and doing politics of nature', *Geoforum*, **39** (1), 98–110.

Ponte, Stefano (2002), 'The latte revolution? Regulation, markets and consumption in the global coffee chain', *World Development*, **30** (7), 1099–122.

Ponte, Stefano and Peter Gibbon (2005), 'Quality standards, conventions and the governance of global value chains', *Economy and Society*, **34** (1), 1–31.

Raynolds, Laura T. (2002), 'Consumer/producer links in fair trade coffee networks', *Sociologia Ruralis*, **42** (4), 404–24.

Slater, Don (2002), 'From calculation to alienation: Disentangling economic abstractions', *Economy and Society*, **31** (2), 234–49.

Uganda Coffee Development Authority (2013), UCDA monthly report for April 2013, available at: http://www.ugandacoffee.org/resources/reports/07%20April%202013%20report.pdf, accessed 23 August 2013.

Viswanathan, Madhu and Rosa A. José (2010), 'Understanding subsistence

Concerned markets

marketplaces: Toward sustainable consumption and commerce for a better world', *Journal of Business Research*, **63** (6), 535–7.
Weiss, Brad (1996), 'Coffee breaks and coffee connections: The lived experience of a commodity in Tanzanian and European worlds', in D. Howes (ed.), *Cross-Cultural Consumption: Global Markets, Local Realities*, London: Routledge, pp. 93–105.
Zelizer, Viviana (1989), 'The social meaning of money: "special monies"', *American Journal of Sociology*, **95** (2), 342–77.

9. Doing green: environmental concerns and the realization of green values in everyday food practices[1]

Hans Kjellberg and Ingrid Stigzelius

INTRODUCTION

Consumers are increasingly challenged to take into account the environmental effects of the food they consume (Halkier, 2010). For instance, the Swedish Environmental Protection Agency estimated that activities related to eating generated 20 per cent of all Swedish greenhouse gas emissions in 2003 (Naturvårdsverket, 2008). Given the recent conclusion of the IPCC that '[l]imiting climate change will require substantial and sustained reductions of greenhouse gas emissions' (IPCC Working group 1, 2013, p. 14), the need to 'do green' in relation to food is likely to become further pronounced in coming years.

Meanwhile, there are already multiple *scripts* available (cf. Akrich, 1992; Shove and Araujo, 2010), which tell consumers what and how to eat to become 'green' food consumers. Such scripts can be found in policy documents, food recipes, green apps, eco-labels and so on. For example, governments in the Nordic countries have sought to guide consumers in making greener food choices by emphasizing their important role in steering production and consumption towards sustainability (Micheletti and Isenhour, 2010). There are also scripts that go beyond buying and eating to address how household spaces are designed for food storage, cooking and recycling. Together, these scripts reflect multiple dimensions of environmental concern, including organic production, local production and reduced carbon footprint. However, since food consumption also encompasses other normative concerns, such as thrift, health, pleasure and care for others, environmental concerns add ambiguity and complexity into everyday life (Halkier, 2001; Kline, 2011; Östberg, 2003).

The purpose of this chapter is to explore how consumers realize green values – 'do green' – in their everyday food practices. We draw on Shove and Pantzar (2005) and others, to investigate how attempts to 'do green' intervene in the integration and coordination of practices related to production, exchange and consumption of food. Our investigation is based on three empirical cases examining: (i) how consumers collectively engage to produce food for themselves; (ii) how a consumer cooperative food distributor constructs a webshop to ease the everyday food purchases for consumers; and (iii) how an NGO seeks to increase consumers' abilities to 'do green' by teaching them 'green cooking'. The cases highlight that individual consumers engage to 'do green' in many different but interrelated food practices. The extent to which consumers are 'doing green' is thus not a discrete variable, but a matter of 'shades of green' jointly produced by these interrelated practices. Further, consumers need not adhere to single traditional roles associated with production, consumption or exchange (cf. Thompson, 2011). Instead, the everyday provision of food becomes a 'crossing place for a plurality of practices' (Halkier, 2009, p. 36; Reckwitz, 2002, p. 256) in which consumers can engage and draw on different modes of economic coordination.

Our main findings are as follows. First, our cases suggest that consumer engagements in food practices are fuelled by multiple concerns, which need to be balanced. Second, other actors are observed to play important parts in consumers' realization of environmental values, both by providing scripts for, and by adjusting situations to 'doing green'. Third, the introduction of green concerns has consequences for other practices in which consumers engage, which complicate their incorporation in everyday life. However, 'doing green' does not appear to reduce the extent to which consumers rely on market exchanges, but rather results in modified such exchanges (in terms of *what* and *how* you buy). Finally, the role of both formal and informal monitoring emerges as central to the realization of green values. The cases underscore the importance of convenience/ practicality as an informal standard against which consumers assess food-related practices.

In the following section, we conceptually elaborate on the challenge of 'doing green' from a practice perspective and generate four heuristic questions to guide our study. We then discuss how we have sought to address these questions empirically, providing details on case selection and data collection. This is followed by three case narratives and a concluding discussion based on our four heuristic questions.

A PRACTICE PERSPECTIVE ON 'DOING GREEN'

One common way of encouraging the production of specific values in society, including green ones, is to rely on markets (Kjellberg and Helgesson, 2010). For example, increasing sales of organic food has been suggested as one way of addressing environmental problems in food production. But while consumers often express positive attitudes towards organic food (Magnusson et al., 2001), sales figures suggest otherwise; the market share for organic food remains around 4 per cent throughout the EU (Klintman and Boström, 2012). One response to this disconnect between attitude and behaviour (Padel and Foster, 2005) is to intensify consumer campaigns under the assumption that the right information will alter behaviour. However, sociological consumer studies reveal that consumers deal with environmental issues in quite complex ways in their everyday lives (Conolly and Prothero, 2008; Halkier, 2001; Warde, 2005). These studies suggest consumers' abilities to 'do green' should be seen in the light of the interrelations between food-related and other practices, and between green and other concerns that influence the organizing of everyday life (Halkier, 2010). This implies that 'doing green' also goes beyond buying organic food (Klintman and Boström, 2012) to include multiple (green) food practices.

Therefore, we approach the issue of how consumers 'do green' from a practice perspective (de Certeau, 1984; Latour, 1986; 1987; Reckwitz, 2002; Shove and Pantzar, 2005). Specifically, we draw on the performative position developed in the sociology of translation (Callon, 1986; 2007; Latour, 1986; 2005), which emphasizes the active production of the social world. As Law and Urry (2004, p. 395) assert: 'while the "real" is indeed "real", it is *also* made'. From this perspective, 'doing green' becomes a question of *actors seeking to realize green values* by modifying various ordinary practices. Following Kjellberg and Helgesson (2010), we define *values* as 'things' that govern practice, for example *ends* considered important to pursue or *means* towards such ends. Our focus is on explicit attempts to alter food-related practices so that they produce environmental values. Borrowing from Thévenot (2002), we consider such attempts to be fuelled by a perceived disconnect between *what is good* and *what is real*. We use the term *concern* to denote this type of perceived disconnect.

Everyday Food Practices

We conceive the food-related activities that consumers engage in as *practices* (Araujo and Kjellberg, 2009; Reckwitz, 2002) (see Figure 9.1). The performance of practices involves and integrates materials, competences

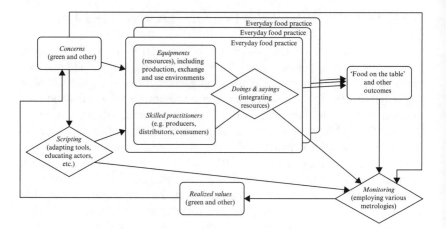

*Figure 9.1   A schematic illustration of the realization of values through
everyday food practices*

and meanings (Shove and Pantzar, 2005). If we consider the generic practice of cooking, this involves various *doings* and *sayings* (Schatzki, 1996) –
reading recipes, weighing ingredients – that are performed using various
types of *equipment* (Shove and Araujo, 2010) – kitchen utensils, a stove.
For many practices there are clearly formulated *scripts* available (what to
do, how, in what order) and many objects designed with such scripts in
mind (Akrich, 1992). Further, practices are performed in particular environments, whose features to varying extents have been adapted to such
scripts. Thus, we may identify specific *production* (Finch and Acha, 2008),
exchange (Kjellberg and Helgesson, 2007) and *use environments* (Burr,
2013), which afford or encourage the performance of certain practices.
In our empirical cases, these environments are illustrated by vegetable
gardens, supermarkets and kitchens, respectively.

Nevertheless, the existence of an adapted environment does not guarantee that a specific practice will be performed, that it will be performed
according to a particular script or that other practices will not be performed. Such matters also depend on the competences of the practitioners, that is to what extent they have been equipped to engage in the
scripted practice (Shove and Araujo, 2010). The performance of a specific
practice further depends on the extent to which the practice is conceived
as meaningful to the practitioner (Shove and Pantzar, 2005). The world
of cooking is full of practices that require experience/knowledge, for
example why a frying steak should be lifted only when turned. Finally, the
performance of a specific practice also depends on whether factors that
may impinge on the situation have been successfully *bracketed* (Callon,

1998; Goffman, 1974) – the smell of burnt food has ended more than one telephone call.

We argue that this conception of practices aptly reflects consumers' engagements with food: specific moves and gestures (e.g. chopping an onion), more or less specialized objects (e.g. pots, pans, knives), varying significance attributed to specific practices (e.g. 'my grandmother always used to. . .'), infrastructural arrangements (e.g. retail store and kitchen layouts) and the variably successful efforts to bracket off other parts of reality (e.g. family members in need of assistance).

Coordinating Multiple Food Practices

The everyday food practices that consumers engage in aim towards resource integration (Vargo and Lusch, 2012; Vargo and Akaka, 2012). Compiling a shopping list, visiting the store and preparing a meal are all practices whose ultimate objective is 'food on the table' (see Figure 9.1). These (integrative) practices involve *co-production*, in which a large number of individual practices become linked, sometimes in the form of joint, simultaneous activity by several actors; always in the form of employed equipment (resources) being the product of practices distributed across time and space (Vargo et al., 2008). In line with previous work on the practices of everyday life (de Certeau, 1984) and proactive consumers (Toffler, 1980), the boundary between production and consumption is blurred.

The links between practices typically involve mediators (Latour, 1994); a family discussion (practice) concerning the menu and responsibilities for cooking (practice) during the next week may result in a written note (mediator) on the refrigerator door, detailing who should do what and when. Potentially, this mediator can enter into the dinner practices over the following days. Through adjustment across practices, complementarity can be achieved, which in turn may render change in one practice difficult without corresponding changes in others. One example would be changing from daily to weekly food purchases, which is likely to require changes in meal planning, transporting and storing foodstuffs.

The practices that need to be coordinated to put food on the table thus involve several actors and several types of situations, including ones that are commonly characterized as production, distribution/exchange and consumption.[2] Coordination between them can be achieved in several ways, for example through markets, hierarchies or cooperative relations. While the choice of method for coordination may not be completely arbitrary – different modes of coordination require different amounts of investments (e.g. in making something tradable) – the location of specific modes of coordination (e.g. market exchange) can be modified (Araujo and Spring, 2006).

Monitoring the Production of 'Green' in Everyday Food Practices

A final issue to address is how to determine that the performance of a given practice produces 'green'. While the ultimate objective of food-related practices may be 'food on the table', other outputs are also produced, such as waste, pride and appreciation. We are interested in how such practices are modified to also produce values that are labelled 'green'. Given our performative stance, there is no definitive list of values that can be subsumed under this label. Rather, the label acts as a metaphorical box that is continuously being filled with diverse contents by actors who employ it (Latour, 1986). To exemplify using one of our cases: when it comes to cooking practices, practitioners sometimes enact *thrift* as an environmental value (reducing waste) and sometimes not (choosing a non-organic vegetable for its lower price).

While this prevents us from defining what 'green' values are at the outset of inquiry, it nonetheless provides a way of approaching the issue (see Figure 9.1). The extent to which a practice, modified to take environmental concerns into account, actually results in the realization of green values depends on the *monitoring* of that practice. The concerns that fuel an actor's engagement in that practice are likely to influence how the actor evaluates the outcome. Due to the multiplicity of evaluation standards that can be applied to determine environmental consequences, for example contribution to our carbon footprint, the outcome is far from certain. As noted by Mallard (1998, p. 594), however, 'precise measurements are never completely true, nor completely conventional, but precisely "conventionally true".' Hence, such evaluations are both *extrinsic* and *intrinsic* (Callon et al., 2002); they are shaped by bringing together standards of evaluation, metrological equipment and outcomes in concrete monitoring. Some monitoring is informal, relying primarily on practitioner reflection, while some is formalized to varying degrees, involving explicit auditing efforts. Monitoring may also be subject to scripting that could introduce priorities among alternative assessment standards (Sjögren and Helgesson, 2007).

Studying Efforts to 'Do Green' in Everyday Food Practices

From the above, we identify four important considerations when exploring consumers' efforts to 'do green'. *First*, efforts to realize green values are fuelled by specific concerns about the environmental consequences of food production and consumption. These concerns, which hinge on a perceived disconnect between what currently is and what would be good, are unlikely to be the only concerns entertained by an actor. *Second*, the concerns of consumers are likely to be influenced by other actors. Some of these 'external' concerns may have been translated into explicit scripts and inscribed into various resources offered to consumers as means towards certain values. *Third*, the performance of specific food practices will depend on and influence other practices, some of which are performed by other actors. *Fourth*, the realization of any green value through a specific practice will depend on how that practice is being monitored.

Based on these considerations, the following four questions are posed in exploring the practical realization of green values in everyday food practices: (1) Which different values and concerns fuel consumer engagements in green food practices? (2) How do other actors seek to influence the realization of green values in those food practices? (3) How does the realization of green values depend on and influence other practices? (4) How is the realization of green values established and reflected upon? It should be noted that these questions serve as interrogating devices; we use them to explore the issue of 'doing green', rather than seeking general answers to them.

HOW WE HAVE STUDIED 'DOING GREEN'

One of the authors conducted three explorative case studies of consumers engaging to 'do green' in food production, food exchange and food preparation. The individual cases were selected for their theoretical relevance (Dubois and Araujo, 2007); they all involve explicit efforts to produce green values in different food-related practices. The specific combination of cases was put together not to provide variation concerning how green values might be realized, but to highlight such efforts in different food-related practices. This makes the cases *complementary* in terms of understanding how green values can be realized in and through the complex of connected practices that puts food on the table.

Empirically, we sought to 'follow the actors' (Latour, 2005) by using data collection techniques that come close to the practices of consumers (Halkier and Jensen, 2011; Warde, 2005). Participant observations, in-depth interviews, a focus group and photo documentation were the primary means used for collecting the empirical material (see Table 9.1). These methods provide accounts that we see as 'enactments of social life' (Halkier and Jensen, 2011, 109), thus reflecting practitioners' performance with others. Combining participant observation of real-life situations with interviews allows us to cover the participants' doings and sayings. More

Table 9.1   Data sources in the case studies

Data sources	Case 1: The Food Park	Case 2: Cooponline.se	Case 3: Climate Clever Food
Written sources	Emails, webpage, diary writing	The webpage	Distributed recipes and brochures, webpage, diary writing
Interviews	Four in-depth interviews with participants and study circle leader (1–2 hours)	Six in-depth interviews with managers and consumers (1–1.5 hours)	One focus group discussion and two in-depth interviews with participants and study circle leader (1–1.5 hours)
Observations	Participant observation of vegetable gardening, photo documentation	Participant observation of food delivery, webpage, screen dumps	Participant observation during cooking, photo documentation

specifically, we used the interview technique 'interview to the double' (Nicolini, 2009), asking the interviewee to explain to an imagined 'double' who is taking their place (i.e. the researcher), exactly what they do so that the double can do the same. This technique gives an opportunity to iden-tify the different doings of a practice, but also portrays the practitioner's image of the practice, unearthing the different normative concerns that guide it. We also employed a combination of autobiography and ethnog-raphy for the participant observations, keeping a diary to detail and reflect upon the practices (Ellis et al., 2011).

The Food Park study is based on participation in a study circle cover-ing an entire growing season. Four in-depth interviews with participants were also conducted. The study of Cooponline.se started with two in-depth interviews with managers at the Coop. Four in-depth interviews took place with customers concerning their motives for and experience of buying food online, and their relation to green food practices. Finally, the study of Climate Clever Food was conducted by participating in a study circle, performing a focus group discussion and two in-depth interviews. Information was also collected from the three respective organizations, including their websites, printed documentation and emails. Finally, photos were taken to document events and material objects in use.

Our analysis involved several iterative steps and can be characterized as a process of 'casing' (Ragin, 1992). First, draft narratives were constructed which aimed to generate rich descriptions of the participating consumers' experiences. Second, the case drafts were discussed against the backdrop of an emerging conceptual focus on the realization of green values in food-related practices. Third, this allowed us to identify several food-related practices in which consumers engaged, along with values guiding them in these practices and associations to and between practices. Fourth, the case narratives were revised and considerably reduced in scope to provide more focused accounts relevant for the paper's objective. Fifth, the four guiding questions were then put to each revised case narrative, and specific observations relating to each question recorded. Sixth, these observations were sorted and turned into four separate subsections, constituting the heart of the concluding discussion. Lastly, based on reviewer comments, we revised the conceptual discussion, adjusted the questions to better reflect our research interest and revisited steps 4 to 6 above.

'DOING GREEN' IN PRODUCTION PRACTICES: THE FOOD PARK

Urban agriculture has been proposed as a means towards more sustainable societies and a way of realizing green values in relation to food (Smit and Nasr, 1992). Basically, urban agriculture involves growing vegetables on your own or together with other citizens in collective allotments. It purports to cultivate a better living place and produce food, often using organic production methods (Delshammar, 2011; Larsson, 2009; Queiroz, 2009). One specific example is The Food Park ('Matparken'), a community garden in Uppsala, Sweden, where people jointly grow vegetables for household needs.

Concerned Consumers Engaging to Produce Green

The Food Park is a bottom-up initiative resulting from a chance encounter between two people interested in urban gardening. The founders wanted to produce organic vegetables for household needs, but scale up production in terms of both area and people involved to increase efficiency. Equally important was a wish to cultivate knowledge of how to grow food in a self-sufficient manner.

> I want to know what I'm doing, to be able to produce a large share of my food if I wanted to. In a way, it's the knowledge of how to do all of this that we acquire in The Food Park, rather than the food itself. And if you want to grow a good share of your vegetable needs, then I think you should do it as efficiently as possible, together with others. My experience tells me that it's much more efficient

to grow at a larger scale. Instead of putting out two plants of broccoli, you put out twenty and a hundred heads of cabbage as well. (Woman 32, co-founder of The Food Park)

The two founders developed their ideas and received permission from the municipality of Uppsala to use an idle field in a suburb, provided that the produce wasn't sold, but used for household needs. The Food Park eventually developed into a politically and religiously independent organization purporting to create a living green urban space, in which citizens participate in constructing and maintaining. Its aims are: 'to increase the interest for organic farming, increase the availability of locally produced food, stimulate a discussion about sustainable food production and at the same time contribute to a meaningful occupation for those who take part in the activities' (Matparken, 2013).

In the spring of 2009, ten people started to cultivate the land at The Food Park. By 2012 there were about 40 people growing food in five groups. Members share all costs for land preparation, irrigation, equipment, seeds and so on and at the same time make the cultivation more fun and effective by growing together. In 2012, The Food Park also housed two study circles with eight participants growing vegetables on two allotments. These circles were arranged together with an educational association to spread knowhow about organic farming. Next we present an account of participating in one study circle and identify a number of production practices, for example sowing and watering. The case study shows how these practices are interlinked and dependent on coordination with both exchange practices (buying things) and consumption practices (storing and using the vegetables).

Planning (Scripting) Food Production

The study circle is designed to teach us organic vegetable production, both in theory and practice, throughout a growing season (March to September). Apart from our circle leader, we are seven women who have joined the study circle for different reasons. We all like the idea of growing together due to limited experience of growing vegetables for household needs. One participant considers it important to be outdoors as a change from her hectic city life, while another one wants to become familiar with more vegetables than the ones she normally buys.

> I want to learn more in general about growing vegetables. To sort of get to know more vegetables than [the supermarket] offers. And then it's good to grow together with others to share the responsibilities. I know I would grow tired of having my own allotment. (Woman 48, participant)

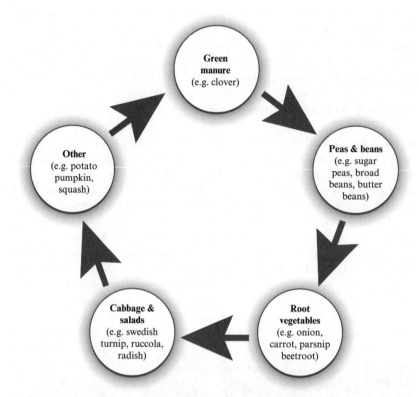

Figure 9.2   The crop rotation system in The Food Park

During the first two meetings we stay inside to learn and discuss various dos and don'ts of organic farming, where for example artificial fertilizers should not be used. Crop rotation is also central to organic farming and works as a natural alternative to pesticides. The Food Park employs a five-year crop rotation (see Figure 9.2), where vegetables with similar properties are grouped together and one patch always contains green manure (nitrogen-fixing plants).

The circle leader has brought books and binders about vegetable and organic farming for further reading. We feel overwhelmed by the volume of factual information, but the circle leader assures us that growing vegetables is a very practical thing and that you learn along the way. However, it is good to plan and reach a common view of what to sow and when. Knowing the seeds' different development times, from seed to finished plant, is essential; a parsnip can take up to 120 days to grow, while a radish only takes 20 days. We will simply not have time to grow some plants! Finally, we are asked if we have particular preferences concerning what to grow. We would then need to order these seeds from a seed merchant. Otherwise we can use what the other groups in The Food Park have already ordered. As beginners we settle for the available seeds, which will ensure a fit with the crop rotation system.

Cultivating the Land and Sowing Seeds

In the beginning of May we meet in The Food Park for the first time. We re-cap the theoretical ideas while sitting by the campfire and then take a tour of the park. We start by putting a spade into the soil to see what it looks like. It is dry on the surface, but more like clay underneath. It is actually called 'rigid clay', our circle leader explains, and is very difficult to handle manually. We therefore feel relieved that a tractor has ploughed the field for us (this is a service that The Food Park procures). We return to the fireplace where our circle leader has prepared soil, trays for the plants and sachets of seeds. We plant different kinds of cabbage and note the names of the seeds (Figure 9.3). After planting everything, one participant takes the tray with her to give it some water and warmth until next time.

Figure 9.3   The ploughed field at The Food Park and participant in the study circle sowing some seeds

Watering and Weeding

Sad news: the cabbage plants didn't make it; they were forgotten in a sunny window! Fortunately, our study circle leader has some extra plants that we can use. In the middle of May we plant cabbage straight into the field, together with onions, carrots, parsley, dill, parsnips, white beets, beetroots, peas and beans. During the summer it is more difficult to meet. Two participants also drop out, leaving only five plus our circle leader. Moreover, few of us had time to maintain our allotment. On June 30, after we all missed a gathering, our circle leader sent us an email urging us to at least weed the root vegetable patch the following Sunday.

During the summer, rain makes us cancel many work sessions. Our water pump is also sabotaged and eventually set alight (see Figure 9.4). One of the participants brings a tent to shelter us from the rain, but it disappears on the night the pump house is burned to the ground. This event triggers a discussion about how to replace the old pump. No one wants to go back to using a petrol-powered generator since it is both difficult to handle and generates noise and pollution. Another option would be to use an electric pump powered by solar panels. However, this would be both

Figure 9.4   The pump house and generator burned to the ground, and some prospering plants

expensive and liable to future sabotage. A third, similarly expensive option would be to connect to the municipal water system.

Harvesting

Despite all our problems, the plants somehow prospered – thanks to nature and some participants with particularly 'green fingers' (see Figure 9.4). Not having distributed the workload evenly between us created an uneasy feeling regarding how much produce each was entitled to. However, given the rich harvest, the real problem was what to do with everything! It was also tricky to know what to harvest when, as one participant explained:

> I usually start by taking a walk [. . .] around the allotment [. . .] to see how it looks. I think and plan a little what I want to pick. And then you just help yourself! But it's a bit difficult, so far it's been difficult to know what to do when harvesting. I need some supervision from our circle leader, for example what will survive the frost and what we can harvest today. It becomes a bit random what stuff you take. I don't know if it is according to the 'state of the art', but you can take what you think is about right. I definitely think everyone has the same right to the vegetables. (Woman 48, participant)

Harvesting is also seen as rewarding:

> You tend to take home quite a lot! I always have two to three bags with me, for example white beet and carrots. And then, when I bike home, I feel awfully good. Because then I feel sort of rich. I've done my shopping. Well, I haven't really shopped, but I've done my work. I can carry home the food. Yes, and it's also a pretty nice bike route! When I bike home I usually think: what shall I do with this now? It's a lot to take care of. (Woman 50, participant)

Storing and Using the Vegetables

Lack of space, time and/or knowledge can make it difficult to handle the harvested vegetables. For example, onions must be left to dry in the open. One participant who lacked space for this put them up to dry in the window instead (see Figure 9.5). Another participant was more concerned about her shallow knowledge about how to use the vegetables. One solution for her was simply to give stuff away.

> I've given lots away, because I thought there was too much I couldn't use 'fresh'. I gave my colleague a cabbage head and some beans – yes, it was a full bag – and some beetroots. He gave me some chanterelles in return. I have enough and to spare. I think it is fun to give as a present, but it's also because I want it to be used fresh. (Woman 48, participant)

Figure 9.5   Onions as curtains: another way of storing vegetables when space is scarce

Even our study circle leader, who really tries to use all the vegetables, finds it difficult to utilize the volumes grown. It also takes time, and she admits that growing your own vegetables and living a normal life easily may conflict.

> At the moment, half of all the food I harvested still lies outside my doorway, stuff that I haven't had the energy to take care of yet. You need to scrub them off first because you don't want to put dirty vegetables into the fridge. It so easily becomes a conflict between everything. [. . .] When I came home from The Food Park I prepared herbal salt from fresh herbs, instead. Luckily, I had some leftovers from the day before, so I didn't need to start cooking as well. (Woman 32, co-founder of The Food Park)

Done Green?

As the growing season came to an end, so did the study circle. As a result of participants dropping out, it proved difficult to cover the costs. However, The Food Park at large seems to grow and prosper, with at least two study circle participants planning to continue their endeavours as urban farmers. They both found the study circle meaningful in terms of learning more about nature and participating in the different seasons and processes involved in food production.

This year [in The Food Park] has been more of a learning period, to see what there is and what you can do with it, a little test rather than to simply get food. I need to learn more about what to do and test what suits my household. [. . .] In general, it's this 'doing' that's been most instructive to me – putting the seeds into the ground, seeing what comes up, and harvesting. To learn the whole process and be part of doing it, not watching it on the telly, but being out there in reality, so to say. (Woman 48, participant)

Our study circle leader suggested that urban agriculture produces many values other than simply getting food on the table. It is also a matter of cultivating knowledge, health and a social sustainability by doing things together. Similarly, the participants invoked a range of values and standards against which they assessed their participation in the study circle, for example, becoming an active part of nature, which is largely independent of the amount of food harvested.

'DOING GREEN' IN EXCHANGE PRACTICES: COOP ONLINE

Food retailers have been put forward as central to the transition towards more sustainable systems for food provision (Belz, 2004; Jones et al., 2008). As part of our exploration of how consumers 'do green' in everyday food practices, we studied one explicit effort to assist consumers towards 'climate clever' food habits undertaken by the Swedish consumer cooperation (KF).[3] This case highlights how the introduction of a new mode of exchange – online food shopping – can involve several, possibly conflicting concerns, and lead consumers towards new combinations of exchange and other food-related practices.

Scripting Consumers' Food Practices

In 2007, the board of KF began to rethink how to facilitate their members' shopping, drawing on their mission statement and a survey from their newly established Internet member panel. The latter had revealed a shortage of time in families with young children, so KF decided to re-introduce online food retailing in an attempt to ease the situation especially for parents.

A year later, KF launched Cooponline.se, an online food store delivering groceries directly to consumers using biogas-fuelled vehicles.

We want to offer you better food habits! Food should be something enjoyable. We cater to those who want to avoid stress, heavy shopping bags and traffic jams. Those who value fresh produce and a wide assortment of organic

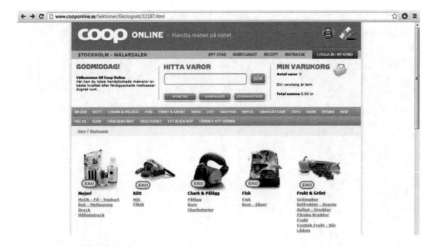

Figure 9.6   The Cooponline.se website with some categories in its organic assortment displayed

products. Those who seek inspiration and news. Those who want to shop in a 'climate clever' way. If we can get more people to calmly plan their grocery shopping, then we have helped more people towards better food habits. That is our vision! (Vision statement, 2008)

The webshop allows consumers to structure their food purchases in several ways. A normal search function (see Figure 9.6) assists if you want to find specific food items. You can also browse various food categories such as dairy, meat or vegetables. If you are indecisive about what fruit and vegetables to buy, you can pick a mixed fruit and vegetable box. For those who have not planned what to buy, there is also a recipe-function and a pre-composed food bag based on a set menu.

Whilst Cooponline.se builds upon KF's core values, it emphasizes the environment, health and ecology to a greater extent than the physical stores. Cooponline.se offers around 600 organic products, which can be found in the ordinary product categories, but also under the heading 'Ekologiskt' (Figure 9.6). Since Cooponline.se is certified by KRAV (an organic label) they can handle fresh organic food manually and avoid pre-packed fruit and vegetables typically found in physical stores. Nevertheless, it is not an organic niche-store, because it also provides conventional food products. 'We don't want to force our customers [to buy organic]', the CEO said. This allows Cooponline.se to cater to different concerns that consumers may have.

Through just-in-time deliveries from suppliers, Cooponline.se gets fresh supplies of bread, fruits, meat and fish in the exact amounts that customers

Figure 9.7   Home delivery of food bags

have ordered. This helps reduce food spoilage and waste – there is simply nothing left in stock when the day is over. Customers can place orders until 24.00, when Cooponline.se tries to optimize the delivery routes for the following day. Between 09.00 and 22.00, biogas fuelled vehicles deliver the goods to the customers' homes (Figure 9.7).

Multiple Consumer Concerns

The interviewed customers revealed several concerns about their current life situation and food practices that led them to try shopping at Cooponline.se. One major motivation for most of them was the possibility of home delivery. Two of the customers did not own a car, for economic as well as environmental reasons. The fact that deliveries were made using biogas-fuelled vehicles additionally spurred some customers, while one customer had not even noted this. Another customer was not able to carry bags because she was recovering from a caesarian birth. She was also excited to try something new and liked the large assortment of organic products.

The product assortment was important to all customers, although in different ways. One customer was particularly keen to support small-scale organic producers. As a result, she bought milk products from a small organic cooperative, rather than from the large dairies.

> It feels much better to support small-scale, organic producers who dare to 'swim against the tide'. [. . .] Some stores don't bother to carry organic alternatives, for example, there's a local Coop close to where I live, where they don't have organic yogurt. Then I get irritated at the entire store! (Woman, 35)

A second customer did not buy any meat products, having both ethical and resource-based objections against meat production. However, he did eat organic chicken, although it was difficult to find in the food stores. A third customer preferred locally produced over organic food, for example when choosing between organic tomatoes from Spain and Swedish tomatoes. She also believed that Swedish producers use less pesticide than foreign ones.

Altered Exchange Practices

The online shopping environment fosters specific buying behaviours based on different scripts (i.e. search through the 'organic shelf' or conventional categories, buy single items or pre-composed menus). This contributed to altered exchange practices both in terms of how and what to buy. For some customers it meant buying more organic products, for others actually less. One customer explained that she now spent only half an hour every week doing her shopping, sitting on the sofa with her laptop. Being more relaxed also made her more price focused: 'it's easier for me to see the price differences now'. Over time she learned that the search results appeared in a specific order, with the most expensive (often organic) products at the top and cheaper ones at the bottom. Her choice of products other than those first appearing on the screen illustrates that consumers can also refuse particular scripts.

At the time of the interviews, two customers still shopped at Cooponline. se while two shopped elsewhere. One of the remaining customers said he used the online and physical stores as complements, topping up in physical stores whatever he could not find online. To him, Cooponline.se had not changed his way of shopping very much, since he was already planning his purchases using weekly shopping lists. However, online shopping had saved him money since it reduced spontaneous purchases. He attributed this to being exposed to fewer offerings than in a physical store. To him, this was a positive effect related to the problem of over-consumption and waste.

Coordinating Exchanges with Other (Green) Food Practices

Food exchange practices are embedded in and affected by a larger set of practices that take place before and after the exchange. One former online customer said one good thing about shopping online had been that it forced them to plan what to eat in advance. Hence, they did not have to ask themselves 'what's for dinner?' every evening while not having the energy to do anything. However, the increased level of planning was not always for the better; changed plans sometimes meant eating somewhere else, leaving them with a surplus of food. Moreover, the ready-made basket of organic vegetables sometimes contained too much of particular vegetables. Hence, the use of specific scripts may sometimes clash with other aspects of everyday life, which in this case led the consumer to reject the script.

Other than simply buying organic products, green food practices can involve a whole different way of thinking about food, including local sourcing, cooking from scratch and reducing waste. These food practices may be motivated by both environmental and economic concerns. Moreover, they connect to concerns about production and use, which affect what and how much to buy. One of the interviewed customers disclosed that her attitude towards food differs from her partner's. She enjoys cooking dishes from scratch, for example using her grandmother's old recipes, and tries to take care of leftovers.

> My boyfriend has more of a 'use-and-throw-away' attitude to food. For example, he buys everything he needs for one dish, cooks it, eats it and then throws away what is left over. (Woman, 35)

Since the municipality where she lives does not offer facilities for handling compostable waste, it becomes even more important for her not to throw away food. This illustrates how some green food practices depend on individual competence (creative use of available food), but also on complementary practices performed by others (handling compostable waste).

Green Food Habits Through Online Food Shopping?

The online customers' reflections about their shopping allow us to further elaborate on the issues involved in producing 'green' through modified exchange practices. It seems that shopping organic food products online and getting them delivered by biogas-fuelled vehicles to your home indeed produces environmental values, as monitored by the customers. But we also note that the customers assess their modified exchange practices using several other standards besides green ones. Similarly to The Food Park case, practicality and convenience in relation to other practices come to the fore in these assessments.

'DOING GREEN' IN CONSUMPTION PRACTICES: COOKING 'CLIMATE CLEVER FOOD'

While food production and distribution have received considerable attention, the role of cooking practices in the transition towards a sustainable system of food provision has also been noted (Velasco, 2008; Videira et al., 2012). Since food preparation practices are likely to have consequences for the demand for food products (cf. Shove and Araujo, 2010), it is highly relevant to include them in an exploration of how consumers 'do green' in everyday food practices. Our third case attends to one explicit effort to educate consumers in more sustainable cooking practices.

Scripting Consumers' Food Practices

The Swedish Society for Nature Conservation (SSNC) is a non-profit NGO that works to preserve Swedish nature (SSNC, 2013). During recent years SSNC has especially acknowledged how food production and consumption contribute to climate change and environmental effects. It is currently developing consumer guides – 'the Green Guide' mobile app, information brochures and website – that provide suggestions on how to become a greener consumer. By empowering consumers, SSNC hopes to make environmental problems more visible, provide good alternatives in the market and inspire consumers to move from words to action (SSNC, 2013). The local Uppsala group of SSNC offered a study circle in the spring of 2013 to inspire its members toward more climate clever cooking: 'cook and eat tasty and climate clever food [. . . and] learn about different aspects of climate clever and environmentally friendly cooking.' (Excerpt from email announcing the study circle.)

Multiple Concerns in a Staged Use Environment

At our first meeting we gathered around the dining table in the home economics kitchen of a local school. The two circle leaders, both board members of SSNC in Uppsala, told us about why they decided to organize the study circle: the climate issue is acute and food plays an important part in it. They had decided to cook vegetarian dishes, since they regarded this as more climate-friendly, and also use as many organic ingredients as possible. In total seven women participated with varying backgrounds and ages, many with a particular interest in environmental and cultural issues. All of us like cooking and joined simply to get some inspiration, learn to cook new dishes and socialize. One woman brought along an exchange student from Italy. They had searched for a course about traditional Swedish cooking but had not found one, and settled on this instead.

The Practice of Climate Clever Cooking

We were served a number of recipes and pre-purchased ingredients, including beans, lentils, carrots, cabbage, lettuce, cold-yeasted bread and desserts based on apples and pears. To provide a cultural food exchange, we later included a traditional Swedish dish (without meat) – potato pancake with lingonberries – and a typical Italian dish that the exchange student introduced – mushroom risotto.

During the three cooking sessions we usually start with a general intro-duction to the recipes, team up in pairs and divide the work between us. We then go to the different kitchen units and try to follow the recipes using the available utensils. The circle leaders help out and answer practical questions such as 'is this the right amount of flour?' Meanwhile, someone sets the table and when the food is ready we sit down to eat (Figure 9.8).

During dinner we discuss what we are eating and its potential climate impact, for example: 'Is organic food necessarily climate friendly?' We

Figure 9.8   The dining table is set!

Figure 9.9   Green devices: milk carton with 'clipper' and a digital kitchen scale

also get advice on how to be more economic and climate friendly in the kitchen, for example by preserving leftovers, putting 'clippers' on milk and cream cartons and using digital scales to get the right amount of each ingredient (Figure 9.9).

After dinner we do the dishes and tidy up. For the first session our circle leader provides empty jars that we can borrow to bring home the leftovers. For the following sessions we are advised to bring our own jars.

Coordinating Cooking with Other (Green) Food Practices

Climate friendly cooking not only depends on the practices taking place in the kitchen, but is also to a large extent connected to the preceding steps in the food chain. The crux is how food in general is produced and transported. One discussion in the circle was about whether rice could ever be environmentally friendly, since the plants produce methane when they are grown in water. We also discussed how to actually measure and quantify if something is climate friendly. Someone suggested giving the various food products a 'plus' or 'minus' based on our intuition. Potatoes and carrots produced in Sweden would get pluses, as would all vegetables grown according to season, while rice and also salad would get minuses, even if organically produced.

As a way of provoking further reflections concerning green food practices, we took some time during the last dinner to discuss the five pieces of advice given in the small pamphlet called '5 ways to eat yourself environmentally clever', published by SSNC, which was given to us together with other climate friendly recipes (Figure 9.10).

Figure 9.10   SSNC pamphlets: 'Recipes for a better climate' and '5 ways to eat yourself environmentally clever'

1) *Indulge in green.* Enjoy a lot of vegetarian food – it is the most important thing you can do to eat environmentally clever. When you occasionally buy meat, organic is the best choice. Or Swedish meat based on uncultivated pasture, that is, meat from animals that have grazed in Swedish natural pastures.

The discussion here centred upon how food is transported, how much meat we eat compared to vegetables and whether it is better to eat frozen or fresh vegetables from a nourishment and waste perspective. One person recommended that we only eat vegetables that are in season, since fresh produce bought during the winter is often grown in energy-consuming greenhouses and/or transported long distances. But then we would not be able to eat any *green* food during the winter, or rely on frozen vegetables that also require energy for freezing. Moreover, fresh vegetables tend to go out-of-date quickly. If you live in a single household it can be difficult to use everything, unless you make lunch boxes for the whole week, as one participant often does.

2) *Switch to organic...* and you will contribute to cleaner water, happier animals, less harmful substances and allow more birds and flowers to flourish. In countries such as Brazil no rainforest needs to be desolated, nor will people get poisoned when they pick your bananas or harvest your coffee beans. In order for you to know that a food product is organic, it is enough that it says 'organic' on the package. Or else you can look for the 'EU-leaf' or 'KRAV' labels.

While many of us agreed it was important to buy organic, we also noted that it is a question of price and availability. As one of the circle leaders put it:

Even though more and more organic products become available, the assortment is still limited and often darn expensive! I was about to buy a couple of orange peppers that I first thought cost 31.90 SEK per kilo, but then I realized the price was per piece. Then I got non-organic ones instead. The question is what it's worth? (Study circle leader)

The study circle leader also asserted that since organic food is produced without pesticides, it would at least keep us from getting *that* on our plates. According to her, organic food also tastes better for some reason she cannot explain.

3) *Smell and taste.* Crazily enough a whole lot of food goes straight into the bin. Plan your purchases and trust your senses more than the 'best-before-date'.

Many of us know that if stored correctly, food products like eggs and milk often last longer than the 'best-before-date'. Besides tasting the food before throwing it away, it is a question of not buying more than you need. One of us admitted that it is easy to fall for special offers like 'Buy 3 for 2!' Another participant thought that people throw away food because it is so cheap. She claimed that she never threw away food, especially after having started to plan every meal in her family on a weekly basis before doing the shopping.

4) *Choose fine fish.* Most of our seas are so heavily fished that our most common food, fish, is about to disappear. Farmed fish is, however, not the solution because fish feed contains a lot of – exactly – fish. So, when you occasionally enjoy a piece of fish, look for these labels: 'KRAV' or 'MSC – Marine Stewardship Council'.

Here we discussed the difficulty of knowing whether eating particular kinds of fish is sustainable or not and also various health issues. One participant has a newspaper clipping on her refrigerator door listing fish that are OK to eat from a sustainable perspective. However, fish stocks around the world change and the lists published by WWF and SSNC are often updated (and sometimes conflict), making it difficult to keep track of things.

From a health perspective we are often recommended to eat fish at least twice a week, particularly fatty fish containing omega-3, such as salmon and Baltic herring. However, these fish also contain various harmful substances, making them unsuitable to eat especially for women of reproductive age. We speculated that farmed fish might be better to eat, but then fish farms contribute to the eutrophication of our seas. We also discussed whether it is better to eat fresh rather than frozen fish, since frozen fish is often transported long distances for packing and then back again for sale.

> 5) *Shop with your muscles.* Your car trip to the food store is likely to be a larger pollutant than your favourite food from the other side of the world. Try to shop without the car from time to time. Carry the food in a *dramaten* [shopping bag on wheels], on the bicycle, or in your arms instead!

Since we all live fairly close to grocery stores many of us already follow this recommendation, even if we occasionally use our cars for a 'weekly shopping'. One participant always walks to the store, using a backpack to carry the food, while another shops on the way home from work riding her bicycle. One of the circle leaders admitted to buying most of the ingredients for the study circle at a large hypermarket (by car), but had today walked to a nearby store using her *dramaten*.

> Yes, I have a *dramaten* since I refuse to destroy my back carrying food. Then I have to put up with looking ridiculous and old-fashioned, but so what! [. . .] Once, however, I tried to squeeze a large pack of toilet paper into it, but I simply didn't succeed. I really wanted to get it in there, but no. It drove me mad! (Study circle leader)

Climate Clever Cooking?

What constitutes climate clever cooking? The experiences from the study circle suggest that there are many ways of becoming more climate clever when cooking. Modifying the resources used is one way of producing environmental values along with your food. This is also quite easily monitored due to the abundance of labels that provide simple ways of keeping track. But as we noted during our discussions, such labels do not guarantee the production of *intensely* green meals. There are always trade-offs to be made, even within what passes as green, for instance between green production and green transportation. Using more vegetables when cooking, whether organically labelled or not, can also be a way of doing green, but offers no guarantee. The amount of energy required for producing and transporting a tomato to a Swedish home varies considerably throughout the year. Reducing waste contributes to 'doing green' even if the dish is not very green itself. The complexity involved in knowing the greenness of what we eat quickly becomes difficult to handle, so we develop various shortcuts to cope.

DOING GREEN: REALIZING ENVIRONMENTAL VALUES IN EVERYDAY FOOD PRACTICES

What are the challenges of realizing green values in everyday food practices? Below, we address each of the four heuristic questions posed earlier in the chapter in the light of our cases.

What Values and Concerns Fuel Green Food Practices?

The cases all suggest several values and associated concerns that fuel the engagements in green food practices. Rather than listing specific values, we present two themes that emerged in response to this question and that run across the cases: (i) the *multiplicity* of values and concerns that fuel actor engagements; and (ii) the resulting need to *balance* such concerns.

Actors in all cases evoke a *multiplicity* of values and concerns in relation to the practices they engage in. The founders of The Food Park express a concern for a lack of knowledge about sustainable food production. Participants in the study circle echo the gap between current and desired knowledge, but also voice other concerns, such as efficiency in production in addition to creating a contrast to hectic city life. In the Cooponline.se case, KF explicitly recognizes a business objective behind its efforts: seeking to attract parents with young children as customers. Since they believe this group to care about health, quality and the environment, these values are emphasized. But the emphasis is tempered by the belief that customers would be sceptical about an offering perceived to limit their choice. The customers, on their part, express a variety of concerns fuelling their engagements, for example saving time and promoting small-scale production. In the third case, the SSNC representatives convey a clear concern fuelling their initiative: how to reduce the climate impact of food consumption. But they also acknowledge thrift as a concern: how to economize on daily food practices. The participants express entirely different concerns, for example how to introduce variety in their everyday cooking and how to teach Swedish cooking to a foreigner.

The second emerging theme is how these multiple concerns can be *balanced* in the performance of a practice; sometimes multiple concerns do not add up in any simple way. In The Food Park, the founders emphasize the need to strike a balance between growing in tune with nature and making things manageable when growing your own food. This was nicely illustrated by the decision to procure the service of a tractor to plough the field. In the case of Cooponline.se, KF explicitly identified the need to balance between creating economic benefits and contributing to a sustainable development. One customer also acknowledged a trade-off between local and ecological production, favouring the former. In the cooking circle, finally, we noted clashes between economy and ecology, as well as between traditional Swedish and climate friendly cooking practices. We will return to this issue when discussing the monitoring of practices, below.

How do Efforts to Script Practices Contribute to Realizing Green Values?

All three cases provide examples of efforts undertaken by other actors to script consumers' everyday food practices. Specifically, they illustrate how *change agents* seek to (i) provide new or altered *scripts*, and (ii) adjust *situations* to better fit particular scripts.

A first example of a script provided for practitioners is that of organic farming. Cultivating in The Food Park not only requires attention to general agricultural *scripts* (for example preparing the soil and watering the plants), but its organic profile also includes crop rotation and bans against artificial fertilizers and pesticides. Beyond this, the whole idea of the study circle is to *script practitioners*; to provide them with skills and competences for engaging in practices that they are unfamiliar with. In the online food store, there is relatively less emphasis on scripting practitioners, although customers need to follow the script for online shopping and are encouraged to plan their purchases in advance. In the third case, the purpose is once again to script practitioners; teaching them how to prepare food that causes less strain on the environment, as illustrated by the folders containing tips towards climate clever food.

The cases also illustrate that scripting efforts do not necessarily target practitioners. The Food Park case provides several examples of efforts to 'set the stage' for vegetable production in line with particular scripts, for example having the tractor plough the field allowed the study circle to focus on other issues. The attention paid to the *situational infrastructure*, specifically the exchange environment, is even more pronounced in the Cooponline.se case. The design of the online shop is part of, and adjusted to, a detailed script for buying food online. For example, specific adjustments include the shortcut to display all organic products. Further, and related to the effort to script practitioners to plan in advance, the store also offers a script for those who fail to plan: the possibility to order a pre-composed basket of food, complete with matching recipes. In the cooking case, there is less emphasis on scripting the environment, although the use of particular *devices*, such as clippers to close packages, is encouraged.

How does the Realization of Green Values Depend on and Influence Other Practices?

Our third question focuses on the performance and coordination of specific practices. A first observation here concerns the need to successfully *bracket* other unfolding events. Some food practices pose relatively strict requirements on practitioners, for example to successfully grow your own vegetables you need to water your seedlings; other things cannot be allowed to interrupt. Similarly, to have Cooponline.se deliver the next day, you need to place your order before midnight. Other practices are more tolerant of disruptions, for example some of the produce from The Food Park stores well.

A second and related observation is that changing a particular practice can have *reverberating effects*, creating a need to alter other practices. If you engage in urban gardening, leaving the city for five weeks in the summer poses problems. But you can develop makeshift solutions, like distributing responsibilities according to a set schedule (a form of bracketing). In the Cooponline.se case, some customers noted that moving from traditional to online shopping required an increased level of planning, while others felt it reduced flexibility. To some extent, the reverberating effects also depend on the available infrastructure. One online customer felt a strong need to manage leftovers and reduce waste since the municipality did not offer facilities for compostable waste. In the cooking circle, it was noted that the use of fresh vegetables required planning and scheduling of cooking to avoid waste.

A third theme emerging from the cases concerns the reliance on different *modes of coordination*. Engaging in urban agriculture did not mean that participants stopped using the market. First, rather than doing away with market exchanges it shifted engagements towards buying other things. Thus, Food Park participants still procure a variety of goods and services, including ploughing service, seeds, tools and so on. Second, to the extent that their production efforts result in food, this is a complement rather than a substitute for buying food. Third, the need to coordinate production and consumption practices cannot be wished away as illustrated by the storage predicaments caused by the rich harvest.[4] One of the participants handled this by evoking other modes of coordination, including gift giving and barter trade.

How is the Realization of Green Values Established?

Our final question concerns how and by whom the realization of green values is monitored. First, when formal organizations engage, *formalized monitoring* ensues. Thus, the association responsible for The Food Park accounts for its achievements in an annual report to its members and through its webpage, for example number of active participants, specific activities undertaken and so on. Cooponline.se, which is run by a much larger organization, also relies on formal monitoring of greenness. The participants in the cooking circle explicitly discussed the challenges of such formalized monitoring: how do you measure if something is climate friendly?

This leads to our second observation, namely that greenness is not enacted as a binary category. As our cases illustrate, everyday food practice involves several interrelated production, exchange and consumption practices, each of which may be performed as more or less green. The combined effect is food practices in varying shades of green, so to speak. While the practitioners are reflective about the trade-offs between different indicators of greenness, they also acknowledge the difficulties of finding workable ways of assessing the overall environmental consequences of their food practices.

Here, *informal procedures* for monitoring value production become important. Participants in The Food Park study circle reflected on the values produced using different standards, for example 'when I bike home [after harvesting] I feel rich'. The use of *multiple standards* to assess outcomes was also evident among the online customers where freedom of choice, time and money spent, amount of waste and increased foresight all figured as standards for evaluation. Here, the use of *rules of thumb* to create monitoring shortcuts also surfaced, for example choosing small-scale organic farmers. Other examples were provided in the cooking circle, for example vegetarian food as a shortcut for green cooking. We also saw how other actors seek to introduce and promote such shortcuts as part of their scripting efforts, for example SSNC's recommendation of various eco-labels as means towards greener cooking.

This takes us back to the issue of *balancing values*. Rules of thumb save time and help you cope with daily activities, but also involve compromises in the realization of values. They introduce biases that may reduce the value produced if assessed against a more comprehensive set of criteria, for example when a locally produced product involves the use of much energy and pesticides. Conversely, their use may be essential to sustain practitioners' efforts to 'do green'; they offer a way of balancing green and other concerns that fuel our everyday life. Multiple concerns do not always require trade-offs, however. In some cases, different concerns align well in everyday practice. The concern for reducing waste, voiced by one online customer, aligned nicely with a concern for thrift. Similarly, the increased planning resulting from shopping online produced several values, for example reduced stress, costs and waste.

CONCLUDING REMARKS

Our exploration of three cases in which consumers explicitly – but not exclusively – sought to realize green values in food practices has underscored the interconnected character of such efforts. First, our analysis suggested that consumer engagements tend to be fuelled by multiple concerns, which result in a need to balance different values, some of which are environmental. Second, other actors play an important part in consumers' realization of environmental values, both by providing scripts for and by adjusting situations to 'doing green'. Third, the introduction of green concerns into everyday food practices has consequences for other practices in which consumers engage, requiring either careful bracketing or complementary changes. Notably, however, 'doing green' did not appear to reduce the extent to which consumers relied on market exchanges, but rather meant that they engaged in modified such exchanges (in terms of format or content). Fourth, the cases illustrated the role of both formal and informal monitoring procedures in the realization of green values. Specifically, they highlighted the centrality of convenience/practicality as an informal standard against which consumers assessed food-related practices. As such, the cases underscored the need to further question how the realization of environmental values is monitored and assessed, and how different standards can be aligned to ease the practical transition to greener food provision.

While reliance on market exchange is not the only way to bridge production and consumption, our cases indicate that it remains important also when other forms of bridging are attempted. There are good reasons for this, most notably the ability of markets to coordinate practices in ways that balance values, for example efficiency in production with variety in consumption. This allows practitioners to escape difficult trade-offs concerning which practices to engage in or which values to realize. That said, markets could be organized to produce many different values, both good and bad (Neyland and Simakova, 2010). Moreover, the standards for evaluating their outputs can change (Reijonen, 2008). This makes it particularly important to entertain concerns about the relative values produced by engagements in production, exchange and consumption practices, respectively. While consumers are typically held accountable for their engagements only in specific dimensions, those dimensions are not fixed, but depend on our collective efforts to establish standards and procedures for assessing and reflecting on the consequences of our everyday practices.

NOTES

1. We are grateful to Debbie Harrison and two anonymous reviewers for valuable comments on earlier versions of this chapter. We would also like to thank the participants in the different case studies who willingly shared their time and thoughts.
2. As noted above, such labels are often misleading from a practice perspective (de Certeau, 1984).
3. KF is a federation of consumer cooperative societies with more than 3 million members (KF, 2013a). It owns several retail companies and operates one of the major Swedish food chains. KF's core values are basically unchanged since its formation in 1899: member owned, innovative, care for humans and the environment, influence and honesty. KF's mission is 'to create economic benefit and [. . .] enable our members to [. . .] contribute to a sustainable development for humans and the environment' (KF, 2013b).
4. Compare the classic observations regarding the functions of middlemen (Alderson, 1967).

REFERENCES

Akrich, Madeleine (1992), 'The de-scription of technical objects', in Wiebe E. Bijker and John Law (eds), *Shaping Technology/Building Society* (Cambridge, MA: MIT Press), 205–24.
Alderson, Wroe (1967), 'Factors governing the development of marketing channels', in Bruce E. Mallen (ed.), *The Marketing Channel: A Conceptual Viewpoint* (New York: John Wiley & Sons), 35–40.
Araujo, Luis and Hans Kjellberg (2009), 'Shaping exchanges, performing markets: The study of marketing practices', in Pauline Maclaran et al. (eds), *Handbook of Marketing Theory* (London: Sage Publications), 195–218.
Araujo, Luis and Martin Spring (2006), 'Services, products, and the institutional structure of production', *Industrial Marketing Management*, Vol. 35, pp. 797–805.
Belz, Frank-Martin (2004), 'A transition towards sustainability in the Swiss agri-food chain (1970–2000): Using and improving the multi-level perspective', in Boelie Elzen, Frank W. Geels and Ken Green (eds), *System Innovation and the Transition to Sustainability* (Cheltenham, UK and Northampton, MA, USA: Edward Elgar Publishing), 97–113.
Burr, Thomas Cameron (2013), 'Market-widening: Shaping total market demand for French and American bicycles circa 1890', *Marketing Theory*, Vol. 14, No. 1, pp. 19–34.
Callon, Michel (1986), 'Some elements of a sociology of translation: Domestication of the scallops and the Fishermen of St-Brieuc Bay', in John Law (ed.), *Power, Action and Belief: a New Sociology of Knowledge* (Sociological Review Monograph; London: Routledge & Kegan Paul), 196–233.
Callon, Michel (1998), 'An essay on framing and overflowing: Economic externalities revisited by sociology', in Michel Callon (ed.), *The Laws of the Markets* (Oxford: Blackwell Publishers and *The Sociological Review*), 244–69.
Callon, Michel (2007), 'What does it mean to say that economics is performative?', in Donald MacKenzie, Fabian Muniesa and Luca Siu (eds), *Do Economists Make Markets? On the Performativity of Economics* (Princeton, NJ: Princeton University Press), 311–57.

Callon, Michel, Cécile Méadel and Vololona Rabeharisoa (2002), 'The economy of qualities', *Economy and Society*, Vol. 31, No. 2, pp. 194–217.

Conolly, John and Andrea Prothero (2008), 'Green consumption: Life-politics, risk and contradictions', *Journal of Consumer Culture*, Vol. 8, No. 1, pp. 117–45.

de Certeau, Michel (1984), *The Practice of Everyday Life*, trans. Steven Rendall (Berkeley: University of California Press) xxiv, 229.

Delshammar, Tim (2011), 'Urban odling i Malmö', Stad och Land (181; Alnarp: Movium, Centrum för stadens utemiljö, Swedish University of Agricultural Sciences (SLU).

Dubois, Anna and Luis Araujo (2007), 'Case research in purchasing and supply management: Opportunities and challenges', *Journal of Purchasing & Supply Management*, Vol. 13, pp. 170–81.

Ellis, Carolyn, Tony E. Adams and Arthur P. Bochner (2011), 'Autoethnography: An Overview', *Historical Social Research*, Vol. 36, No. 4, pp. 273–90.

Finch, John H. and Virginia L. Acha (2008), 'Making and exchanging a second-hand oil field, considered in an industrial marketing setting', *Marketing Theory*, Vol. 8, No. 1, pp. 45–66.

Goffman, Erving (1974), *Frame Analysis: An Essay on the Organization of Experience* (New York: Harper & Row).

Halkier, Bente (2001), 'Consuming ambivalences: Consumer handling of environmentally related risks in food', *Journal of Consumer Culture*, Vol. 1, No. 2, pp. 205–24.

Halkier, Bente (2009), 'A practice theoretical perspective on everyday dealings with environmental challenges of food consumption', *Anthropology of Food*, available at: http://aof.revues.org/6405, accessed 19 June 2014.

Halkier, Bente (2010), *Consumption Challenged. Food in Medialised Everyday Lives* (Farnham: Ashgate Publishing Ltd).

Halkier, Bente and Iben Jensen (2011), 'Methodological challenges in using practice theory in consumption research. Examples from a study on handling nutritional contestations of food consumption', *Journal of Consumer Culture*, Vol. 11, No. 1, pp. 101–23.

IPCC Working group 1 (2013), 'Climate Change 2013: The physical science basis. Summary for policymakers', (Stockholm: Intergovernmental Panel on Climate Change).

Jones, Peter, Daphne Comfort and David Hillier (2008), 'Moving towards sustainable food retailing?', *International Journal of Retail & Distribution Management*, Vol. 36, No. 12, pp. 995–1001.

KF (2013a), 'About KF', available at: http://www.coop.se/Globala-sidor/In-english/, accessed 18 April 2013.

KF (2013b), 'Our values', available at: http://www.coop.se/Globala-sidor/OmKF/Kooperativ-samverkan/Vara-varderingar/, accessed 18 April 2013.

Kjellberg, Hans and Claes-Fredrik Helgesson (2007), 'The mode of exchange and shaping of markets: Distributor influence on the Swedish post-war food industry', *Industrial Marketing Management*, Vol. 36, No. 7, pp. 861–78.

Kjellberg, Hans and Claes-Fredrik Helgesson (2010), 'Political marketing: Multiple values, performativities and modes of engaging', *Journal of Cultural Economy*, Vol. 3, No. 2, pp. 279–97.

Kline, Stephen (2011), 'Book reviews, Bente Halkier, Consumption Challenged: Food in Medialised Everyday Lives', *Journal of Consumer Culture*, Vol. 11, No. 3, pp. 385–87.

Klintman, Mikael and Magnus Boström (2012), 'Political consumerism and the transition towards a more sustainable food regime: Looking behind and beyond the organic shelf', in Gert Spaargaren, Peter Oosterveer and Anne Loeber (eds), *Food Practices in Transition* (New York: Routledge).

Larsson, Maria (2009), 'Stadsdelsträdgård. Plats för gemenskap och kreativa processer', (Swedish University of Agricultural Sciences).

Latour, Bruno (1986), 'The powers of association', in John Law (ed.), *Power, Action and Belief: A New Sociology of Knowledge* (London: Routledge & Kegan Paul), 264–80.

Latour, Bruno (1987), *Science in Action: How to Follow Scientists and Engineers Through Society* (Cambridge, MA: Harvard University Press).

Latour, Bruno (1994), 'On technical mediation – philosophy, sociology, genealogy', *Common Knowledge*, Vol. 3, No. 2, pp. 29–64.

Latour, Bruno (2005), *Reassembling the Social. An Introduction to Actor-Network-Theory* (Clarendon Lectures in Management Studies; Oxford: Oxford University Press).

Law, John and John Urry (2004), 'Enacting the social', *Economy and Society*, Vol. 33, No. 3, pp. 390–410.

Magnusson, M. et al. (2001), 'Attitudes towards organic foods among Swedish consumers', *British Food Journal*, Vol. 103, No. 3, pp. 209–26.

Mallard, Alexandre (1998), 'Compare, standardize and settle agreement: On some usual metrological problems', *Social Studies of Science*, Vol. 28, No. 4, pp. 571–601.

Matparken (The Food Park) (2013), 'Statutes of the non-profit organization Matparken', available at: http://matparken.se/index.php/component/content/article/8-matparken-1/20-stadgar-matparken-ideell-foerening, accessed 15 April 2013.

Micheletti, M. and Isenhour, C. (2010), 'Political consumerism', in K. Ekström (ed.), *Consumer Behaviour, A Nordic Perspective* (Lund: Studentlitteratur).

Naturvårdsverket (2008), 'Konsumtionens klimatpåverkan', (Stockholm: Naturvårdsverket).

Neyland, Daniel and Elena Simakova (2010), 'Trading bads and goods: Market practices in fair trade', in Luis Araujo, John H. Finch and Hans Kjellberg (eds), *Reconnecting Marketing to Markets* (Oxford: Oxford University Press).

Nicolini, Davide (2009), 'Articulating practice through the interview to the double', *Management Learning*, Vol. 40, No. 2, pp. 195–212.

Östberg, Jacob (2003), 'What's eating the eater? Perspectives on the everyday anxiety of food consumption in late modernity', doctoral thesis (Lund University).

Padel, Susanne and Carolyn Foster (2005), 'Exploring the gap between attitudes and behaviour: Understanding why consumers buy or do not buy organic food', *British Food Journal*, Vol. 107, No. 8, pp. 606–25.

Queiroz, M (2009), 'Urban agriculture/agricultural urbanity. Om stadsodling, urban och peri-urban agrikultur, för en mindre klimatbelastande och energikrävande matproduktion', (Swedish University of Agricultural Sciences (SLU)).

Ragin, Charles C. (1992), '"Casing" and the process of social inquiry', in Charles C. Ragin and Howard S. Becker (eds), *What is a Case? Exploring the Foundations of Social Inquiry* (Cambridge: Cambridge University Press), 217–26.

Reckwitz, Andreas (2002), 'Toward a theory of social practices: A development in culturalist theorizing', *European Journal of Social Theory*, Vol. 5, No. 2, pp. 243–63.

Reijonen, Satu (2008), *Green and Fragile. A Study on Markets and the Natural Environment* (Copenhagen Business School).

Schatzki, Theodore R. (1996), *Social Practices: A Wittgensteinian Approach to Human Activity and the Social* (Cambridge: Cambridge University Press).

Shove, Elizabeth and Luis Araujo (2010), 'Consumption, materiality, and markets', in Luis Araujo, John H. Finch and Hans Kjellberg (eds), *Reconnecting Marketing to Markets* (Oxford: Oxford University Press), 13–28.

Shove, Elizabeth and Mika Pantzar (2005), 'Consumers, producers and practices: Understanding the invention and reinvention of Nordic walking', *Journal of Consumer Culture*, Vol. 5, No. 1, pp. 43–64.

Sjögren, Ebba and Claes-Fredrik Helgesson (2007), 'The Q(u)ALYfying hand: Health economics and medicine in the shaping of Swedish markets for subsidised pharmaceuticals', in Michel Callon, Yuval Millo and Fabian Muniesa (eds), *Market Devices* (Oxford: Blackwell), 215–40.

Smit, Jac and Joe Nasr (1992), 'Urban agriculture for sustainable cities: Using wastes and idle land and water bodies as resources', *Environment and Urbanization*, Vol. 4, No. 2, pp. 141–52.

SSNC (2013), 'About us', available at: http://www.naturskyddsforeningen.se/om/om-oss, accessed 2 May 2013.

Thévenot, Laurent (2002), 'Which road to follow? The moral complexity of an equipped humanity', in John Law and Annemarie Mol (eds), *Complexities: Social Studies of Knowledge Practices* (Durham and London: Duke University Press), 53–87.

Thompson, C.J. (2011), 'Understanding consumption as political and moral practice: Introduction to the special issue', *Journal of Consumer Culture*, Vol. 11, No. 2, pp. 139–44.

Toffler, Alvin (1980), *The Third Wave* (New York: Bantam Books).

Vargo, Stephen L. and Melissa Akaka (2012), 'Value cocreation and service systems (re)formation: A service ecosystems view', *Service Science*, Vol. 4, No. 3, pp. 207–17.

Vargo, Stephen L. and Robert F. Lusch (2012), 'The nature and understanding of value: A service-dominant logic perspective', in Stephen L. Vargo and Robert F. Lusch (eds), *Special Issue: Toward a Better Understanding of the Role of Value in Markets and Marketing* (*Review of Marketing Research*, Vol. 9: Emerald Group Publishing), 1–12.

Vargo, Stephen L., Paul P. Maglio and Melissa Archpru Akaka (2008), 'On value and value co-creation: A service systems and service logic perspective', *European Management Journal*, Vol. 26, pp. 145–52.

Velasco, Ignacio (2008), 'More sustainable cooking technologies: A case study in rural kitchens in Michoacan, Mexico' (Lund University).

Videira, Nuno et al. (2012), 'Background paper on sustainable food consumption and growth', 1st multinational knowledge brokerage event on Sustainable Food Consumption (Lisbon).

Warde, Alan (2005), 'Consumption and theories of practice', *Journal of Consumer Culture*, Vol. 5, No. 2, pp. 131–53.

10. Concerned markets: facing the future, beyond 'interested' and 'contested' markets

Franck Cochoy

Let's start from a self-evident truth: talking about 'concerned markets' necessarily amounts to proposing a new type of market. Doing so reminds us that, since Adam Smith, the market has been the subject of a strong tension between its singular and plural forms. Economics worked hard to define the market as a unique, homogeneous, nature-like entity (Latour, 2014). But since then social scientists, marketing scholars and ordinary actors have never ceased to insist on the plural dimension of real markets, that is 'marketplaces' as local, empirical spaces and interfaces where goods and services can be exchanged for a payment. On the one (invisible!) hand, we have 'The market', as a universal, ahistorical and abstract exchange mechanism; on the other (visible (Chandler, 1977)!) hand(s) we have several markets, innumerable markets, too many markets for them to be named (industrial and consumer markets; markets for cars (Kjellberg, 2012), markets for love (Kessous, 2012), markets for. . . everything).

However, and as this book nicely demonstrates, concerned markets are much more than just another type to be added to the list. Contrary to all the other forms of markets, concerned markets are defined neither by a particular type of good or service nor by the refusal of the market institution; concerned markets rather point to all kinds of markets and the concerns which may arise from them or about them. Indeed, talking about concerned markets first evidences a strong concern for the market itself and markets themselves, for what they are, for what they do, for what they should be, for what they should do and for how they could be transformed to do so. I would say that concerned markets emerge each time there is a concern about or inside markets. In this respect, and as I will show, one would understand the contribution of this book better by defining 'concerned markets' as a third form of market which stems from the opposition between what I would call the 'interested market' and what Philippe

Steiner and his colleagues recently named 'contested markets' (Steiner and Trespeuch, 2013; Steiner, 2014).

CONCERNED MARKETS: AN OUTCOME OF THE OPPOSITION BETWEEN THE INTERESTED MARKET AND CONTESTED MARKETS

The Interested Market

The 'interested market' is built on the economic motive of human self-interest. Adam Smith and the liberal tradition described the market as a mechanism governing human conduct much like the laws of physics. Seen in this light, one understands better the positivist view of economics, with its mathematical modelling approach and representation of economic matters as 'matters of fact' rather than 'matters of concern' (Latour, 2014).

However, it should not be forgotten that the same interested market is inherently concerned, at least in its beginnings. As Albert Hirschman (1977) brilliantly showed, economic science is nothing but the answer to a political concern: the market was conceived as an emancipatory and even revolutionary tool, as a way of escaping the Old Regime's absolutism and arbitrariness. Conceiving economic conduct as governed by natural laws was a means towards reducing political domination over the economy.

The concern about the evils of the Old Regime was fuelled by the concern for other values, like freedom, individual success and entrepreneurship: the 'market world' is an 'order of worth' in itself, as Boltanski and Thévenot (2006) demonstrated. Smith's genius was to propose that, by converting dangerous human passions into the single motive of economic self-interest, and by showing that self-interest is oriented toward things rather than people, social order could be preserved and the common good attained without resorting to the old schemes of religious and State controls. Hence, we should not forget that 'liberty' is at the core of 'liberalism': the 'objective' interested market was constructed as a weapon for freeing individuals from political constraint. To establish such freedom, Smith invented the radical demarcation between economic facts and political concerns; 'A self-regulating market demands nothing less than the institutional separation of society into an economic and political sphere' (Polanyi, 2001, p. 71). Along such a view, the distinction between 'nature-like economics' and 'human politics' is just a particular avatar, adapted to social issues, of the separation between science and politics so well described by Bruno Latour in *We Have Never Been Modern* (1993).

Contested Markets

We all know what happened. The project of realizing this 'interested market utopia' was implemented and, as for any utopia, the implementation failed to fulfil the utopian promises. The market idea faced a series of fragmentation, hybridization and contradiction processes.

The realization of the market idea gave rise to a multiplicity of markets rather than a single one. This multiplicity rests on the hybridization between the global market ideals and local constraints, which rather defined each enactment of the market system as a special combination (or *agencement* (Callon et al., 2013)) of economic, social and political resources. Latour (1993) showed that the modernist official separation between nature and culture favoured the backstage proliferation of hybrids combining the two, such as AIDS, GMOs and so on.

Economic matters did not escape this hybridization. Under the large umbrella of the market economy, 'free' markets have been endlessly framed, controlled, ruled, designed: any market object is 'hand-made' but not by one, two or even three hands, but by at least four. That is, the single invisible hand of the market mechanism (of course), but also the visible hand of the State, the visible hands of managers and the visible hands of market mediators (marketers, advertisers, standardizers and so on). This inescapable hybridization process raised a series of equally inescapable contradictions: the game of freedom built an iron cage where free market individuals were eventually trapped (Weber, 1997 [1905]); the competitive game led successful market entrepreneurs to grow into corporate giants (Chandler, 1977). In the end, big capitalism emerged as the perverse effect of liberalism.

The 'interested market' also gave rise to 'contested markets', a notion recently proposed by Philippe Steiner and Marie Trespeuch (2013; see also Steiner, 2014). The authors define contested markets as 'markets where the products bought and sold are morally contested', such as the markets for child adoption, human organs, funeral services, prostitution, GMOs, money games and so on. (To a certain extent the market for education addressed by Guus Dix in the present book is a good candidate for joining this category; see below.)

If I might rely on a French pun, I would say that the proponents of contested markets are also concerned, if by concerned ('concernés') we mean dismayed ('consternés'). That is, these scholars express a concern 'about' markets; for the values they convey, for their legitimacy and moreover for their social and moral effects, beyond that of market theory and ideology. They distinguish two specific worlds, the social and the economic, and they worry about the colonization of the first by the second. It seems to me that this stream of thought may be regarded as a legacy of the Polanyian tradition, with its legitimate concern (in the sense of 'worry') for marketization and commoditization processes and their consequences. Like the critics of modernism (Latour, 1993), Polanyi revealed the fallacy of the separation between natural markets and human politics. He showed that markets, far from being the natural phenomena economics portray, were actively constructed by the very State they were supposed to oppose. More importantly, Polanyi showed how markets colonized social life, by 'marketizing' commodities such as land, money and labour (that is 'human beings themselves' in Polanyi's terms (Polanyi, 2001, p. 71)), and provoked a series of social disasters, like the weakening of social ties, the exploitation of labour and so on. In the same vein, the analysts of contested markets focus on the dangers of extending markets to commodities such as drugs, pornography or money games. In particular they focus on the impact of such marketization processes on 'fragile populations', such as the children who may encounter alcohol or pornographic movies, or the non-smokers exposed to the smoke of others' cigarettes (Steiner, 2014).

Concerned Markets

The opposition between 'the interested market' and 'contested markets' calls for a reassessment of what the market is, or rather what markets are. It is such a reassessment that the present book, with its focus on 'concerned markets', proposes.

I tend to see matters of 'concerned markets' as a relevant, thoughtful and helpful outcome of two ideas, one from Bruno Latour and the other from Michel Callon. Latour first introduced the distinction between 'matters of fact' and 'matters of concern' in order to propose a new way to look at 'things' (that is entities which combine objective and moral dimensions). For Latour (2004), the unquestioned 'facts' of science can (and even should) be discussed not because of their 'social' or 'constructed' character, but because of the concerns they embody and raise at the same time. For example, issues such as global warming or the proliferation of GMOs are both matters of fact and matters of concern.

Callon developed a similar reasoning for economic matters. First, in focusing on the performative rather than constative aspect of science, Callon encouraged economic sociologists to leave the somewhat unproductive debate about the truthfulness of economic theories (the economy as 'matter of fact') and instead to concentrate the discussion on their social effects (the economy as 'matter of concern') (Callon, 1998a). Second, and in line with this point of view, Callon suggested that economics is better judged on the moral value of what it produces than on the accuracy of its descriptions. Based on this idea, he invited us to examine what kind of market *agencements* could take care of the populations which are the stakeholders or the leftovers of contemporary market games – what he calls 'concerned groups' (Callon et al., 2009) or 'orphan groups' (Callon, 2007).

Thinking in terms of 'concerned markets' is a means to go further, because the notion helps in acknowledging the inescapability of markets, and more importantly proposes a way of dealing with it. Markets are inescapable not only because the refusal of contested markets leads to the emergence of their clandestine equivalent (Steiner, 2014), but also because concerns are *inside* rather than outside markets. As this book's introduction states clearly and relevantly, the distinction between the social and economic worlds is blurred; nothing in the present world is purely social or economic, and any market entity presents itself as a hybrid form which combines matters of fact and matters of concern, a state of affairs acknowledged by Philippe Steiner, who nicely talks about the 'intricacy of morality and exchange within [market] devices'.

Linus Johansson Krafve's chapter in this volume gives an excellent example of such intricacy: the voucher system whereby any patient may pay for the services of their choice among publicly authorized care providers is a clear combination of the market choice system and the public concern for 'neutral', universally accessible and State controlled healthcare services. But if markets are inescapably hybrid entities, we should admit that 'caring' about them (being concerned) is more appropriate than 'contesting' them.

Similarly, if any market entity combines matters of fact and matters of concern, the central challenge is not how to contest markets, tracing the unfindable border between market and non-market spheres or designing alternatives; instead it is to find the proper combination of elements, that is the right 'market *agencement*', to cater to the various concerns that are being raised (Callon et al., 2013). In the remaining pages of this chapter I would like to stress how the different chapters of the book address such issues.

MARKETING AS CREATING AND MANAGING CONCERNS

First, several contributions clearly show that the enactment of a plurality of concerns in market settings consists in shifting matters of fact – products 'as they are' – into matters of concern – products as what they should or should not be; in many cases, 'goods' should be better named as 'bads'

(Neyland and Simakova, 2010; Latour, 2014)! Enacting matters of concern in a market is about 'heating' the cold, unquestioned, taken-for-granted market objects (what Callon et al. (2002) call 'goods') into hot, debated, uncertain market entities (what the same authors call 'products'). As noted in the introduction of the book, this heating process is not the monopoly of critique; it does not come from the outside of markets only; rather, it often emerges from within the market itself, either because market actors know all the benefits they may gain from the 'digestion' of critique (Boltanski and Chiapello, 2007), or because they find an immediate interest in raising concerns.

The latter case is best illustrated by Frank Azimont and Luis Araujo's chapter on the production and marketization of functional foods, that is 'foods which claim a specified benefit'. What the authors' fascinating account illustrates is that producing and selling such foods rests on a double process of first heating up, then cooling down the market objects. The foods are heated up, in the sense that marketers work hard to raise a concern for health beyond the unquestioned matter of fact of nutrition. The factual aspect of foods is thus reopened; the plain character of each product is questioned; a scientific inquiry is conducted about what components could be added, removed or transformed to increase the healthy character of food. But after having been heated up and redefined, the product is once again 'cooled' down in order to transform the new matter of concern (health) into a matter of fact (healthy food). By means of 'investments in form' (Thévenot, 1984), in the present case relating to the implementation of a mix of scientific studies and marketing campaigns, the company builds 'credibility' around the rhetoric of 'proven positive effects'.

All in all, the development of 'medical marketing' appears as an excellent example of how social concerns can be incorporated into objects and discourses in order to be industrialized, commoditized and marketed. Azimont and Araujo thus convincingly show that concerns are a way to create new markets. If healthy food is one good example of such process, other cases abound, for example Jürgen Hauber and Chantal Ruppert-Winkel's chapter about the market for maize as a source of energy, and Kjellberg and Stigzelius' chapter about the market for organic and sustainable food.

Of course, the marketization of concerns may also develop from an external critique of market actors and/or products. However, typically such critique is later 'digested' by market actors themselves, as D'Antone and Spencer's example of palm oil wonderfully demonstrates. Here, the critique of palm oil 'reheats' the product in showing that it is not made of just a particular type of vegetable oil (oil as an 'obvious', taken-for-granted matter of fact), but also of several concerns, for example deforestation, healthcare threats, and so on.

Far from fighting the critique, market actors paradoxically seize palm oil contestation as an opportunity to redefine the product, proposing several quality schemes aimed at differentiating palm oil according to its more or less 'sustainable' character. What is remarkable in this case is that instead of being heated up and then cooled down, the product becomes hotter and hotter as the process of 'upward' quality competition unfolds.

First, a Swiss retailer sets up a standard for sustainable palm oil with the help of the WWF NGO. Nestlé then counters this initiative by stressing some forgotten concerns in the competitor's scheme and proposing an enhanced standard. Other actors soon enter the game and raise additional concerns, such as the fate of wild animals. This calls for a more radical 'palm free movement', or, reversely, the interests of local palm oil producers, which condemns the sustainable rhetoric as the mere expression of Western interests. Apart from their differences, what these examples show is that market preferences and values are never given; rather, they are 'given to': they are built, shaped, exchanged and communicated to market actors as possible product qualities, so that social concerns and market competition become one and the same.

A CONCERN FOR CONCERNED MARKETS

As we understand, moral concerns and market interests, instead of being antithetical, often go hand in hand – the invisible hand of the market in the visible hand of social actors – to the point that it becomes hard to distinguish which is which. As D'Antone and Spencer nicely note, 'what is defined as a "concern" by other market versions is often motivated by interests of different actors'. This confusion between interests and concerns is pervasive in most of the chapters presented. For example, the resistance of teachers' unions to the introduction of market-like incentive systems in Dutch education may be seen as the defence of a broad concern for education, or as the expression of the teachers' corporatist interests (Dix). The same is true of coffee producers whose concern for their children's education may obviously be read in terms of family interests (Onyas and Ryan). It is also clear in the case of German maize producers, which deliberately position themselves on either of two markets (cattle food and energy production) depending on the money they can make from each of them (Hauber and Ruppert-Winkel).

On the one hand, this confusion echoes Adam Smith's astute conversion of passions into interests (see above), then his old pretension to anchor the common good to the expression of individual conflicting interests. But on the other hand, most of these chapters also stress an interesting disjuncture between private interests and the common good, and therefore demonstrate that 'concerned markets' are precisely about finding the means to rearticulate the two.

A wonderful and counter-intuitive example of this is given by Ronika Chakrabarti and Katy Mason in their case study about the recovery of a local community of farmers after a tsunami destroyed their island. The authors paradoxically show that in some circumstances, concerns may be raised about self-proclaimed concerned markets. On the one hand, Western companies and management scholars have invented the 'bottom of the pyramid' approach to markets (BoP), which is put forward as intimately connected to a concern for people with very low incomes in underdeveloped countries. Observing that this population lacks access to market goods, the BoP framework proposes to fill the gap by making goods and services accessible to them.

On the other hand, the authors nicely demonstrate that this approach starts from the wrong side of the pyramid: even if concerned with its bottom, the BoP strategy works top-down. As a consequence, in designing Western solutions for the third world, it promotes a 'matter of fact' rather than 'matter of concern' approach, which proves not to be flexible, interactive and imaginative enough to meet local unpredictable needs. By contrast, Chakrabarti and Mason promote a true bottom-up approach, whereby even hard matters of fact such as scientists' certainties about land fertility are challenged by the concerns of local ordinary people.

The authors describe a 'rebirth' experience from a situation in which nothing exists any more: no institutions, no welfare, no economy and no markets. They present a collective experiment inspired by Dewey's inquiry and aimed at designing solutions where scientists, instead of pushing *a priori* solutions, just help people articulate matters of fact and matters of concern. They do so in establishing a boat service in order to reach a distant market, identifying an affordable fertilizer and learning how to develop skills in fish farming and goat management.

If I come back to these details, it is because they clearly evidence that in that case (maybe despite the authors!) the 'concerned market' approach surprisingly enacts the original market mythology and utopia, which starts from no State, just individual small-size actors, a mistrust regarding any centralized entity that cares about the others from far away (see the criticism of the BoP approach), and a symmetrical faith in local initiatives and entrepreneurship. This chapter shows that in some cases the disappearance of the market equals the disappearance of life, and that sometimes going back to life conversely goes through the market.

That said, it is also important to stress a big difference: here, the enactment of the market does not rest on isolated 'interested' and competing
initiatives, but on a collectively 'concerned' experiment. In this sense, this
case is also a good example of how markets can be acceptable and even
useful, provided that actors find the proper *agencement* of market and
social elements. Here, hybrid forums and collective experiments, which
prove able to gather and bridge laymen and experts' knowledge on a
symmetrical basis (Callon et al., 2009), can efficiently articulate private
interests and the common good.

FROM CORN FLAKES TO FLEX CROPS:
CONCERNED MARKETS AS VALUING ENTITIES

Since concerned markets combine social and economic matters, the
articulation of values and prices is at the core of their functioning. There
is no better word than 'valuation' to encompass these two notions. This
is because the word both means setting a price (evaluating) and attributing value (valuing), which has two sub-meanings: defining the qualities
of goods (Karpik, 2010) and relating them to an order of worth (Stark,
2009). The book shows that in concerned markets, these three dimensions
of valuation procedures are closely interrelated. The chapters describing
concerns in the markets for maize and coffee provide good examples of
such articulations.

Historically, maize was an ordinary good, with no other concern
attached to it than economic interest (even if it later received some mater-
ialistic values in terms of health, for instance). As such it was just a commodity among many others sold on the interested market (Chandler,
1977). But Jürgen Hauber and Chantal Ruppert-Winkel tell us the fascinating story of the conversion of corn flakes to flex crops, that is the shift
from corn as mere food (here for cattle) to corn as food or energy.

It is the introduction of a particular value, the need for renewable
energy for the protection of the planet, which succeeds in splitting a single
product into two very different commodities, the 'interested' vs. the
'concerned' corn. 'Flex crops are crops like soya, palm oil, sugar cane or
maize that can be used for the production of food or energy'. But valuing
as 'defining' (maize as food vs. maize as fuel) and valuing as 'politicizing' (maize as an economic good vs. maize as renewable energy) is closely
linked to valuing as 'pricing': splitting a single product into two different
goods allows the attribution of a specific price to each of them.

In Jürgen Hauber and Chantal Ruppert-Winkel's case, maize as food
receives no other price than the flexible and 'spot' price of the interested

market, whereas maize as energy receives a fixed and long-term price attributed by concerned political authorities. What is fascinating is then to discover that the concerned market for energy remains closely subordinated to the interested market of food. That is, the producers' decisions to sell their goods on one market rather than the other, via long-term contracts or spot-market sales, apparently depend only on their economic calculations, with no concern for the moral value of each type of product. We thus understand that valuing products (defining, politicizing and pricing them) is not a matter of deciding whether to rely on market or political frameworks, but a problem of finding the right *agencement* that can help the actors to attain their economic and political goals.

The case of coffee addressed by Winfred Onyas and Annmarie Ryan is both very similar and very different. It is very similar to the extent that coffee is also a single product split in two, with the same type of pricing mechanisms and calculations. That is, coffee is produced either as dry-processed or washed, and, just like flex crops, each form of coffee is connected to a particular market and pricing system: dry-processed coffee is sold to traders on the spot market, whereas washed coffee is sold through contracts signed with the Good African Company (GAC), ensuring the buyer a higher and more stable price. Just as for maize farmers, coffee producers can choose whether to sell in one market or the other.

But in Onyas and Ryan's case, and despite GAC's proclaimed concern for the promotion of local coffee – the company's name points at its 'Good' and 'African' character – it seems clear that coffee, whether washed or not, and contrary to what we observed with maize as food or as a means to save the planet, remains a standard 'interested' commodity, with no particular concern attached to it (except the very economic and technical concern for material quality). Symmetrically and in contrast to maize producers driven by economic interests, coffee producers express strong social concerns: they complain about the GAC restricting their price scheme to economic and technical dimensions and forgetting higher social stakes, such as the need for the farmers to earn a decent wage and care about their children's education.

Once again, by comparing the maize and coffee cases we glimpse the working of concerned markets: these markets consist in attaching some values to market *agencements* from the outside, when designing the market (see maize), or from the inside, when contesting them (see coffee). The two cases show that the success of such attachments is by no means guaranteed: it depends on power asymmetries between the actors and their ability to properly 'marketize' concerns (see maize, where farmers have the strongest position) or 'concernize' markets, to coin a word (see coffee, where the local producers still lack power).

FROM RESISTANT ACTORS TO REFLEXIVE SCIENTISTS

The last case helps us define concerned markets as markets that prove capable of internalizing the critique levelled at them (coping with moral externalities, or framing the overflow of concerns, to speak in Callon's terms (1998b)). Acknowledging such processes is a good way to understand that politics is not 'around markets' but at the core of the market game. It also helps us appreciate that market actors are far from being the mechanical incarnation of an average economic man following a universal rational calculation scheme. Instead, they are reflexive and proactive players who may act according to several patterns, whose actions may be fuelled by diverse concerns (i.e. material, identity or moral 'scripts' (Darr and Pinch, 2013)), and who contribute not only to the functioning of markets in accordance with specific rules, but also to the design of these very rules and to the markets themselves.

There is no better example of such 'concerned behaviour' of market agents than Guus Dix's chapter on the experiment conducted in the Netherlands to 'incentivize' teachers in the Dutch education system. This experiment performs the neo-liberal views of New Public Management (NPM) policies which, inspired by principal–agent theory, hold that improving the performance of teachers goes through a pure 'interested market' approach based on quantifying the results and paying bonuses to the agents who perform best (let's note, however, that if the experiment was fully faithful to its source of inspiration, it should also punish the laggards! (Andreoni et al., 2003)). Guus Dix could have noted that education itself is largely based on such schemes with grades, diplomas and awards (and sometimes punishments); hence, it is the inefficiency of incentives that leads NPM proponents to correct them by supporting their further development!

What the experiment shows is that the incentivizing scheme doesn't produce good and bad performances only, but also resistance. To phrase it in accordance with our typology, framing education as an 'interested market' ironically shifts it into a 'contested' one. The resistance to this experiment takes two forms. The first consists in refusing the scheme: only 40 schools out of a total of 8.000 applied to the scheme. Moreover, the experiment provoked 'the largest strike in the history of the union', based on contested market-like arguments according to which knowledge is not and cannot be a marketable good.

The second type of resistance, not evidenced in the present experiment but observed in similar cases, consists in perverting the scheme by shifting interest into opportunism, that is its *reductio ad absurdum*: '[in the US], teachers could deliberately manipulate the test scores by keeping certain students out of the test' (see the fourth season of the American series *The Wire* for an excellent illustration!). In other cases, 'fraudulent schools in America [. . .] received large sums of money for fake increases'. The lesson is well known (except by some economists?): the more you rely on principal–agent theory to prevent actors' opportunism and control their behaviour, the more the actors become opportunistic and out of control (Gomez, 1996).

The main merit of Guus Dix's case is to help us go beyond the mere opposition between interested and contested markets. The content of and reasons for critique are far less important than its presence: behind the development of critique we indeed discover that ordinary actors are not just object-like agents equipped with a nature-like interest; they also prove their ability to be 'concerned' in the sense of 'reflexive'; they inter-act with the devices that are meant to play on their objective nature and/ or objectify them and, in so doing, they shift matters of fact into matters of concern. Hence, the question of the marketization of education is not just about playing the game (interested market) or refusing it (contested market); it is also about questioning and reinventing the rules of the game itself (concerned market).

However, it is very important to note that ordinary actors do not have the monopoly of 'concerned' reflexivity. Economists themselves are also capable of being reflexively concerned about 'what "what they do" does'. Of course, on the one hand, relying on the old and somewhat question-able scheme of principal–agent theory may be seen as a lack of concern for what economic science can produce. But on the other hand something is produced, and the experimenters show a concern (in the sense of an awareness and preoccupation) for what they obtain: for instance, they fear the division of the educational field into good schools on the one side and bad ones on the other. They also care about the effects of individualized versus team bonuses. As a consequence, dealing with concerned markets also requires us to be sensitive to concerned economics; as we learned from Callon (1998a), economic matters (the economy) are largely the performative effects of economic concerns (economics).

Dix tells a story of an attempt to perform the theory of rational eco-nomic players at a time when, ironically enough, other mainstream econo-mists have relaxed their assumption of rationality, that is their faith in the efficiency of pure interested markets. For instance, behavioural econo-mists tried to reconcile free choice and public concerns: recognizing that most people are not well informed about what is in their best interest, but still believing that the market freedom deserves to be kept, they invented the nudge theory. This is a way to favour choices that are congruent with public concerns without imposing on individual freedom ('nudging' people consists for instance in placing vegetables before the French fries in school restaurants and thus increasing the consumption of the first type of food without limiting or constraining the pupils' choice (Thaler and Sunstein, 2008)).

Philippe Steiner describes how the economist Alvin Roth designed a computerized platform for organ gift-giving, which does not rest on the price mechanism but on an algorithm that allocates the organs in accordance with the receivers' expressed preferences for a given organ, or a priority position on the waiting list (Steiner, 2010). We could also invoke environmental economics and Ronald Coase's market for pollution permits, which is one of the best examples of how economic externalities (pollution) and moral concerns (protecting the environment) can be internalized and framed by market mechanisms (Coase, 1960). Several other examples can be found in this book, such as the case of health economics and its concern for fairness and competitive neutrality, which led the Swedish county under study to shift from capitation (i.e. reimbursement based on the average expected cost of listed patients) to Diagnosis Related Groups (i.e. reimbursement based on the diagnosis profile of the care centre's population) (Johansson Krafve).

But reflexive market concerns are not restricted to laymen and economists; they are also shared (or disputed!) by marketers and other social scientists. In this respect, one should pay tribute to the broadened concept of marketing in the late 1960s/early 1970s (Kotler and Levy, 1969; Lazer, 1969). This opened a space for a concerned managerial approach to exchanges in general, along the idea that the marketing expertise could be extended to non-profit organizations and social causes (Cochoy, 1998).

As marketing scholars with a reflexive, concerned approach to markets, several authors of this book share this legacy, for instance when they wonder about the force and deceptiveness of medical marketing (Azimont and Araujo), participate in collective market design experiments (Chakrabarti and Mason), care about the environment (D'Antone and Spencer; Kjellberg and Stigzelius) or neglected populations (Onyas and Ryan). What is important at this stage is not to decide which expertise is the most appropriate, but to show that markets are full of concerned agents, ranging from laymen to economists and other scientists.

Beyond concerned markets, there is also a market for social concerns and concerned theories which all compete to define the proper moral approach to markets. The present book is the best evidence one could give of the existence of such markets; it is the honour of the editors and authors not to limit their agenda to the analysis of concerned markets but to be concerned themselves: the contributors to the present collection explicitly push the translation of the ANT approach from market think-ing to market design. Indeed, if sciences are performative, the science which describes this performativity benefits from a privileged position to defend its own performative power, relevancy and social usefulness. For an example, see Chakrabarti and Mason's proposal of a 'market design' approach based on outdoor participatory experiments where laymen and scientists collectively deliberate in order to identify relevant solutions to market concerns (Callon et al., 2009).

CONCERNED CONSUMER BEHAVIOUR: SOLUTION OR 'SCAPEGOAL'?

There remains a need for more precision about how to develop market pol-itics: what concerns should be implemented into market *agencements*, with what effects, and so on. As I have already stated, 'concerned behaviours' are not restricted to market scientists; on the contrary they are widely shared by ordinary persons. For example, see Kjellberg and Stigzelius' rich ethnographic account about how Swedish environmentally-conscious consumers try to 'do green' in growing their own organic vegetables from a shared garden, buying sustainable food from an online store using biogas-fuelled delivery trucks or learning 'climate clever' cooking together with an environmentalist NGO.

Doing green shows that being concerned means being connected, affected and worried, to retrieve the excellent categories established in the book's introduction. It means being connected, to the extent that each concerned actor traces some connections between the general concern he or she cares about, and his or her personal situation and action. It also means being connected to the extent that the same person often develops social ties with other people who share the same concern and willingness to act. Being concerned means being affected and thus committed, to the extent that each concerned actor supposes that he or she can do something that matters, and engage in an action that contributes, even modestly, to reshaping the world.

Last but not least, being concerned means being worried, to the extent that each concerned actor feels a moral burden, experiences the sentiments of fault and guilt, as if he or she lost his or her consumer innocence, as if he or she left the abundance of the interested market. This abundance is to the consumerist world what the Garden of Eden was to Eve, before she accessed knowledge by eating the forbidden fruit, just like the consumer who, after decades of overconsumption, becomes aware of the environ-mental and social threats the planet is facing. But this biblical analogy raises another unexpected concern about the meaning of concerned market behaviour. Are 'doing green' and all other forms of political consumerism/ethical consumption (Dubuisson-Quellier, 2013; Cochoy, 2011) perhaps the modern equivalent of the Middle Age trade in indulgences, that is, a premonitory and paroxysmal form of concerned market?[1] Let's remind ourselves that this profitable trade allowed any sinner to obtain partial or total pardon from sins against a payment to the Catholic Church. Similarly, does not doing a 'little something' for the environment redeem one's feeling of guilt for overconsumption?

The problem (and advantage!) with doing green (and engaging in any similar concerned practice) is that its real contribution to the fulfilment of the concern at stake is very hard to estimate from the individual point of view. Kjellberg and Stigzelius subtly address this measurement dilemma: on the one hand, they acknowledge that 'the realization of any (green) value through a specific practice will depend on how that practice is being monitored', but on the other hand, they underline that such monitoring goes through 'rules of thumb' measurements, that is procedures whose 'workability' is obtained at the expense of an obvious lack of reliability. Given this uncertainty, a marginal but individually costly contribution (in terms of time and commitment) may be experienced as an important one, and may lead people to forget all the other aspects of their life which do not fit their sustainability agenda.

For example, Kjellberg and Stigzelius mention that their concerned gardeners experienced difficulties in doing green during the summer holiday season, since many of them were travelling. Where did they travel? Did not some of them travel by plane to the other side of the world, consuming more than a ton of CO_2, and thus ruining in seconds a year of hard but anecdotal concerned work in the community garden? We don't know the answers for sure, but the fact that we don't nicely shows how focusing on one local concerned market behaviour can work as the 'scapegoal' that helps us forget the vast array of unsustainable behaviour that surrounds it.

This cognitive process parallels on the demand side what may be observed on the supply side with the behaviour of large corporations, even if what is involuntary in one case is generally purposeful in the other. For instance, British Petroleum, despite its core pollutant activity, displays a strong commitment for environment preservation; Philip Morris, despite its cigarette business, supports actions for preventing the young public to smoke as part of its corporate social responsibility policy (Cochoy, 2014); and so on.

Hence a dilemma: on the one hand, given the severe threats that the planet is facing, being concerned is mandatory, something has to be done. As Latour vehemently argues, we have entered the age of the '*anthropocène*', that is the moment when, for the first time in the globe's history, humans' actions transform the planet, in particular as a result of the blind implementation of the nature-like laws of interested markets and capitalism. Contesting markets has its virtues (Dubuisson-Quellier, 2013); it is even necessary when markets deal with goods full of moral deadlocks such as drugs, organs, pornography and so on (Steiner, 2014), but it may be not enough to address today's wider challenges.

Hopefully, transforming markets by being concerned is still possible. If humans interact with nature, malicious interactions may indeed be replaced by beneficial ones (Latour, 2014). From this point of view, any concerned behaviour doesn't hurt and is welcome. On the other hand, given the scope of the problems to be solved, one should carefully develop a 'meta-concern' for the proper allocation of concerned behaviour. As Kjellberg and Stigzelius put it, we should find 'how multiple concerns can be balanced/aligned/coordinated'. In other words, we should avoid the possible 'scapegoal' effect of some actions, and rather imagine which 'moral scripts' should orient our conducts (Darr and Pinch, 2013); we should define which undertakings we – market laymen and scientists – could and should engage in together for the development of a sustainable economy and society. This book is a collective and welcome invitation to do so.

NOTE

1. I owe this image to Vincent-Antonin Lépinay who evoked it during an informal conversation at the margins of a conference held in June 2007 at Cerisy-la-Salles on Bruno Latour's work.

REFERENCES

Andreoni, J., W. Harbaugh and L. Vesterlund (2003), 'The carrot or the stick: Rewards, punishments, and cooperation', *The American Economic Review*, 93(3), 893–902.

Boltanski, L. and E. Chiapello (2007), *The New Spirit of Capitalism*, London & New York: Verso.

Boltanski, L. and L. Thévenot (2006), *On Justification: The Economies of Worth*, Princeton: Princeton University Press.

Callon, M. (1998a), 'Introduction: The embeddedness of economic markets in economics', in M. Callon (ed.), *The Laws of the Markets*, Oxford: Blackwell, pp. 2–57.

Callon, M. (1998b), 'An essay on framing and overflowing: Economic externalities revisited by sociology', in M. Callon (ed.), *The Laws of the Markets*, Oxford: Blackwell, pp. 244–69.

Callon, M. (2007), 'An essay on the growing contribution of economic markets to the proliferation of the social', *Theory, Culture & Society*, December, 24(7–8), 139–63.

Callon, M., P. Lascoumes and Y. Barthe (2009), *Acting in an Uncertain World: An Essay on Technical Democracy*, Cambridge, MA: MIT Press.

Callon, M., C. Méadel and V. Rabeharisoa (2002), 'The economy of qualities', *Economy and Society*, 31(2), 194–217.

Callon, M. et al. (eds) (2013), *Sociologie des Agencements Marchands*, Paris: Presses de l'Ecole des Mines.

Chandler, A.D. Jr (1977), *The Visible Hand, The Managerial Revolution in American Business*, Cambridge, MA: The Belknap Press of Harvard University Press.

Coase, R.H. (1960), 'The problem of social cost', *Journal of Law and Economics*, 3(1), 1–44.

Cochoy, F. (1998), 'Another discipline for the market economy: Marketing as a performative knowledge and know-how for capitalism', in M. Callon (ed.), *The Laws of the Markets*, Oxford: Blackwell, pp. 194–221.

Cochoy, F. (2011), 'Political consumption revisited: Should we resist "consumers' resistance"?' in K. Ekström and K. Glans (eds), *Beyond the Consumption Bubble*, London: Routledge, pp. 112–24.

Cochoy, F. (2014), 'Cigarette packages: The big red chevron and the 282 little kids', in N. Thrift, A. Tickell and S. Woolgar (eds), *Globalisation in Practice*, Oxford: Oxford University Press, pp. 165–70.

Darr, A. and T. Pinch (2013), 'Performing sales: Material scripts and the social organization of obligation', *Organization Studies*, 34(11), 1601–21.

Dubuisson-Quellier, S. (2013), *Ethical Consumption*, Winnipeg, Canada: Fennewood Publishing.

Gomez, P-Y. (1996), *Le Gouvernement de l'Entreprise, Modèles Economiques de l'Entreprise et Pratiques de Gestion*, Paris: InterEditions.

Hirschman, A.O. (1977), *The Passions and the Interests: Political Arguments for Capitalism Before its Triumph*, Princeton, NJ: Princeton University Press.

Karpik, Lucien (2010), *Valuing the Unique: The Economics of Singularities*, Princeton, NJ: Princeton University Press.

Kessous, E. (2012), 'Des liens marchands au lien amoureux: Le marché de la rencontre sur Internet', in F. Cochoy (ed.), *Du Lien Marchand, Essai(s) de Sociologie Economique Relationniste*, Toulouse: Presses Universitaires du Mirail, pp. 321–41.

Kjellberg, H. (2012), 'Moi, ma Thunderbird et les autres: Une affaire de collection', in F. Cochoy (ed.), *Du Lien Marchand, Essai(s) de Sociologie Economique Relationniste*, Toulouse: Presses Universitaires du Mirail, pp. 295–319.

Kotler, Ph. and S. Levy (1969), 'Broadening the concept of marketing', *Journal of Marketing*, Vol. 33 (January), pp. 10–15.

Latour, B. (1993), *We Have Never Been Modern*, Cambridge, MA: Harvard University Press.

Latour, B. (2004), 'Why has critique run out of steam? From matters of fact to matters of concern', *Critical Inquiry*, 30(Winter), 225–48.

Latour, B. (2014), 'On some of the affects of capitalism', lecture given at the Royal Academy, Copenhagen, 26 February.

Lazer, W. (1969), 'Marketing's changing social relationships', *Journal of Marketing*, 33(1), 3–9.

Neyland, D. and E. Simakova (2010), 'Trading bads and goods: Market practices in fair trade', in L. Araujo, J. Finch and H. Kjellberg (eds), *Reconnecting Marketing to Markets*, Oxford: Oxford University Press, pp. 204–23.

Polanyi, K. (2001), *The Great Transformation, The Political and Economic Origins of Our Time*, Boston, MA: Beacon Press.

Stark, D. (2009), *The Sense of Dissonance. Accounts of Worth in Economic Life*, Princeton and Oxford: Princeton University Press.

Steiner, P. (2010), 'Gift-giving or market? Economists and the performation of organ commerce', *Journal of Cultural Economy*, 3(2), 243–59.

Steiner, P. (ed.) (2014, forthcoming), *Contested Markets*.

Steiner, P. and M. Trespeuch (2013), 'Maîtriser les passions, construire l'intérêt: Les jeux d'argent en ligne et les organes humains à l'épreuve du marché', *Revue Française de Sociologie*, 54(1), 155–80.

Thaler, R.H. and C.R. Sunstein (2008), *Nudge, Improving Decisions about Health, Wealth and Happiness*, New Haven and London: Yale University Press.

Thévenot, L. (1984), 'Rules and implements: Investment in forms', *Social Science Information*, 23(1), 1–45.

Weber, M. (1997 [1905]), *The Protestant Ethic and the Spirit of Capitalism*, London: Routledge.

Index